Nation, State, and Territory

Nation, State, and Territory

Origins, Evolutions, and Relationships

Volume 1

GEORGE W. WHITE

With Cartographic Work by
EMILY A. WHITE

ROWMAN & LITTLEFIELD PUBLISHERS, INC.
Lanham • Boulder • New York • Toronto • Plymouth, UK

ROWMAN & LITTLEFIELD PUBLISHERS, INC.

Published in the United States of America
by Rowman & Littlefield Publishers, Inc.
A wholly owned subsidiary of The Rowman & Littlefield Publishing Group, Inc.
4501 Forbes Boulevard, Suite 200, Lanham, Maryland 20706
www.rowmanlittlefield.com

Estover Road, Plymouth PL6 7PY, United Kingdom

Copyright © 2004 by Rowman & Littlefield Publishers, Inc.
First paperback edition 2007

British Library Cataloguing in Publication Information Available

The hardback edition of this book was cataloged by the Library of Congress as follows:

White, George W., 1963–
    Nation, state, and territory : origins, evolutions, and relationships / George W. White ;
with cartographic work by Emily A. White.
        p. cm.
    Includes bibliographical references and index.
    1. Nationalism—Europe. 2. National state. 3. State, The. 4. Group identity—
Europe. 5. Political geography. 6. Europe—Boundaries. I. Title.
    JC311.W463 2004
    320.1—dc22
                                                                    2004014114
ISBN-13: 978-0-7425-3025-6 (cloth : alk. paper)
ISBN-10: 0-7425-3025-6 (cloth : alk. paper)
ISBN-13: 978-0-7425-3026-3 (pbk. : alk. paper)
ISBN-10: 0-7425-3026-4 (pbk. : alk. paper)

Printed in the United States of America

In memory of
Lucas Baldwin Gibbons
for having brought light into all of our lives

Few people are capable of expressing with equanimity opinions which differ from the prejudices of their social environment. Most people are even incapable of forming such opinions.

It is theory that decides what can be observed.

The important thing is to not stop questioning.

—Albert Einstein

Contents

Figures

Acknowledgments

I would like to express my appreciation to Professor Glynn Baugher and Ruth Linholm for their thoughtful and meticulous editing. Professor Baugher's unique knowledge of the English language, especially its word origins, is invaluable. I am indebted to my wife Emily for the cartographic work, her general help with the entire project, and her understanding for the amount of time this project consumed. I thank my mother, Yvonne, for sharing her library and knowledge of European royalty. My appreciation goes to Britta Ricker for her help in the final manuscript preparation. I also want to thank those of you with whom I attended conferences, who provided me with great intellectual stimulation, gave me feedback on my presentations, and with whom I had many informal discussions.

1

Introduction

Love your country. Your country is the land where your parents sleep, where is spoken that language in which the chosen of your heart, blushing, whispered the first word of love; it is the home that God has given you that by striving to perfect yourselves therein you may prepare to ascend to him.

—*Giuseppe Mazzini*

As we begin the twenty-first century, globalization is a much talked and written about subject. As it batters down all sorts of boundaries at every geographic scale imaginable, it seems to be the predominant force driving politics, economics, and culture, all other paradigms beaten down before it. It seems to be creating a single, monolithic global economy, global political structure, and global culture. With the uniqueness of politics, economics, and culture eroding, it seems that the study of differing ideologies and systems is becoming increasingly irrelevant. Certainly when Communism began to collapse in Eastern Europe in 1989 and was soon followed by the dissolution of the Soviet Union in 1991, much of the interest in Communist ideologies and economic practices evaporated. Those seeking prominence by trying to be in the forefront of that which was to come looked for a new paradigm. With his provocatively entitled book *The End of History and the Last Man* (1992), Francis Fukuyama suggested that the recent spread of liberal democracy constitutes "'the end point of mankind's ideological evolution' and the 'final form of human government'" (xi). Interestingly, Fukuyama looked backward as much as forward in that he asked whether Georg Wilhelm Friedrich Hegel (1770-1831) and Karl Marx (1818-1883) were correct in thinking that human society evolved and would one day reach a final stage and no

1

longer need to evolve any further. Fukuyama was not concerned about globalization per se, but his ideas ran parallel to the apparent processes of globalization in that the world was becoming increasingly homogeneous. Fukuyama simply restricted himself to the notion that liberal democracies were taking over the world rather than showing an interest in all the myriad nuances of globalization.

The establishment of new liberal democracies around the world turned out to be very problematic. Yugoslavia disintegrated amid the violence of fervent ethnic nationalism. Cultural differences lay at the root of conflict in the Caucasus, Chechnya, Rwanda, Southwest Asia,[1] and numerous other conflicts. Though Communism faded, the world seemed to be a more violent place as old "ethnic hatreds" seemed to be bounding to the forefront and causing much misery. Samuel Huntington's book *The Clash of Nations and the Remaking of the New World Order* (1996) garnered much attention as Huntington argued that the fundamental source of conflict in the world would be cultural differences, not ideological or economic ones. Though many would not argue that culture is a source of conflict, Huntington's argument was oversimplified in that he saw little connection between culture and ideology and economics. Moreover, he divided the world up into eight highly generalized civilizations, describing the cultures of these civilizations as unproblematic and essential without recognizing the fluidity and overlapping character of identity. Not surprisingly, Huntington's ideas were attacked. Yet Huntington, like Fukuyama, is widely read by many because the interest in the new global order and the desire to be the one to identify the new global order, or at least be there when the global order is discovered, remain strong. Indeed, the concern with globalization is consuming the energies of people, from academics to pundits.

While globalization deserves attention, it is by no means making older phenomena and processes irrelevant. Indeed, if globalization is an unrelenting force reshaping international politics, restructuring economic relationships, and homogenizing cultures, many individuals and peoples are threatened by it, resisting, and fighting back. Terrorism, which is on the minds of many and is now perhaps garnering as much attention as globalization itself, may be a sign of that resistance. It means that terrorism, like globalization, increasingly may be a new reality, but it also may be the response of well-established paradigms of identity. Thus the more globalization seems to homogenize, the more many individuals and peoples resist. Ironically, globalization is intensifying some people's senses of identity. Of these identities, national identity figures prominently. Eventually, globalization may completely dissolve and dissipate national identities, but in the meantime nationhood continues its role as a fundamental layer of human identity, as it ever was. Indeed, many conflicts, like the ones noted above, continue to be between nations and have little to do with globalization. Thus, the study of nationhood's dynamic character remains important and a key to understanding the road that humanity has yet to travel.

In order to understand how peoples protect their national identities—from globalization or otherwise—it is important to understand the character of nationhood and whence it derives its character. Nationhood is a human construct. Derived from cultural characteristics, it is fluid and highly malleable, overlapping other layers of human identities. Such an idea is generally accepted by those who study the phenomenon. However, given less recognition is the idea that culture is inextricably intertwined with the concepts of place and territory, not deterministically but as human constructs themselves. As it is difficult, even counterproductive, to separate language and religion from politics and economics, it is likewise counterproductive to separate these characteristics from place and territory. Using the term *nation* as a synonym for such words as *country* and *state* rather as a human group identity, and *country* and *state* as a politically organized territory shows that human identity is closely tied to place and territory. Indeed, the term *nation-state* reflects the intimate bonds of people and place.

At a basic level, the nation-state ideal derives from the belief (assumption for some) that human beings are fundamentally and naturally divided into social groupings known as nations. As essential—ideally indivisible—social units, nations must then govern themselves because only they know what is best for themselves. The ideal is the social equivalent of the Western notion of the individual who, as indicated by the very nature of the word, is indivisible. Therefore, it is believed that individual rights are inalienable and the individual, knowing what is best for him- or herself, has the right to participate in his or her own governance. While individuals cannot realistically form and govern their own states—each comprised of a single person—nations can and ideally must do so. Thus, self-governance—as expressed in the possession of a state—is essential to nationhood and also the link to territory, for how can a nation govern itself without control over a territory of its own? Through the need for self-governance nations are tied to states and the term *nation-state* emerges. Hence, the dissolutions of the Soviet Union and of Yugoslavia were driven by nations within these states who felt that their rights had been violated and that the only way to protect their rights and to cultivate national identities was to proclaim political, and therefore territorial, independence. Continued conflicts in Northern Ireland, Southwest Asia, Russia (specifically Chechnya), and numerous others strike at the heart of nations' needs to achieve self-governance through territorial sovereignty, namely, the establishment of independent states. The persistence and intractability of these conflicts derive from overlapping claims to territory.

Nations' striving for control of their own territories is by no means a recent phenomenon. Indeed, since the rise of modern nationalism more than two hundred years ago, many of history's great conflicts have been marked by it. In the twentieth century alone, the dissolution of empires in Europe after the First World War, the rise of fascism (an extreme variation of nationalism), and European decolonization following the Second World War all were driven by the need of nations to control their own territories. The dissolution of the Soviet Union, Yugoslavia, and Czechoslovakia in the 1990s, among others, and the continuing conflicts over territory elsewhere have been merely new incarnations of this nationalist principle.

Because most of humanity subscribes to the nation-state ideal by belonging to one of the world's nations, the recent struggles of some nations to control their own territories with their own sovereign governments have elicited some sympathy from those in independent and secure nations. Yet the disparity between the number of nations and the number of states in turn creates a major disjunction between the spatial distribution of nations and the spatial distribution of states. The earth contains as many as 5,000 nations yet is divided into only approximately 200 states! Because international relations are already very complicated with 200 states, the prospect of some 5,000 nations is forbidding. Moreover, because the earth's entire land surface is already allotted, new states would have to be carved out of current ones. Therefore, in spite of any underlying sympathies for those nations wishing to have their own states, the independent and secure nations' have a vested interest in maintaining the status quo concerning the world's political map. Witness the initial refusal of various national governments to recognize the declarations of independence by many of the substate units of both the Soviet Union and Yugoslavia. The United States government even refused to recognize the declarations of independence by the Baltic states—although the United States had never acknowledged their absorption into the Soviet Union in the 1940s. When the German government finally broke ranks more recently and recognized the independence of Slovenia and Croatia, it was condemned by other governments.

The prospect of a world with 5,000 states and the inevitable loss of territory of current states is reason enough to explain why political leaders are reluctant to recognize independence movements of subjugated nations. In fact, the recognition of another nation's right to independence may not in principle be the issue; recognition is withheld to forestall an even more difficult question: Which nation receives which territory as part of an indepen-dence declaration? When governments were forced to accept the dissolution of the Soviet Union and Yugoslavia, they took the position that former re-public boundaries within these states should serve as the boundaries of the new independent states. Because most of these boundaries were unjust or flawed representations of the nation-state ideal, this response was not an an-swer to the question but an attempt to stave it off.

The question of territory is so complicated and delicate that if the right answer is not given, violence will erupt. Yet in some cases, there may be no right answer. Not surprisingly, most political leaders avoid at all costs the issue of drawing new political boundaries. Nonetheless, it can be the only path to peace. Hence policy makers often find themselves staring at maps and facing a near-impossible task: reordering the political map in such a way to please everyone involved while at the same time keeping at bay the biased participants and their often unreasonable demands.

A brief survey of new boundary proposals in regions such as the former Yugoslavia and the Southwest Asia demonstrates that the diplomats charged with the tasks were unequipped to handle their assignments. Their approach typically tried to provide objective solutions for subjective problems. Be-cause conflicts often are characterized by emotionalism and subjectivity, ob-jectivity is embraced in the false belief that it will solve conflict.

Some disputes certainly could use an infusion of objectivity, but the de-sire to treat all issues in an objective manner has led to unfortunate conse-quences. The first and most dangerous mistake that any political leader can make is to believe that ethnic groups and/or nations can be defined objec-tively. Indeed, the illusion of objectivity can be so strong that mediators be-gin from the assumption that group identities are clear and unchanging; therefore, it is easy to identify the number and locations of members of a group simply by taking a census. Censuses are a favorite tool of diplomats because objective criteria such as language use and religious affiliation are tallied. Moreover, since this data can be mapped, diplomats believe that they can then use this information to determine "appropriate" boundaries for na-tion-states. This process seems straightforward and objective, and hence is believed to be appropriate. Unfortunately, it fails to identify all members of ethnic groups and nations. Using the "objective" characteristics of an ethnic group or a nation to map out the distribution of such groups often excludes individuals who consider themselves to be members of a particular group, and includes individuals who do not consider themselves to be members of a specific group. Not all French speakers consider themselves to be French, even in Europe. By the same token, not all who consider themselves to be

French actually speak French. This may be less true today than in the past, but groups such as the Alsatians preferred to be part of the French nation rather than the German one when they spoke their native Germanic language.

Despite relentless attempts to objectively define ethnic groups and nations, such efforts are doomed to failure because ethnic and national identities are not objective phenomena. Ethnic groups and nations are composed of human beings, and the human condition is not an objective one. Feelings and emotions are major components of what it is to be human and thus are key components of any form of human identity as well. Therefore, any examination of human beings, from the individual to large social formations such as nations, must take into account the subjective nature of human identity. Furthermore, the subjectivity of ethnic and national identities is rooted in the fact that human social identities are dynamic and overlapping, not static and discrete as often treated. Many social groups evolve into nations, and nations themselves evolve through their own internal dynamics. Many ethnic groups and nations come into being through stereotyping and persecution. Others are also shaped by governmental manipulation. The varying experiences of social groups make each ethnic group and nation essentially unique though they share many commonalities. In addition, the varying experiences of social groups are further complicated by self-perception. Identity is not merely the result of experience but also of self-perception. How social groups—not to mention individuals—perceive their experiences and hence themselves accounts for much of the subjective nature of ethnic and national identity. The scholar Fredrik Barth recognized the subjective nature of human identity when he argued that we must understand the way in which each group defines itself because a group's identity is derived largely from its self-perception (Barth 1969, 14). Others have agreed, noting that ethnic and national identities are more subjective than objective (Kohn 1955; Anthony Smith 1983; Symmons-Symonolewicz 1985; Colin Williams 1985). There is growing consensus that those who consider subjective components are closer to capturing the nature and dynamics of ethnicity and nationalism than those who have focused exclusively on objective criteria (Alexander Murphy 1988, 15). Therefore, our understanding of ethnicity and nationalism can best be enhanced by a further refinement of our understanding of their subjective components.

Place and territory are two key subjective components of identity that have been considered separate and distinct from human identity. Beyond the fact that human beings occupy places and territories, little acknowledgment has been given to the relationships, even strong emotional bonds, that we have with particular places. This lack of recognition has persisted though our vocabularies contain words and expressions that illustrate these strong passionate attachments. "Homesickness" for example is a word that expresses a depression through a longing for one's home; home can be a place as small as an individual dwelling or as large as an entire country. In a similar vein, "territoriality" describes the protective attitude that humans exhibit toward places; and, like homesickness, it is a very emotional and subjective human expression. If places and territories were separate and distinct from the human condition, and thus outside the realm of human identity, then they would be meaningless to us. We would move from place to place without ever feeling the loss of separation from or the need to protect certain places, and we would not have any concept of homesickness or territoriality. Clearly this is not the case; indeed, quite the opposite is true. Places and territories have deep meaning for us, indicating that human identity is in some way derived from them.

Place and territory also are qualities of group identities as well as individual ones. If an individual can feel a homesickness for an entire country, it follows that this feeling will exist in large numbers as well. The same is true of territoriality. Groups can express a collective need or desire to protect "their" portion of the earth's surface. Both of these phenomena illustrate that group identities also derive from place and territory.

These strong emotional bonds that connect individuals and groups to places and territories may be nonrational but are not irrational. At the most basic level, places and territories contain the natural resources that people need to sustain themselves. Economic analyses measure the amount of actual or potential resources contained around the world. However, the importance of place and territory goes much further. Human beings are diverse; we are differentiated by culture, and culture varies from region to region. It does not exist independently of place. Groups organize and shape the places and territories they inhabit to reflect their attitudes, values, sense of history—in essence their cultures. This expression of group culture in the landscape is daily reinforced in the individual members of the group. Hence places and their unique cultural landscapes in turn influence and mold the attitudes and values of their inhabitants (Relph 1976; Tuan 1974). This continual process of action and reaction represents a significant aspect of human identity at all levels. Hence "place" has become as much a part of human identity as language, religion, or shared history, and likewise we often feel as passionate about protecting our "place" as we do about our language, our religion, or our history.

This protectiveness of place, expressed in the term *territoriality*, manifests itself forcefully within groups, and in sometimes unpredictable ways. Keeping in mind that places and territories contain not only natural resources but also the cultural landscapes of group identity, then the expression of territoriality is moreover the expression of a group's need to protect its language, its religion, its essential identity. Understanding this aspect of territoriality makes its virulent and often violent expressions less unpredictable.

Because we as human beings simultaneously subscribe to many levels of identity—as an individual, a member of a community, and part of a nation—place and territory have meaning for us at all of these levels. Likewise, we express territoriality at all of these levels, but to varying degrees. The nation-state era in which we currently live has had a tremendous impact on the nature of human identity and the way in which we express territoriality. Because the nation-state ideal professes the belief that humanity is fundamentally divided into nations, our national identities have come to take precedence in our lives. While we obviously have not abandoned our individual, community, or ethnic identities, we often sacrifice our individual, community, and ethnic needs to those of the nation.

The world's current state system, composed primarily of nation-states, exists to ensure that our national identities take precedence in our lives, particularly when national identities serve the needs of the state. This state system allows us to negotiate, arbitrate, and even litigate territorial spaces at smaller scales of identity—at the individual, community, and ethnic levels; hence transgressions of territorial spaces at these levels of identity tend to be less violent. On the other hand, the world's state system has no higher level of government that can effectively compel a given nation to act against its own best interest, even for the benefit of all nations. Nations are free to exert their control over territories but are limited to the resources that they can marshal to accomplish this. Because many nations identify with territories that overlap one another, their attempts to assert control of a territory as they define it often result in discord, and sometimes lead to armed conflict. Armed confrontation may seem futile, but nations often feel that they must have sovereignty over their territories if they are to preserve and maintain their national identities. In Southeastern Europe, many nations feel that their identities have been violated because their territories have been continually transgressed by other nations. Not surprisingly, conflict has been persistent in this region.

Nations being territorial or having other subjective qualities is not new. Nevertheless, the subjective components of national identity frequently are not addressed because they are difficult to measure, whereas it is easier to grasp objective criteria. Measuring something more concrete such as language use or religious affiliation is attractive because it is seemingly easier to accomplish and less controversial than analyzing the emotional bonds that nations have with particular places and territories. Geographers too have great difficulty "mapping" these subjective components and likewise prefer to map more tangible criteria.

Despite the inherent problems in trying to map a subjective component of national identity like emotional attachment to place, we must endeavor to do so in order to truly understand the nature of nationalism and thereby be able to resolve territorial disputes between nations. One of the intended contributions of these volumes is to propose a method for accomplishing this task. The emotional attachments to and the significance of places and territories can be judged by the roles that they play for a nation, by the feelings a nation expresses toward them, and by the efforts a nation undertakes to protect them. In a more systematic manner, the significance of places and territories can be judged by looking at three indicators: site identification, landscape description, and the "tenacity factor." Site identification denotes the locations of institutions (e.g., seats of government, printing presses, educational and religious centers) and historic sites (e.g., battles, birthplaces). Landscape description identifies important places as expressed in literature (frequently in poetry), visual art, and music. Besides specific sites, landscape description can refer to broad categories of places such as mountain ranges, valleys, and rivers. Both site identification and landscape description create a spatial distribution of places important to a nation. In other words, they help to define and thus delineate a nation's territory. In order to ascertain just how significant particular places are for a nation, the "tenacity factor" is employed. The tenacity factor looks at the history of a group's determination to protect or seize individual places or pieces of territory. Southeastern Europe is a region of continual conflict; numerous wars, alliances, and proclamations by national governments demonstrate the zeal of nations in protecting or seizing particular places or territories.

The identification and mapping of significant places are intended to elucidate the place component of national identity. When complete, however, it will provide another benefit by contributing to our understanding of the nature of territorial disputes. In short, territorial conflicts and their level of intensity between nations are in direct proportion to the significance of the contested territories to the nations' identities. This should not be surprising, but current methods of analyzing territorial disputes have not been able to draw this conclusion because they do not take into account the significance of place. As a partial consequence, many analyses also have not been able to predict the locations and intensities of territorial conflicts. The identification and mapping of significant places will help to accomplish these goals.

Recognizing that place and territory represent significant aspects of national identity helps to explain the cause and intensity of territorial conflicts; however, this is only a start. Beyond merely identifying significant places and territories, we must address why they come to be significant, and what can be done to solve or even prevent these conflicts. To address these issues, we must discuss how states and temporal processes have shaped the very idea of nation.

States are not merely passive corollaries to nations but forces unto their own. The spatial networks of states, characterized by their political boundaries and their communication and transportation pathways, direct the movement of individuals. Hence, states play an active role in influencing who will bond together in large social groups like nations and similarly help to determine the place and territories to which people will develop strong emotional attachments. States have been such pervasive forces that they have instilled state-centered thinking within many people. As nations strive to gain states, we tend to presume that the existence of a state implies the existence of a nation by a similar name. Thus, many assume the existence of the French nation because there is a French state and that a Nigerian nation lives within the Nigerian state. Such is not always the case, as with the example of Nigeria. States, however, bestow citizenship, which is a layer of social identity like ethnicity and nationhood. Furthermore, because we live in the nation-state era, states without corresponding titular nations are threatened with disintegration. To legitimize and perpetuate themselves, states will cultivate a sense of national identity among its citizens. Often, the nation-building projects of states will fail. For example, the Yugoslav state disintegrated before a significant number of that state's citizens adopted a sense of Yugoslav nationhood. However, despite internal conflict, Nigeria still exists; only time will tell if the Nigerian state will be able to cultivate a Nigerian national identity among its citizens. Though the task is daunting, state-centered thinking and other states aid in the process. In Afghanistan and Iraq, for example, Afghani and Iraqi national identities are very tenuous at best as ethnic groups remain hostile to one another. Crucially, the Afghani and Iraqi governments are ineffective. However, the global community of states, having no desire to allow Afghanistan and Iraq to disintegrate despite the seemingly intractable ethnic and religious conflicts, is working to make the Afghani and Iraqi governments functional again. If effective Afghani and Iraqi governments are constructed, they will certainly begin cultivating senses of Afghani and Iraqi national identities respectively and from their very start because their legitimacy and longevity will depend on it. Many states have taken the idea of the nation-state and flipped it around to state-nation. It is an indication of the power of states in shaping human social identity and the emotional bonds that nations develop with place and territory.

Historical processes too have been an active force and have contributed to the uniqueness of national identities and the distinctive self-perceptions of nations. The concept of the modern nation is a very recent phenomenon in human history, and many places become significant upon being recast in a nationalist framework. Understanding how this recasting takes place gets at the very heart of any national identity and thus explains why certain places and territories become significant.

When modern nationalism emerged some two hundred years ago, it began with the premise that humanity was fundamentally divided into nations. A few corollaries soon followed, culminating in the idea that every nation must have its own state if the world were to enjoy everlasting peace—thus formulating the nation-state ideal. These fundamental ideas still characterize the doctrine of nationalist ideology, but they cannot stand alone, either now or when first formulated. A myriad of ancillary concepts had to accompany these simple ideas to make the nation-state ideal a viable sociopolitical system. Some of the crucial issues that still needed to be addressed were how a nation was to be defined and how a nation's territory was to be delineated. As nationalism grew, however, many of the accompanying concepts did not grow directly out of the original doctrine. Instead, the basic concept of the nation crystallized around many ideas from the past, from previous conceptions of the earth and ideological systems. Thus these earlier ideas became enmeshed in the concept of nation, serving as many of the ancillary concepts to make the nation-state ideal a reality.

Many of the prenationalist ideas embedded within the nation-state ideal relate to the meaning of place and the political organization of territory. The nation-state ideal has logical implications here, but the actual attitudes that nations hold toward place and territory deviate considerably. These attitudes are holdovers from the time that dynastic imperialism reigned supreme but persisted into the era of nationalism and even provided a trunk for the nation-state to firmly graft itself onto. From medieval times and earlier, the human mind found it convenient to draw political boundaries along physiographic features such as rivers and mountain ranges. At the time, they marked the limits of the power of dynastic rulers who then treated their lands as personal possessions. However, as society evolved, these boundaries took on new meanings. In short, they became the containers in which modern nations and states evolved. This evolution has differed around the world, resulting in many regional variations. In general terms within Europe, the conception of territory and its political arrangement emerged differently in the empires of Western Europe than it did in the empires of Central and Eastern Europe.

When nationalism emerged in Western Europe, it was within the context of the Enlightenment, which was noteworthy for the emphasis it placed on rational thought and the rights of the individual. In contrast to the imperial order of states and their territories, the nationalist ideal in the context of Enlightenment philosophy implied a reordering of political control over territories to create numerous small states. Small territories ensure the rights of the individual better than huge and sprawling empires. The actual delineation of such territories is to a large degree irrelevant because individuals have rights no matter where they live or what their individual cultural characteristics may be. This conclusion, however, was rarely discussed as a serious issue for nationalists at the time. Security was more important to Enlightenment thinking than common cultural characteristics.[2] Hence, the interest in states' political boundaries lay in the desire to provide security. The delineation of political boundaries along rivers and mountains ranges was thought to provide the greatest security. With many of the imperial boundaries already delineated in such a manner, few calls were made to redraw boundaries. The concept of nation was framed directly within the existing territorial order, which was accepted as a given. Thus empires were simply redefined as nation-states. The French empire, for example, became redefined as the French Republic, with no call to redraw its boundaries as implied by the new ideology of nationalism expressed in the context of Enlightenment philosophy.

When nationalism spread to Central and Eastern Europe, this process could not be replicated easily. First of all, individual rights did not have a strong tradition in these regions. Instead, more emphasis was placed on the collective group, which came to be defined by common cultural characteristics such as language and religion. This idea implied a philosophy much different than that of the Enlightenment. In fact, it developed into a system that became known as Romantic philosophy, and it called for a much different territorial arrangement of states than Enlightenment philosophy. In short, Romanticism implied the redrawing of boundaries according to the distribution of nations, supposedly defined by language and religion. This task may seem simple today because many national identities have evolved to the point that they clearly are distinguishable from one another. At the time, however, national identities based on shared cultural characteristics were more a notion than a reality. Cultural characteristics continually changed across the landscape with few obvious and neat breaks that could serve as political boundaries. Therefore, the practice of drawing political boundaries was not a straightforward one.

Some Central and Eastern Europeans, such as the Germans and Russians, could define their new national territories in the same manner as Western Europeans, by redefining their imperial states as new nation-states. Unfortunately, circumstances did not allow this process to take place for most in either region. Quite simply, most did not have existing imperial states of their own that could be recast as new nation-states. Yet imperialism and its political ordering of the landscape was just as much a legacy for these peoples as it was for Western Europeans. Central and Eastern Europeans even experienced the process of redefining imperial territories as national ones; they lived in imperial states under the control of groups who were developing policies to do just that. Consequently, many Central and Eastern Europeans found themselves persecuted and treated as unwanted minorities. As they experienced discrimination, they began to develop a national consciousness and in turn also began to feel alien to the empires in which they lived. Not all developed a national consciousness through discrimination. Some developed group awareness simply through the diffusion of the nationalist idea from Western Europe. Nevertheless, they too could no longer identify with the empires in which they lived.

The need for secession became obvious. Yet the choice of territory for such an act was not obvious because Central and Eastern Europeans lacked their own imperial states to redefine as their new national states. This was a problem that their Western European counterparts never had to confront. The philosophy of Romanticism, however, provided a means for solving this; in addition to language and religion, Romanticism emphasized "shared history" as a unique characteristic of peoples. This emphasis on history allowed those who were developing a national consciousness to reach into the past, to times of great empires of their ancestors. Those empires were then resurrected so that their territories could serve as the bases for modern nation-states. In other words, in contrast to Western Europeans who had existing empires that they could redefine, many Central and Eastern Europeans had to add one step to the process of defining national territories by resurrecting defunct empires. This process also avoided the problems associated with drawing political boundaries according to cultural characteristics when the cultural landscape was in constant transition. It also avoided addressing the fact that imperial governments had manipulated people's identities for so long and to such a degree that language use and religious adherence were not an accurate measure of an individual's or a group's identity. Despite the added step in defining their national territories, Central and Eastern Europeans had defined their territories just like Western Europeans in that they chose dynastic imperial territories with borders that followed physiographic features that predated modern nations. Moreover, though it is remembered that Romantic philosophers placed great stock in using language and other cultural characteristics to define nationhood, it should not be forgotten that notions of naturally defined territories framed by physiographic boundaries such as rivers and mountains played a large role in defining language and other cultural characteristics in the minds of Romantic thinkers. Thus, Romantic thinkers, much like Enlightenment thinkers, continued to rely on older conceptions of political-territorial ordering though their understandings of such orderings had changed.

Analyzing a phenomenon such as the modern nation and state tempts us to examine them in their pure ideological forms. Doing so, however, presents two major dangers: first, that the role that technological innovations and new scientific discoveries played in bringing about modern nations and states will be overlooked; second, that competing and previous ideological structures and institutions will be mistakenly de-emphasized or even disregarded. This error must be avoided, for the national idea did not arise out of a temporal and spatial vacuum. Technological innovations and new scientific discoveries shaped the development of both the national idea and state mechanisms as they matured. Most noteworthy were the Industrial Revolution, the idea of race, and environmental determinism. At the same time, both new and old paradigms vehemently opposed the new idea of nation while the pervasive character of state mechanisms grew in strength. Prominent among the new and old paradigms were Marxism, established religion, and old dynastic imperial forces. The latter two, which were the old paradigms, had been strong forces in shaping the world's political and social landscape. The national idea ascended suddenly and rapidly but did not easily sweep aside dynastic imperialism or established religion. At the same time, it had to contend with Marxist ideas.

Of the new and old paradigms, imperialism's political structures and institutions were most deeply entrenched. One look at Europe's political map in the early twentieth century illustrates that imperialism was still a powerful force despite more than a century of nationalist agitation against it (see figure 1.1). Imperialism finally collapsed, but it would be a gross oversimplification to say that the national idea and the modern state wholly supplanted it. During the struggle against imperialism, both the national idea and the modern state were still in their formative years. Many facets of nationalist ideology were not yet formulated, and historical circumstances did not allow nationalism to develop logically and purely from its own premises. Elements of pre-

EUROPE ON THE EVE OF THE FIRST WORLD WAR

—— 1914 Boundaries

Territory lost by the Ottoman
Empire in 1912/1913

Bulgarian Territory lost to
Romania in 1913

1 - LUXEMBOURG
2 - MONTENEGRO   3 - ALBANIA

0   500 km

NORWAY

SWEDEN

Baltic
Sea

North
Sea

DEN.

RUSSIAN

EMPIRE

NETH.

BELG.

GERMAN

EMPIRE

FRANCE

SWITZ.

AUSTRO-HUNGARIAN

EMPIRE

ROMANIA

Black
Sea

ITALY

Adriatic Sea

2

SERBIA

BULGARIA

3

GREECE

Aegean
Sea

OTTOMAN

EMPIRE

Mediterranean
Sea

Figure 1.1 Europe on the Eve of the First World War

vious cultural and ideological systems were taken up by it and enmeshed within it. For instance, imperialism's territorial order remained meaningful and largely intact in the minds of people, and served as an important link to the past which even nationalists could not reject. The basic dimensions of imperial states also provided the framework for modern states. The national idea triumphed and the modern state emerged, but describing the national idea's victory as one in which it deposed imperialism is not accurate. A more apt analogy would be the petrification process: in the end the new material of stone comes into being as the old wood vanishes; however, this new material is in the form of the old. Such was the case with the national idea's triumph over imperialism and the rise of the modern state. They were a new material in the form of the old, and that form was the territorial order.

The concepts presented in this volume are not a rejection of, nor a radical departure from, current ideas. Rather they grow out of and extend existing concepts. What has been lacking in studies on nationalism is the strong recognition that nations derive their identities to a large degree from particular places and territories, and that control of these is often essential to maintaining a healthy sense of national identity. Failure to give full recognition to this aspect of nationhood has prevented a thorough understanding of the nature of many territorial conflicts. To address these deficiencies, chapter 2 begins by laying out what is already known about forms of human identity, with greatest emphasis placed on that of the nation and its dynamic and evolving character. From there, the place and territorial components of identity are discussed. These are significant for several reasons. First, they provide groups with the natural resources necessary for basic human survival. In addition, they are essential from a cultural perspective because they enable groups to express their identities in landscape. This expression plays an important role in transmitting group characteristics to individuals and to succeeding generations. Groups also must have the ability to enact laws to maintain and cultivate their identities. Laws, however, are effective only within certain geographical spaces, and territory is a form of geographical space that enables groups to formulate the laws and policies necessary to their identities. The significance of territory is underscored by a phenomenon known as territoriality, which exists at all levels of identity but is strongest at the national level—not surprisingly, considering that we live in the nation-state era. The significance of place and territory reflects this phenomenon, but it is a difficult thing to measure and map. The chapter ends with a discussion of indicators that can be used to accomplish this task.

Chapter 3 considers the role of the state in shaping, even creating, national identity. The state's governmental policies and practices demand particular behaviors and knowledge of its citizens and likewise inculcate its citizens with certain ideas of their shared history, language, and culture. The state's spatial networks of communication and transportation in conjunction with its political boundaries direct the flow of ideas, goods, and people, in turn helping to determine who comes together to form a nation and what regional variations in culture will be amalgamated into a national culture. The relationship between states and nations is not deterministic. Though states shape nations, ideally states serve nations, as indicated by the very structure of the term *nation-state*. Nations then employ state mechanisms to further nationalist goals, both inside and outside the states that nations possess. As dynamic forces, both nations and states influence each other. The latter part of the chapter explores this dynamic relationship and how it shapes nations' understandings of their territories.

Chapters 4 and 5 take up the historical dimensions of the national idea and the modern state in an effort to understand how certain places and territories came to be significant to particular nations in Europe. These historical dimensions are vital to consider because the national idea and the modern state did not evolve independently of what came before them. Chapter 4 begins by considering medieval views of the world, governing structures, and the conceptions of territory. It then traces the evolution of these views, structures, and conceptions with particular consideration of the influence of technological innovations and new scientific discoveries. The Treaty of Westphalia in 1648 marks the time when nations and states are first identifiable by modern understandings, but the chapter continues to trace their development through the Enlightenment and then to the Romantic period at the end of the eighteenth and beginning of the nineteenth centuries, the time when modern nations and states become recognizable by today's understandings. The chapter illustrates how modern nations and states have embedded within them many older ideas, many of which are found as far back as medieval times and earlier. Chapter 5 picks up the story in the nineteenth century. At that time, nations and states are not yet fully cast. The Industrial Revolution, the idea of race, and environmental determinism play major roles in shaping the national idea and the development of states. The national idea also is formed by its adversarial relationship with the new Marxist idea and the old structures of dynastic imperialism and established religion. The competition is bitter and often intense. In the twentieth century, the national idea triumphs and the modern state develops into a pervasive force, but both are products of their historical development. Most notably, modern nations and states are framed to a large degree, though it varies by case, by the old dynastic imperial territorial order.

George Santayana once stated that it seemed "a dreadful indignity to have a soul controlled by geography." I cannot be completely sure of what he meant, but his statement seems to echo a narrow understanding of geography and its processes. It reflects the popular notion that geography is nothing more than the arrangement of mountains and rivers, that mountains and rivers in turn are nothing more than commodities to be possessed and bartered. Certainly such sentiments are seen in the statement that "Patriotism is often an arbitrary veneration of real estate above principles" by George Jean Nathan. However, geography is more than knowing the arrangement of mountains and rivers. If language is more than scribbles on paper and utterances of hairless primates, and if religion is more than the opium of the people and the refuge for those who do not understand science, mountains and rivers are more than piles of dirt and flowing water. Moreover, mountains and rivers are only a few elements in the geographies that we create and live in. Sense of territory and emotional attachment to place are both much broader and much deeper elements of the human experience. They, like language and religion, are worlds of meaning and the very fabric of the human condition, from that of the individual to that of large social groups like nations. Just as nations can wrap their identities around languages and religions, nations too can house their identities in place and territory and become as fanatical about protecting their places and territories as they do about preserving their languages and religions. Indeed, it is often important for nations to control the places that define this identity. In those cases where effective control is achieved, a healthy and peaceful national psychology will emerge, but in cases where that control is not achieved, conflict with neighboring ethnic groups and nations will persist. Therefore, knowing the place component of group identity tells us much about national identity and helps us to understand many of the conflicts that arise between nations.

Just as place and territory are more than locations, maps too are more than images. Too frequently maps are treated like wallpaper, doing little more than filling space on the wall behind a news anchor's head or taking up space in the front or the end matter of books, serving as some gray matter of dead space. All too often, news anchors will cover some news event like one concerning the Palestinians or the Kurds while presenting a simplistic map of Southwest Asian countries. With neither the Palestinians nor Kurds represented on such political maps, viewers are not given the spatial distributions of these peoples. They are not only deprived of knowing these peoples' locations, but are also deprived of tools that would help them better understand the conflict. Indeed, maps are not wallpaper but analytical tools. Just as a picture is worth more than a thousand words, maps too are a medium that provides for an understanding that mere text—or words—cannot convey. The maps in these volumes have not been shunted to the back or the front to get them out of the way. They are integrated into text where they are positioned to help the reader understand the points being made. The reader is invited to look at these maps intently and not just glance at them. Ideally, the maps should lead to realizations that would not be possible otherwise, including a greater appreciation for sense of territory and emotional attachment to place.

Notes

1. I prefer to use the term *Southwest Asia* rather than the ethnocentric term *Middle East*.

2. Though many Enlightenment thinkers made reference to common culture, they thought of it in terms of common political philosophy rather than common language or religion.

2

Nations as Spatial Entities

Mist blowing round some headland, somewhere in your memory
Everyone is from somewhere—even if you've never been there.
—Jethro Tull, *Another Christmas Song*

The idea of nation is a pervasive force in modern human society and has been studied by the practitioners of many disciplines. Sociologists, anthropologists, and political scientists have illuminated nationhood from their disciplinary perspectives. Historians and geographers too have contributed to the understanding of nationhood. After all, nations are phenomena that exist in time and space, meaning that temporal and spatial processes shape nations. Unfortunately, outside the field of geography, the spatial attributes of nations are frequently ignored in many studies of nations. The tacit recognition given to the fact that nations occupy spaces does not qualify as genuine inquiry into the spatiality of nations. To truly recognize that nations have spatial qualities is to recognize that spatial processes and interactions contribute to the development of national identities (Karl Deutsch 1969; Soja 1971). While general principles underlie spatial relationships, the exact nature and intensity of these relationships differ geographically, making the character of places and territories unique. The uniqueness of places and territories in turn contributes to the uniqueness of national identities.

In a broad sense, "place" and "territory" are spatial components of nationhood because they both shape and are shaped by their human inhabitants. More specifically, place and territory have many important nuances as well. Of these is the notion that certain places and territories become significant to nations, that nations develop strong emotional

21

bonds to these places and territories—what Yi-Fu Tuan calls *topo-philia*[1]—and that nations can become very protective of these places and territories—a phenomenon known as territoriality. Thus the spatiality of nations is multiplex. This chapter focuses on and elucidates the spatial components of nationhood in detail. Unfortunately, the term *nation* often is used with a lack of clarity, making it too difficult to discuss it in a spatial context without first clarifying the concept of *nation* in its entirety. Therefore, this chapter begins with some clarification of the term *nation* so that the concepts of place and territory can be understood more easily.

Definitions of Nation

The word *nation* is frequently spoken and written on a daily basis in a wide variety of contexts—from politics and economics to weather and sports. Both across and within these broad subjects, the word *nation* is used in a variety of ways, sometimes referring to peoples, other times to countries, occasionally to both at the same time (Gyeke 1997, 77-114), and most often applied unclearly. Consequently, the word *nation* has been interchanged with terms like *tribe, race, ethnic group, state,* and *country.* Though meanings of these words are overlapping to varying degrees, a careless interchange of these terms muddles not only their meanings but also the reporting and research of issues that employ these terms. Therefore, it is important to sort out the differing meanings of these concepts before they can be used effectively.

    Tribe generally refers to small groups of people of common descent and strong kinship ties. Because European colonialists used the term to refer to a primitive stage of human social development, thereby legitimizing their control over many tribes on the basis that Europeans were culturally superior, many peoples have rejected the term *tribe.* To show their equality with European nations, many of these peoples insist that they too are nations just like the European peoples. Though tribal identity is not inferior to national identity, tribal identity is different from national identity. However, the current practice of substituting the term *nation* for *tribe* broadens the concept of nation and also makes it more complicated if not more convoluted.

    Race, too, complicates the concept of nation. It is bound to the idea that human beings are grouped according to common genetics. The practices of racial hygiene and eugenics, though not invented by the Nazis but enthusiastically embraced by them, should have discredited the idea that humans can be divided up easily into racial groups.[2] Recent research also shows that more than 99 percent of human DNA is shared with chimpanzees, demonstrating that the genetic differences between human groupings must be biologically insignificant if humans are so closely related to other primates. Recent DNA evidence, for example, shows that the English are mostly of Celtic origin (Wade 2003). This scientific discovery refutes the long-held English belief that the English are genetically Anglo-Saxon because their language and culture are derived from Anglo-Saxon culture. The study of language and culture led the English to believe that the Angles and Saxons displaced the native Celts. However, science now suggests that the Celts remained and adopted Anglo-Saxon culture. It means that the English are genetically much more closely related to the Welsh, Scots, and Irish than any of these groups have previously thought. This situation illustrates that racial differences are cultural constructions—more in the mind's eye than in the genes.

The term *ethnic group* is most commonly and openly interchanged with nation. Deriving fròm the Greek word *ethnos*, meaning "common descent," ethnicity has the same original meaning as nation (Connor 1978, 386). Without having been used pejoratively or tragically like the terms *tribe* and *race*, ethnicity and ethnic group have become vibrant concepts as people show pride in their various ethnicities. "Common descent" also carries with it certain biological-racial undertones that connect it with the term *nation*, which derives from the Latin *nationem*—meaning *breed* or *race* (Connor 1978, 381). It is perhaps then not surprising that the terms *race, ethnic group,* and *nation* were used as synonyms for one another in the nineteenth and much of the twentieth century. Popular usage of the terms *ethnic group* and *nation* frequently still reflects the notion that ethnic groups and nations have a genetic basis.

"Common descent" may suggest some biological origins, but it also suggests common culture with language and religion frequently identified as the defining cultural characteristics. It would seem necessary for people to speak the same language to live together as a unified group. Indeed, many ethnic groups and nations have a name that is the same as the language they speak. For example, the French speak French, the Spanish speak Spanish, and the Japanese speak Japanese. Likewise, with religion profoundly shaping the worldview of individuals, it would also seem necessary for a group to have the same religious beliefs. However, the reality of identity is not so simple as the theories derived from such deductions or popular perceptions. A one-to-one correlation does not exist between language and/or religion and national identities around the world. English, for example, is the mother tongue for a number of nations, with not all English speakers considering themselves to be part of a single English nation; the same situation exists for a number of other languages, such as French, Spanish,[3] and German. By the same token, not all nations have a single language. Belgians, Swiss, and Americans, for example, are polyglot nations. In regard to religion, Christians have not bonded into a single nation, and neither have Muslims, Buddhists, or Hindus though each group has distinct worldviews and associated cultural practices and traditions.

Language and religious belief are not as concrete and clear-cut as they seem. First, in the case of language, though such peoples as the Germans, French, and Italians supposedly united around their common German, French, and Italian languages respectively, these peoples have spoken these languages only recently in their histories. For centuries, educated Germans preferred to speak French or Latin and scoffed at any German who actually spoke German (Ergang [1931] 1976, 20-39, 140-176). When Martin Opitz (1597-1639) wrote a book arguing that Germans should speak the German language, he wrote in Latin because few literate Germans would have understood it had it been written in German.[4] In 1789, only about 50 percent of the French spoke French and only 12 to 13 percent spoke it correctly by the language standards of the time; in 1860, only 2.5 percent of the population in Italy spoke Italian regularly (Hobsbawn 1990, 60-61). In general, the ruling classes of European countries spoke languages such as Latin and French, considered to be either sacred or appropriate for the upper classes. It meant that the upper classes could converse with one another across Europe but not very well with the people in the lands they ruled. The ruled classes spoke localized languages that varied greatly from place to place. Modern linguists may classify these languages as dialects of languages such as German, French, and Italian. However, mutual intelligibility—which theoretically facilitates communication, the transference of ideas, and the rise of common culture—hardly existed. Illiterate peasants were generally unaware of the linguistic commonalities of what they spoke and knew less of the literary languages that represented what they spoke—that is if such standards existed at all. The cases of the Germans, French, and Italians—which are more the rule than exception—contradict the argument that language is the genesis of national identity as their national languages developed so late in history. Similarly, other peoples have adopted new languages but still identify themselves as distinct peoples. Few Irish, Scots, and Welsh speak Irish, Scots, and Welsh but do not feel one with the English though they speak English.

Second, though languages and religions are depicted clearly in books, actual language and religious practice are much more complicated. Many people are multilingual, engage in mixed religious practices, and are part of families who practice more than one religion. As one moves over earth space, that is from place to place, language and religious practices frequently change slowly with no clear boundaries. Academics draw sharp and distinct boundaries for languages and religions, and governments are quick to go along with these classifications or create their own, but these clear-cut classifications often mean nothing to the people concerned. Two people who are classified as speaking the same language—either by linguists or governments—may not realize that they speak the same language and may not bond together once they realize that they speak the same language. Such is also true for religious belief. For example, Protestants and Roman Catholics are both classified as Christians because both groups share the common belief that Jesus of Nazareth is the messiah. However, despite this common belief that distinguishes these fellow Christians from people with other, much different, religious beliefs, it is not uncommon for Protestants to call themselves Christians but not include Roman Catholics as they apply the term. Such practice reflects a Protestant view that Roman Catholics are not fellow Christians but believers in a different religion. In this case, as in many cases, popular perceptions vary greatly from actual relationships that supposedly define situations.

The problematic use of language and religion to determine ethnicity and nationhood is illustrated by the small town of Karapchiu in Ukraine, which lies along the Romanian border. Romanians, Ukrainians, and Russians live together in this town of less than one thousand people. It would be a mistake to assume that each of these peoples differentiates one another by language though separate Romanian, Ukrainian, and Russian languages exist. Living together, the Romanians, Ukrainians, and Russians adopted many of one another's cultural practices. For example, the Romanians of the village shifted over to speaking Ukrainian while the Ukrainians converted from Roman Catholicism[5] to Orthodoxy, like their Romanian neighbors. Though these three peoples in this town now speak the same language and practice the same religion, they nevertheless see themselves as three distinct peoples. How one hooks one's horse up to a wagon is the telling factor. The Romanians hook their horses up on the right side of the wagon, the Ukrainians on the left, and the Russians in the middle. The positions of the horses relative to the wagons wear ruts in the roads differently, creating problems for those with dissimilar practices and consequently setting each group apart from another.[6] In this farming community, the way in which one hooks one's horse up to a wagon is more profound than one's language or religion and more indicative of one's identity. The case of Karapchiu is not meant to argue that wagon hitching is the basis of identity. Rather it is used as a further example that language and religion are not as definitive as they seem because language and religion classifications are not as neat in real life as in academic distinctions. People will shift their language use, will speak many languages, convert to other religions, and adopt other cultural practices without changing their identities.

The problematic nature of language and religion shows that it is nearly impossible to define ethnic groups and nations by objective criteria. Defining criteria exist but lie almost exclusively in the subjective realm as ethnic groups and nations (and also tribes and races) are largely self-perceived. Benedict Anderson poignantly illustrates the self-perceived nature of nationhood with the term "imagined community" (Anderson 1991) with not all nations defining themselves in the same way. The key to understanding any particular nation's identity comes from an appreciation of how nations conceive of themselves with their uniquely defined sets of traits and not in a preoccupation with a generic set of individual cultural traits that can supposedly define all nations. Even though nations share many similar attributes, the meaning and significance of individual attributes vary from nation to nation. Even when nations latch onto phenomena such as language and religion, language and religion become significant only because individual nations have perceived them to be so. The French, for example, may define themselves in terms of their language as demonstrated by the language laws that they have crafted to protect their language. However, Serbs and Croats speak essentially the same language but differ according to religious belief. In yet another case, Americans define themselves according to ideas of democracy and capitalism. In the same way that the French protect their language for fear that its poor use threatens French national identity, Americans are highly protective of their democratic symbols (e.g., flags) and feel threatened by Communism to a degree that other nations do not. The American case also illustrates that ideology is just as much a defining national characteristic as language or religion. Thus, studies that narrowly focus on the measurable cultural attributes completely miss the point of language and religion as a characteristic of nationhood. Simply identifying who speaks what language or practices which religion does not indicate a person's national identity.

Ethnic groups and nations have many similarities in that they are defined by distinctive sets of subjectively perceived cultural attributes. Despite their similarities, ethnic groups and nations have their differences. First, ethnic groups do not always exhibit self-awareness as nations do

(Connor 1978, 390). Ethnic groups are often conceived of and defined by outside observers, such as academics, nations, and states, whereas nations express a strong sense of unity. Second, ethnic groups do not possess, or strive to possess, a genuine political self-government. Therefore, ethnic groups do not have their own states or struggle to establish them for themselves. Consequently, while "national struggle for independence" and "nation-state" are necessary conditions of nationhood, the concept of ethnic group has not spawned the same corollary concepts of "ethnic struggle for independence" and "ethnic group-state." Indeed, when an ethnic group develops the desire for political self-government, it has by definition become a nation.

Modern nations' desire for self-government sets nations apart from ethnic groups in another way. Self-government requires sovereignty over territory, expressed in the form of a state. Nations need to craft their own laws to protect their culture, but laws apply to people only via territory and do not follow people wherever they travel. Not surprisingly, nations that do not have sovereignty over territory struggle to establish their own states. Such struggles are commonly very persistent and violent as stateless nations feel that they are vulnerable and may also feel that their national rights are violated until they obtain their own states.

Nations may define themselves in varying ways that are not simple and straightforward. Yet despite the breadth of self-definitions, it is possible to construct a definition of *nation* based on the characteristics identified thus far. One created by Konstantin Symmons-Symonolewicz is all-encompassing and very applicable to the nations of the world. Symmons-Symonolewicz defines a nation as

> a territorially-based community of human beings sharing a distinct variant of modern culture, bound together by a strong sentiment of unity and solidarity, marked by a clear historically-rooted consciousness of national identity, and possessing, or striving to possess, a genuine political self-government. (1985, 221)

The Dynamics of Nationhood

Nations may differ from racial groups, tribes, and ethnic groups but coexist and overlap with these other forms of identities, making identity multilayered for most individuals. Racial groups, tribes, and ethnic groups frequently exist as subgroups within nations. Some nations, such as Americans, are composed of many racial and ethnic groups. Americans will identify their ethnicities, for example, in such combinations as African American, Irish American, Japanese American, etc. The first word indicates ethnicity and the second nationhood. Such terms indicate that nations can be multiethnic. Despite the cultural differences of the differing ethnicities, peaceful coexistence occurs because they accept, even desire, the same laws of American nationhood. Because nationhood is very political, one way to distinguish between ethnicity and nationhood is to identify where an individual's political loyalty lies. In times of crisis, such as war, the various ethnic groups will pull together as Americans to protect their laws and their land.

Though many ethnic groups may live as minorities of nations, a number of ethnic groups—such as the Jews and the Arabs—can be found as members of many different nations.[7] They may be larger than nations, but their ethnic and national identities are likewise distinguished by their political loyalties. Thus Arabs, for example, will go to war with one another if their varying national identities come into conflict. The loyalty and cohesiveness of national identity overweigh the shared cultural characteristics of ethnicity.

The overlapping of national identities with racial, tribal, and ethnic identities occurs because nations will often derive their characteristics from one of these other forms of identity. For example, when racial groups, tribes, and ethnic groups become politicized, they will develop senses of nationhood as they develop the desire for self-governance and their own states. A number of nations trace their origins or tie their identities to particular racial, tribal, or ethnic characteristics.

The interplay between national identities and racial, tribal, and ethnic identities is also fueled by other factors. Groups' perceptions of themselves evolve over time. Group identity also evolves with stereotyping and persecution and by government manipulation.

Evolution from Within

In broad terms, as time and historical experience progress, nations' perceptions of themselves will evolve. Americans, for example, have become increasingly inclusive over time. In the late eighteenth century, American nationhood was restricted to white males. In time, the definition of "white" expanded, as illustrated in the book *How the Irish Became White* (Ignatiev 1995). Following the experiences of the Civil War, new migrations of peoples, and a great host of other events, other racial groups and women became fully fledged Americans. By the late twentieth century, Americans became concerned with expunging Eurocentric views from American society.

Not all nations become more inclusive as their perceptions of themselves evolve. Some become more exclusionary. This situation, for example, occurred with the rise of Nazi Germany. Most ethnic Jews within Germany accepted German national identity and did not feel that their religious beliefs and cultural practices disqualified them from being part of the German nation. The Nazis, however, redefined German identity, and conflict resulted. It is important to note that the Jews did not exclude themselves but were, in fact, excluded. Ted Rogane[8] best illustrates this point when he said, "Up until 1933, my mother was a German. All of a sudden, Hitler comes to power and you are not a German—you are a Jew" (Mortenson 1992, C1).

If racial, tribal, and ethnic groups are excluded or simply do not share the same sense of belonging or the desire for self-government with their host nations, tension will arise, often resulting in the rise of a separate national consciousness among members of these groups. The tensions that arise between racial, tribal, and ethnic groups on the one hand, with nations on the other hand, often come about when a dominant national group redefines the national identity in a way that contradicts the identity of one or more of its racial, tribal, or ethnic groups. For example, the continual exclusion of Jews in Europe led to the rise of a Jewish national consciousness among many Jews, known as Zionism.

The Jewish case is a poignant one but not a unique one. The redefinition of national identities by dominant groups and the resultant exclusion of ethnic minorities continue to serve as an important catalyst for the development of new national identities today. French speakers within Canada do not believe that their language disqualifies them from being Canadian. The poor treatment that they have received from English-speaking Canadians, however, has led to the emergence of a national consciousness among many French speakers. The rise of national consciousness in turn is leading to demands for political self-government. Similarly, some English speakers within the United States are trying to make English a necessary characteristic of American nationhood. While Spanish speakers do not feel disqualified from being American because they may not speak English, continued exclusionary treatment, particularly in the form of legislation, may cause Spanish speakers to reject American identity and develop a new national consciousness.

These cases illustrate that tribal, racial, ethnic, and national identities are not simple, unchanging givens. These forms of identity are very dynamic, with tribal, racial, and ethnic groups existing within nations, among nations, and often evolving into nations. Nations even contribute to the changing character of tribal, racial, and ethnic identities because national identities are ever changing themselves. As national identities change, they cause reevaluations of identities within ethnic groups.

That tribal, racial, and ethnic groups and nations are closely related is illustrated by the interchangeable use of the terms without clear recognition of their distinct differences. Ironically, adherence to any form of these identities on the part of an entire population is often treated as excluding the other. Consequently, arguments arise, for example, as to whether a particularly named group is a tribe, race, ethnic group, or nation. However, American Hispanics show that identity is not so black and white as 48 percent identified themselves as "white," 42 percent said that they were "some other race," and 6 percent claimed to be multiracial in the 2000 census of the United States (U.S. Census Bureau 2001). Despite such surveys that show the complexity of identity, arguments continually arise as to whether such groups as the Jews, Scots, Catalans, etc., are ethnic groups or nations. Evidence is collected to support either argument, but no recognition is given to the possibility that some Jews, Scots, Catalans, etc., have a corresponding national consciousness while others have an ethnic identity within another nation. For example, individual Jews with a national consciousness (i.e., Zionists) want their own nation-state (i.e., Israel), while ethnic Jews who accept another national identity want to be in the nation-state of their appropriate national identity (e.g., Jewish Americans want to be in the American nation-state). By the same token, Scots with a national consciousness want an independent Scottish nation-state but ethnic Scots are content to stay within Great Britain. In other words, an entire population does not have to be classified as exclusively an ethnic group or a nation. Moreover, the numbers within a population that subscribe to either an ethnic or a national identity are likely to be ever changing, depending on the evolving political, economic, and social circumstances that affect them.[9]

On those occasions when tribal, racial, or ethnic groups develop national consciousness, they are confronted with being within the states of other nations. Before long, members of these emerging nations realize that full nationhood cannot be achieved without political independence, a condition which can be achieved only with sovereignty over territory. When this realization occurs, the struggle for an independent nation-state begins. At any given moment in modern history, the world has fully developed nations with political self-rule and territorial sovereignty, nations striving for it, and nations still in their embryonic state. The world's nations are not static and fixed, but evolutionary, with some nations being very mature and new ones being born before our eyes.

Some researchers do not recognize that the desire for political self-rule and territorial sovereignty are necessary conditions for nationhood (Gallagher 1995, 717-18; Seton-Watson 1977, 1; Shafer 1972, 18). They point to multinational states such as the United Kingdom and Spain. These examples, however, do not refute the aforementioned characteristics of the term *nation* but, in fact, confirm them. To simply point out that Scots, Welsh, and English coexist within the United Kingdom and that Basques and Catalans live with the Spanish in the same state is to paper over the tensions that exist among these peoples. Such a conclusion also ignores that the most discontent among these peoples (i.e., Scots, Welsh, Irish, Basques, and Catalans) and the ones calling for political self-rule and territorial sovereignty are the ones who call themselves nationalists. The attempt to use the United Kingdom or Spain as a refutation likewise fails to take into account that not every individual among the Scots, Welsh, Irish, Basques, and Catalans has expressed national consciousness though these peoples are collectively dubbed nations. Also, looking at the political map and noting that Great Britain and Spain are multinational is treating nationhood as a static concept and not recognizing that an evolutionary process is unfolding which, in fact, may require a redrawing of the political map to accommodate the nationalist aspirations of these peoples, thus proving that the desire for political self-rule and territorial sovereignty are necessary conditions for nationhood.

Stereotyping and Persecution

People in one place may think of themselves in a particular way but are forced to think of themselves differently when living in other places among other people(s). For example, Japanese, Chinese, and Vietnamese peoples are unlikely to see their cultures as closely related to one another as they live in East and Southeast Asia. However, Japanese, Chinese, and Vietnamese living as ethnic minorities in Europe or North America may find that the dominant groups around them see little difference between them and generally stereotype them as "Orientals" or "Asians." Such stereotyping may be offensive, but surrounded by ethnic groups with differences much greater than differences between themselves, Japanese, Chinese, and Vietnamese may then see commonalities, develop a broader identity, and accept a term such as *Asian*. The bond is likely to be hastened if surrounding groups—seeing little difference between them—persecute them.

The development of an "Asian" group from stereotyping and persecution is hardly a unique circumstance. Mexicans, Nicaraguans, and Argentineans may feel that they have little in common until they live as minorities in the United States, where they have come to accept "Latino" and "Hispanic" identities. In the case of indigenous Americans, they did not move to a new land but found themselves minorities as European settlers came to outnumber and overpower them. Though these indigenous peoples had their own tribal names, they were labeled with "Indian" and later "Native American"—as *America* is a European name. At some level, however, they came to accept these categorizations.

Not all individuals passively accept the broad labels placed upon them. Many actually embrace the categorizations and actively pursue pan-movements to unite those who fall under such conceptions. Noteworthy, pan-movements frequently begin among people who live as minorities in other lands. For example, few people from Africa attended the first Pan-African Congress—held in 1919. Most were from the West Indies and the United States, and the congress was held in Paris. Later Pan-African congresses also had very few representatives from Africa[10] (Du-Bois 1970, 372-87). Author Richard Rodriguez notes the following about Hispanics:

> The interesting thing about Hispanics is that you will never meet us in Latin America. You may meet Chileans and Peruvians and Mexicans. You will not meet Hispanics. If you inquire in Lima or Bogotá about Hispanics, you will be referred to Dallas. For "Hispanic" is a gringo contrivance, a definition of the world according to European patterns of colonization. (2003, B11)

Some of these identities may not be fully formed ethnic or national identities. If so, it would not be because they are "artificial" but because they are still in their embryonic or infant stages. They show that ethnic groups and nations are not fixed and unchanging entities existing from the beginning of time but rather the result of the grouping and regrouping of individuals as peoples in differing combinations and expressions as time progresses. They also indicate that many taken-for-granted groups are products of similar processes. For example, Germans are the outcome of the coalescing of Bavarians, Hessians, Prussians, and a number of other peoples who likewise have not lost these other forms of identity but now see them as parts of a greater whole rather than wholes by themselves as their ancestors conceived of them. Italians, too, resulted from the merging of Venetian, Tuscan, Sicilian, and a variety of other identities. It means that the Pan-Slavic,[11] Pan-Arab, and a number of other pan-movements—some of which have yet to be conceived of—may some day evolve into identities that are as cohesive as any other currently existing ethnic or national identities.

Governmental Manipulation

Governmental manipulation works hand in hand with stereotyping and persecution. Dominant ethnic groups and nations will employ governmental mechanisms to persecute and categorize minorities according to their stereotyped views of these minorities. For example, the South African government created identity categories of "white," "black," "colored," and "Asian" under its policies of apartheid (Poulsen 1995, 232-35) and slotted people according to its perceptions of what these categories meant. It is important to understand that the South African government not only racially discriminated, but it also determined which racial categories would exist and who would belong in them. In addition, the South African government not only persecuted tribes but altered tribal categories and identities (Desmond 1971). It fabricated tribal names by both slicing up and splicing together existing tribal names. It then pasted these names on designated "homelands" and forced people into these homelands, dividing some existing tribes as they were sent to different homelands while grouping other tribes together.[12]

Governmental manipulation is not confined to peoples falling under the jurisdictions of state governments. Many state governments will manipulate peoples within other states to destabilize opposing governments. During the First World War, the Allied powers—particularly the United States under the leadership of Woodrow Wilson—fueled national consciousness by promising national self-determination. Such promises contributed to the demise of both the Austro-Hungarian and Ottoman empires. In the latter case, the British government sent T. E. Lawrence (a.k.a. Lawrence of Arabia) to Southwest Asia (a.k.a. the Middle East) to promote Arab nationalism. More recently, George Bush fanned Kurdish nationalism in the 1991 Gulf War in an attempt to topple Saddam Hussein within Iraq. The legacy of these governmental manipulations is still felt today. Though these national identities may have emerged on their own without manipulation by outside governments, these manipulations give rise to certain questions: Would these nations have suffered as many tragedies had they not been manipulated, and would the characters of these nations be what they are today had they not been manipulated? For example, after the Kurds rose up against Saddam Hussein, many of them

were slaughtered. Certainly, such an experience had a profound and perhaps an adverse effect on the Kurdish national psyche.

Nations versus Countries and States

It was noted earlier in this chapter that the term *nation* is frequently applied to countries and states, including nation-states. For example, both
France and the French are called nations. It is also not uncommon to hear
nation applied to both a people and a country or state in close juxtaposi-
tion. For example, statements are made to the effect that "It rained across
that nation as the nation mourned its loss." One example of this varied
use of the term *nation* is seen in the book *Yugoslavia: Death of a Nation*
(Silber and Little 1997). The title seems to apply the term to a country:
Yugoslavia. However, the following text also calls Yugoslavia a state
and uses the word *nation* in other ways:

> As Communism declined in the late 1980s, Yugoslavia, was, in many
> ways, better placed than any other Communist state to make the transi-
> tion to multi-party democracy, either as a single state, or as a group of
> successor states. There was a real chance for Yugoslavia to take its
> place in a new and, at that time, hopeful community of European na-
> tions. (26)

> The [SDS] party repeatedly declared that Izetbegović was not entitled
> to preside over the Serbian people, because under his leadership Bos-
> nia-Herzegovina supported Slovenia and Croatia in their wars against
> Yugoslavia. This policy, they argued, would leave the Serbs scattered
> across several separate states. The nation would be vulnerable to ex-
> termination said a Party statement of July 11. The SDS deputies said
> their boycott precluded them from respecting any decision taken by
> Parliament, which was now comprised of only two nations—Muslims
> and Croats. (212-13)

I hesitate to single out Silber and Little for their muddled usage of the
term *nation* because such usage of nation can be found almost everywhere and because their book is otherwise well written. However, it is
precisely the mainstream character of their book that so fittingly illustrates how the term *nation* is so commonly and confusingly applied.
    The ambiguous use of *nation* derives in part at least from how the
usage of the term developed. When *nation* became part of the English
language in the late thirteenth century, it clearly referred to those who

were blood related. However, by the seventeenth century, nation was applied to the inhabitants of a country regardless of a shared breed or race (Connor 1978, 381; Raymond Williams 1976, 178). Thus, though the term continued to refer to groups of people, the common denominator of this identity became territory. From there, it is understandable the term *nation* was later applied to countries. Though the popular practice of interchanging *nation* with such terms as *country* and *state* lacks clarity and is avoided by academics who research nations and nationalism, popular usage of the term indicates that nations are somehow tied to territory. Indeed, most nations receive their names from places. For example, the French, Swiss, and German nations derive their names from places (e.g., France, Switzerland, and Germany), not languages.[13]

The inappropriate substitution of *nation* for such terms as *country* and *state* is also reinforced by the ideology of nationalism. Modern nationalism advocates a world in which the spatial extent of political units is coterminous with the spatial distributions of nations (Connor 1978, 381-82; Gellner 1983, 1-7). Reality does not conform to this principle of nationalist ideology because many political units (e.g., states) contain multiple nations (albeit with tension), and a number of nations are distributed across two or more political units (see figure 2.1). Nevertheless, the belief in "one people-one state" leads many to assume that the existence of a state implies the existence of a people with a similar name. Because the world's political map, for example, contains a Somalia, a Zaire, and at one time a Yugoslavia, many would assume that there are or were Somalian, Zairian, and Yugoslavian nations. People and state become linked so closely together that they essentially become indistinguishable and, therefore, are used interchangeably. Some of the best examples are the names of organizations such as the International Monetary Fund, the International Court of Justice, and the United Nations. The presence of the term *nation* in the names of these organizations implies that the basic building blocks of these organizations are peoples, and that these organizations are to serve peoples. On the contrary, members of these organizations are states, not nations.[14] While it is true that the member states nominally represent nations,[15] nations without states are not represented. Describing these organizations for what they are, their names should be the "Interstate Monetary Fund," the "Interstate Court of Justice," and the "United States"! Governments of multinational states also encourage the interchange of the terms *nation* and *state*. Such substitutions promote the idea that the government and state exist to serve a single nation with the same name. This gives legitimacy to the governments of states with diverse and disunited populations, thereby helping

Chapter Two

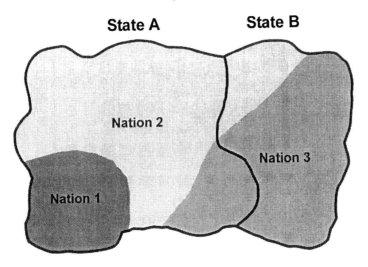

Figure 2.1 Nations and States
Illustration showing examples of the kinds of spatial disjunctions that can exist between nations and states.

such governments to perpetuate themselves.

The inappropriate substitution of the term *nation* for *country* and *state* actually illustrates the close link between people and place. While many researchers consider the temporal development of nations, few realize that nations develop spatially as well. Nevertheless, the concept of place and territory manifests itself in some form in many definitions of nation (Alter 1994, 1-15; Benedict Anderson 1991, 7; van den Berghe 1981, 61; Stalin 1994, 19-20). Konstantin Symmons-Symonolewicz's definition of the modern nation, which begins with the phrase "territorially-based community," is just one example.

The Significance of Place and Territory

Place and territory are significant to nations for two major reasons. First, they contain within them the natural resources that contribute to the particularities of human culture. The emphasis here is on quality, not quantity, which often leads us to unsubstantiated conclusions about self-sufficiency and security. Quality of natural resources focuses more on the spatial variations within nature and how they in turn contribute to the varying character of human identity from region to region. Second, place and territory are important from the cultural perspective as well. Nations express their identities in the cultural landscape of places and territories. In turn, identities are reinforced in the members of the nation and passed on from generation to generation through the cultural landscape. Because nations derive their identities from the natural and cultural environments, nations need to have sovereign political control over place and territory. Sovereignty means the ability to enact and enforce laws to protect and cultivate national identity. Because laws need to be tied to place and territory to be effective, nations need place and territory to enact and enforce laws that protect their natural and cultural environments.

Natural Resources

At one level, place and territory are significant because they contain the natural resources that sustain human life. We obviously cannot survive without air, water, and food. Because place and territory provide us with these necessities, our lives are connected to place and territory to such a degree that we are dependent on them. This dependency, however, is not limited to mere survival, for our luxuries are likewise derived from the resources of place and territory. Resources then are a common denominator for all societies, from the most primitive to the most extravagant.

Resources are not the same everywhere. Some places and territories obviously contain more than others, and the kinds of resources vary as well. Human beings have been acutely aware of the areal differences in the quality and quantity of resources for time immemorial. The uneven distribution of the earth's resources is at the source of many conflicts that have arisen between and within human societies. Not surprisingly, modern analysts, including many geographers, have become preoccupied with the location of resources. Resource location is certainly significant, but locational analysis of resources is often pursued on the assumption that humans, whether individuals or societies, struggle for resources simply to improve material conditions, usually characterized as basic human greed when not directly related to survival.

The conclusion that human beings struggle for resources out of greed has overshadowed the other significant attributes of resources. What is forgotten is that the particular resources of places and territories fundamentally shape human culture. We human beings, of course, have the ability to use resources any way we choose, resulting in groups with varying cultural characteristics despite similar availability of resources. Therefore, the argument here is not for environmental determinism but for cultural possibilism. Nevertheless, despite the ability of human beings to interpret their natural environments differently, they can create material cultures only from the possibilities that particular natural environments offer in each place and territory. This means that the spatial variations that exist in culture are partially tied to the spatial variations of natural resources. So from the perspective of natural resources, the uniqueness of place and territory is an attribute of ethnic and national identities.

That each place and territory contains within it different resources is seemingly more important prior to the rise of advanced technology that characterizes modern society. Nevertheless, while modern technologies may allow human beings to break free from the restrictions presented by the limited resources found in each place and territory, the uneven and varied distribution of resources in the world has not become insignificant to human culture. Many cultures, despite their modernity, still reflect the characteristics of particular natural environments. David Sopher points out that Jewish culture, for example, is largely derived from the natural environment of the Eastern Mediterranean. He shows that Jewish holidays are tied to the seasonal rhythms of the Eastern Mediterranean environment which in turn resulted in particular agricultural practices, diets, and lifestyles (Sopher 1967, 5, 19-21).[16] In other words, if Judaism had originated in another place in the world, it would have developed into something much different than it is today. Furthermore, even though Jews are found all over the world, they still have many cultural characteristics that are derived from the Eastern Mediterranean environment. No wonder then that modern Zionists chose the Eastern Mediterranean for a modern Jewish nation-state. The nation-state ideal requires only an independent state with sovereignty over territory; a specific territory is not required. Zionists even had offers of territory in other countries but rejected them in favor of the territory of ancient Israel (Glassner and Fahrer 2004, 15). The Eastern Mediterranean obviously continued to have meaning for Zionists, even though their ancestors had been separated from it for many centuries. Not to recognize this meaning requires one to ask why Zionists chose the resource-poor and politically hostile Eastern Mediterranean for a modern Jewish state.

The significance of place and territory for the natural resources they provide plays a key role in modern societies. Take the French, Swiss, and Japanese, for example, three of the wealthiest and most technologically advanced nations in the world. All three of these nations have the ability to import just about any product they desire, thereby having the ability to reshape their cultures in any way they choose. Despite this ability, however, these nations continue using the products that were originally developed in their national territories. In cuisine alone, the French, the Swiss, and the Japanese have not given up their traditional foods for more globally consumed products like Coca-Cola, hamburgers, and pizza. Even though these nations certainly have increased their consumption of these products, it is still difficult to imagine these nations without their traditional foods that they developed in their national territories. Moreover, even though these nations can import many of their traditional foods from other areas of the world more cheaply than they can produce them at home, they tend not to. These nations, as well as others, show a preference for the types of products that have been traditionally grown in the home territory; they even show a bias for the actual products that they grow at home. Not only is wine a part of French culture, the French prefer to drink wines from France instead of buying cheaper wines from other countries.

Nations often profess that the products grown at home are superior to similar ones grown abroad, in foreign places and territories. Such beliefs can be attributed only to cultural particularities because they cannot be substantiated by rational scientific means. Nevertheless, nations subsequently will subsidize their home producers at great economic expense to protect them from foreign competition. Such subsidies are not rational from an economic perspective, yet even the wealthiest and most capitalistic nations subsidize certain home industries. Often it is in the name of protecting jobs, but the money could be more wisely spent developing competitive industries. Moreover, such subsidies are directed at industries producing goods in the home territory that are fundamentally a part of the national culture.

Emphasizing traditional foods is a concrete way of illustrating the importance of place and territory for the natural resources they provide. Other material traits in national cultures demonstrate linkages to the natural resources of particular places and territories. Many festivals and other celebrations may be tied to the natural environment. Combining diet with the myriad material traits of a nation, one sees the importance of place and territory: it becomes hard to imagine how the various nations of the world could be as they are if they had developed in places other than the ones where they have had a long-standing relationship with the natural world. Would French national identity still be what it is if it had developed in the tropical rain forests of South America? Would the Swiss nation still have the same character if it had developed on an island archipelago in the South Pacific? Would Japanese culture be what it is if it had developed in the deserts of North Africa? It is impossible to say exactly how the identities of these nations would have developed if they were born and had matured in these other natural environments. Only an environmental determinist would pretend to know how. Yet it is clear that these national identities would have developed differently in different natural environments. Therefore, from the perspective of natural resources alone, because place and territory shape the material traits of national cultures, they must be components of national identities as well.

Cultural Landscapes

Place and territory are significant to human identity beyond providing the natural resources that sustain human life and shape culture. They are crucial from a purely cultural perspective as well. As Edward Relph notes, places are

> profound centres of human experience. There is for everyone a deep association with the consciousness of the places where we were born and grew up, where we live now, or where we have had particularly moving experiences. This association seems to constitute a vital source of both individual and cultural identity and security, a point of departure from which we orient ourselves in the world. (1976, 430)

Place and territory as cultural phenomena are not passive, however. They contain the idea of the cultural landscape, which is an important medium for human beings "to embody their feelings, images, and thoughts in tangible material" (Tuan 1977, 17). This means that cultural identity is expressed and even invested in the landscape, making the cultural landscape a basis for common identity for members of a group. It is even possible to gain important insight into the characteristics of a cultural group by examining the group's landscape. The amount of space that a cultural group allocates to activities (e.g., economic, political, social, religious), as well as the locations assigned to these activities, reveals much about a cultural group's values and beliefs. Investigations of the cultural landscape illustrate that "place" is not separate and detached from the human condition but actually "an organized world of meaning" (Tuan 1977, 179) that is very much a part of human identity.

Reading the cultural landscape is an important means of understanding the character of a nation's identity; however, the cultural landscape has even greater significance: it plays a key role in the development of a common national consciousness among individuals. The particular spatial arrangements within the cultural landscape of a nation's territory dictate the movements and interactions of individuals, making such movements and interactions unique to the members of a nation, thus the basis of a common identity. In other words, as Peter Taylor notes, "Every social organization has its created space so that the spatiality is part of their being" (Taylor 1993, 84). Thus, the assertion "America is an automobile society" implies that the distinctive spatial arrangements found within the United States have led to social interactions and relationships which separate Americans from other nations.

In addition to contributing to the rise of a national identity with a certain character, the cultural landscapes of a nation's territory serve to maintain the national identity among individual members and to transmit the national identity to succeeding generations. Donald Meinig illustrates this aspect very well with the following: "Every mature nation has its symbolic landscapes. They are part of the shared set of ideas and memories which bind people together" (Meinig 1979, 164). Therefore, although language, religion, shared history, and even common ideology are often touted as common ingredients for a national identity, these national characteristics must be expressed in the cultural landscape.[17]

Nations that base their identity on a particular language need to be able to write their language in the cultural landscape: on street signs, on buildings, on billboards, etc. Nations cultivate their languages partly through this medium. Not to be able to do so, to have to use a foreign language, would be too repressive to the nation. Nations that have their own religious beliefs must be able to build places of worship and mourning, erect monuments of religious significance, and express their religious beliefs in myriad subtle ways in the landscape. Nations that cannot express their religious beliefs in the landscape and create landscapes to practice their religion's beliefs likewise are repressed. A sense of shared history and political ideology is also reflected and invested in the cultural landscape. Monuments are the obvious examples, but names of streets, buildings, plazas, parks, and even cities are also an important part of a nation's cultural landscape of history and ideology. Individuals learn the history and ideology of their nation when they are young; then, the expressions of history and ideology in the landscape serve as constant reminders of specific histories and ideologies and even make historical events and figures and ideological figures and beliefs more concrete, thus more real.[18] A nation unable to express its history and ideology in the landscape is in danger of losing these aspects of its identity. Territory then, with its cultural landscapes, "comes to be viewed as the repository of shared collective consciousness, the place wherein memory is rooted" (Williams and Smith 1983, 503). Moreover, the landscape of a nation's beliefs plays an important role in inculcating the national identity into individuals long after the formal educational experience of youth. As a constant, three-dimensional, visual reminder, the cultural landscape reinforces the shared national identity within the psyche of every individual on a daily basis, even transmitting the nation's characteristics from generation to generation.

The significance of place and territory is illustrated every time a dispute arises concerning the placement or treatment of some element in the cultural landscape. The inhabitants of a city can become incensed if a public place receives a name or becomes the location of a monument or artwork that does not reflect their identity. Likewise, the shift in identity requires the reconstruction of the cultural landscape before the identity shift can become complete. The world witnessed this process in the last decade as Communism was rejected in the former Soviet Union and Eastern Europe. Monuments to the Communist ideology were systematically destroyed, and street names, plaza names, and even city names that reflected Communist beliefs were changed immediately. Additionally, in non-Russian countries of the former Soviet Union and Eastern Europe, the landscape was filled not only with elements of Communism but also with reminders of foreign domination.[19] Vast sums of money were spent in destroying these landscapes, and much more was invested in building new monuments and other elements in the landscape that reflected the new sense of national pride. From the rational economic perspective, such behavior was, and is, perplexing. The economies of these countries were in shambles, and huge investments were needed to correct the situation, making the investments in monuments seem frivolous. For these nations, however, the Communist landscapes did not reflect their identities. For some, these landscapes were even constant reminders of past oppression. Thus East Europeans put great effort into destroying the Communist and other landscapes because it was necessary to eradicate Communism and foreign domination from their national identities. At the same time, these peoples spent vast sums of money constructing new landscapes as a necessary means of building new national identities. The energy that East Europeans have put into reconstructing their cultural landscapes illustrates how people and place are closely linked, even intertwined.

Both Natural and Cultural

Place and territory are significant and form a part of human identity, including national identity, because they provide the natural resources that sustain human life and they contain the cultural landscapes that both express human identity and reinforce various forms of group identity within individuals. Even though natural resources and cultural landscapes are two different phenomena that can be discussed separately, only a fine line separates them.[20] Aside from natural resources, human beings become very accustomed to the natural landscapes of places and territories, each with its own seasonal rhythms, climates, geomorphologies, and vegetation. These natural elements become engrained in the human psyche. In turn, human beings, including nations, begin to appreciate these natural landscapes not just for their resources but for their aesthetic beauty and begin to incorporate this sense of aesthetic beauty into poetry, art, and literature. Natural landscapes then become much like cultural landscapes in that we as human beings become very accustomed to them, and they in turn become meaningful to us, to such a degree that we begin to identify with them. Place then is composed of both culturally created and natural elements, intertwined and inseparable for human identity:

> [Place] is made up of experiences, mostly fleeting and undramatic, repeated day after day and over the span of years. It is a unique blend of sights, sounds, and smells, a unique harmony of natural and artificial rhythms such as times of sunset, of work and play. The feel of a place is registered in one's muscles and bones. (Tuan 1977, 183-84)

Though we as human beings appreciate the natural environment for its aesthetic beauty, we also interact with it, bestow our values upon it, and treat the earth's landscape like a canvas or a piece of wood, shaping it into something that has great meaning to us. The new blend of natural and human landscape reflects our efforts, aspirations, and dreams. It even reflects our identity, who we are and what we believe. And just like the canvas and the piece of wood, it is worth a lot more than the raw material we first possessed.

George Stewart noted that "Once, from the eastern ocean to the western ocean, the land stretched away without names. Nameless headlands split the surf; nameless lakes reflected nameless mountains; and nameless rivers flowed through nameless valleys into nameless bays" (1945, 3; also quoted in Loy 1989). Though we take place-names—also toponyms—for granted, it would seem very odd to live in places without names as Stewart describes. Indeed, few such places exist for humans have named just about every feature on earth's landscape. The naming of places is a fundamental way that we as human beings interact with territory and make it part of human identity. Toponyms then tell us about cultures and the kinds of bonds peoples have developed with particular places. Central and Eastern Europe is one of those interesting regions of the world because it also has allonyms—multiple names for given features (Randall 2001, 105). These allonyms are interesting because they indicate how different peoples view the same places, and how they have developed bonds to these places for differing reasons though they can also develop new group identities through their shared bonds of the same places. Far from advocating a world with nameless places, Stewart notes how the naming of places becomes part of and a reflection of human identity: "Men came at last, tribe following tribe, speaking different language and thinking different thoughts. According to their ways of speech and thought they gave names, and in their generations laid their bones by the streams and hills they had named" (1945, 3).

The belief that place and territory are inextricably linked with human identity is reflected in human speech in a number of ways. One of the most illustrative examples of this link is the adage "You can take the boy out of the country but you cannot take the country out of the boy." This adage, and its many variations which name specific places and territories, gives tacit recognition that we as human beings derive much of our identity from particular places. The influence that place has on our beliefs and personalities becomes obvious when we go to new places. We often behave awkwardly because we do not know the people or the course of events in these new places. We fit into new social groupings only when we have lived in new places long enough to have developed a full appreciation for the qualities of these new places, meaning that our identities have been reshaped by these new places.

A second example of human speech illustrating that place and territory are qualities of human identity is the first question usually put to a stranger: "Where are you from?" The answer to this question often reveals more about a person than the answer to any other question, a multitude of images and information. To say that one is from California, New York, or Georgia (or Germany, India, or China on another scale) reveals much about one's identity. Even in places like Northern Ireland where religious adherence seems to be the primary means of group identification, children in the Protestant and Catholic ghettos also pose this same question first. While the children are interested in religious affiliation, they determine it by identifying place of residence. On the other hand, if the answer to this question is a place or territory outside of Northern Ireland, then religious affiliation becomes unimportant, and volunteering one's religious belief is treated as a non sequitur. The children prefer to hear about other characteristics of the stranger's place of origin.[21]

Just as human identity is multilayered in the sense that we are indi-

viduals, members of families, communities, cities, provinces, and countries as well as members of social and religious groups and the like, our
identities are likewise tied to places and territories of differing geographic scales. Guntram Herb and David Kaplan apply the term *nested
identities* to the varying geographic scales of human identity (1999). One
illustration of nested identities comes from Bruce Feiler's book *Walking
the Bible*:

> As we sped along, I began to feel a certain pull from the landscape, and
> I realized that this trip had begun to affect me some place deep in my
> body. It wasn't my head, or my heart. It wasn't even my feet. It was
> someplace so new to me that I couldn't locate it at first, or give it a
> name. It was a feeling of gravity. A feeling that I wanted to take off all
> my clothes and lie facedown on the soil. At once I recalled my grand-
> mother's funeral and the gulping ache I felt when they tossed a handful
> of soil on her coffin: "From ashes to ashes, from dust to dust." Not until
> this car ride, staring at this soil, did I fully understand what that phrase
> meant. Adam had been made from dust; his name is derived from the
> word *adama*, earth. "For dust you are," God says to Adam, "and to dust
> you shall return." Here was the source of that soil, I realized, and at that
> moment I had to resist the temptation to leap out and touch it.
>
> So where did this feeling come from? For most of my life, my reli-
> gious identity was not connected to a particular place, and certainly not
> to any place in the Bible. As a fifth-generation American Jew from the
> South, I had a strong attachment to Judaism, but one based on family,
> community, ethics, public service; not spirituality or mysticism. And
> not on any deep-seated attachment to the Promised Land. Instead, I was
> attached to the South, and like many Jewish southerners, I struggled be-
> tween a religion that gave me a sense of identity and a place that made
> me feel at home.
>
> I always believed that I was able to venture far afield in my life be-
> cause I had a strong sense of family and a stronger sense of place. I
> wasn't looking for a new way of life, or a new place to call home.
> . . . What happened to me that afternoon in Turkey was that some ill-
> defined part of me, some homeless portion of my consciousness that I
> hadn't even realized was looking for a home suddenly found a place
> where it felt comfortable and surged forward to down anchor. Here was
> a piece of land—completely alien, yet completely familiar—that
> seemed to draw me to it in a way I never thought possible outside my
> hometown. It's as if my internal zip code were being recalibrated, as if
> my genes were being jiggled and respun.
> . . . This feeling triggered a question that would stick with me for the
> remainder of our travels. Was I imagining this connection because of a
> lifetime of biblical associations, or was this ground somehow part of

me already? Was I reacting to a spirit that existed in the place, or did that spirit exist within me? Was it in my DNA? (2001b, 30-32)

Basic human vocabulary also reveals strong emotional bonds that we humans have for particular places and territories—or *topophilia,* in turn illustrating that human identity is partially derived from place and territory. On the positive side, we have words like *home* and its derivations such as *hometown* and *homeland.* In contrast to the word *house,* which simply connotes a physical structure, *home* has deeper meaning, referring to the experiences, memories, and people that make up such a place.[22] Personified terms such as *motherland* and *fatherland* recognize that places and territories give us life, nurture and provide for us, and even protect us, making us who we are. Albert Schweitzer stated that living in one's ancestral homeland is "the most basic of all human rights" (Jordan 1996, 171). Not surprisingly, we refer to places and territories with our strongest words of endearment. In fact, "to die for one's country"[23] is one of the most noble and heroic sacrifices that one can make. To evade military service is treated with intense scorn, not only by governments but by members of the nation who believe it necessary to risk one's life to protect one's country.

On the negative side, we have words such as *homesickness,* which refers to a deep emotional longing for places and territories from which we are separated. This separation often results in profound feelings of despair and despondency. Even those of us who move and eventually adjust to new places and territories often feel that there is still "no place like home." Permanent separation from homeland makes one an *exile,* which most of us would consider a dreaded fate. Euripides even said that "There is no greater sorrow on earth than the loss of one's native land." The trauma of separation has molded exiled literary writers who have provided humanity with great works which eloquently express the significance of place to the human condition. As Andrew Gurr points out,

> In consequence of this separation from home in space as well as time, the writer characteristically centres his attention not so much on his sense of history (that was the preoccupation of the stay-at-homes of whom Yeats is perhaps the greatest example), as on his sense of home as a unit in space and time together. For the colonial exiles the search for identity and the construction of a vision of home amount to the same thing. (1981, 11)

Alienation from a cultural or physical home has radical effects on the writer's mind as well as his choice of theme. Joyce's life and art, inseparable as they are, make a kind of paradigm for the non-metropolitan writer in this century. Exiled by what might be called the mutual consent of the exile and the society sending him into exile, he spent his life obsessively rebuilding his home in his art. The characters in *Dubliners . . .* reappear in *A Portrait* and *Ulysses*. The geography is narrow and exact. . . . With Joyce, as with many other writers, the distance of exile only intensified the faithful minuteness with which the home was recorded. (1981, 15)

The power of place and the preoccupation that exiled writers have with their homelands as they attempt to hold on to their identities are echoed by Jan Vladislav as well:

With some effort, or nostalgia, we can evoke our country's true geography. Slowly but correctly, we can redraw its faded contours. . . .

Our home is the place from which we originate, and toward which we turn to look from an ever-increasing distance. Our home is a point in time which we have lost, but can always rediscover, along with details which we would not even have noticed *then, on the spot.* . . . This is not only a question of individual memory but, for a man's home, fixed in time, is shaped not only by his own history, but also by the histories of those who surround him, by his family and his tribe, and by the palpable history of tilled fields, of ancient villages and new cities, and above all by that changeable, unfathomable, mythic reservoir of his native language.

A man's native village can be engulfed by the waters of a dam, a city can be razed to the ground by bombs, a landscape can be rendered unrecognizable by the creative as well as the destructive activity of man. But one thing never changes. We never stop carrying within us this meeting place with ourselves, with all our successive and abandoned selves, this place of recognition, of acceptance or rejection of ourselves and the rest of the world. Perhaps that is the hell which each of us is said to carry in his heart. But if our hell is there, so too is our paradise. . . . *To live one's own life* means to protect a home within oneself, an elusive yet real home. It means to provide a refuge for one's personal history, one's family traditions, one's language, one's ideas, *one's native land.* To live an alien life, even if only a few feet from his place of birth, is to lose all of this. To accept an alien life is to accept an alien death—and that is notably the lot of those forced into exile.

. . . The state has at its disposal only one means of imposing a foreign existence on a man who wants to lead his own life: exile is a death penalty in effigy which aims at destroying everything that makes up man's life, his history, his particular language, in brief, his *home,* and makes a foreigner of him everywhere. Only the man who is determined to refuse to live an alien, imaginary life is immunized against such a sentence, for it cannot reach his world. This path may lead to self-deception, suffering, and tragedy, but it will not destroy him. His native land, which has made him and which allows him to live his own life to the end, cannot be stolen from him. This native land, which a man cannot abandon and which even more cannot be stolen from him, is not a hope, but a certainty, on which each one of us can rely, wherever we may be, whether in our home town or ten thousand miles away. (1990, 14-16)

Just as negative as exile and one of the greatest fears of individuals is *homelessness,* a form of placelessness. Homelessness not only represents a total loss of power within society, it even represents a total loss of identity: homeless people are treated as if they do not exist. Often such people are even stripped of the word *people* and simply referred to as *the homeless.* Without places of their own, homeless people have "no place in society."[24]

Because human identity is so closely tied to place and territory, the destruction of places and territories is an integral part of the expulsion and/or annihilation of individuals and peoples. If, for example, religion is the basis of a group's identity, then the destruction of places of worship and other sacred sites is tantamount to the destruction of the group's identity. If a strong sense of history is important to a group, then the destruction of that group's historical sites, memorials, libraries, and other places of historical significance is a means of eradicating that group. One group also cannot successfully supplant another group if the original group's places stand as a testimony to their existence. In practical terms, the new group cannot successfully cultivate its own identity within the landscapes of those they drove off—at least not without modifying those places. Quite simply, they require different places of worship, their own historical monuments, and their own language landscapes. Likewise, historical revisionists cannot successfully impress their new histories upon society if the old group's places remain as continual visual contradictions. Thus the destruction of places is fundamental to genocide and "ethnic cleansing," not just an unfortunate by-product of them. Andras Riedlmayer noted this point when he described the destruction of cultural sites in Bosnia-Herzegovina in the 1990s: "We are still told that 'ancient hatreds' are what fuel this destruction, but that is not true. The history that is being erased, both buildings and documents, speak eloquently of centuries of pluralism and tolerance in Bosnia. It is evidence of a successfully-shared past that the nationalists seek to destroy" (1995a, 1). In fact, Riedlmayer illustrates this point in the titles of some of his works: *Killing Memory: Bosnia's Cultural Heritage and Its Destruction* (1994), *Killing Memory: The Targeting of Bosnia's Cultural Heritage* (1995a), and "Erasing the Past: The Destruction of Libraries and Archives in Bosnia Herzegovina" (1995b).

Territoriality

Because human identity is derived from, expressed, and even invested in place and territory, it logically follows that we as human beings become very protective of the places and territories that define our identities. Indeed, we need to be able to exert some degree of political control over place and territory if we are to obtain and exploit natural resources and maintain the natural and cultural landscapes that shape and define our identities. Place and territory are necessary even for governance, which entails the ability to enact and execute laws. Because all laws have to be tied to place and territory to be effective and meaningful, the possession of place and territory is necessary for governance. This need we have to exert some degree of control over and to protect place and territory is referred to as *territoriality*.[25]

Territoriality exists at all levels of human identity, from that of the individual to that of the nation. At the individual level, territoriality is commonly called personal space. Personal space includes the envelope of air surrounding our bodies as well as the places that we require for our various activities (workplaces, living spaces, etc.). Because our individual identities are tied to the small spaces that we occupy while going about our daily lives, it is not surprising that we exhibit a protectiveness over our personal spaces, cautioning others not to violate them. Our protectiveness is often demonstrated by nameplates, signs, and other markings that make it clear to others that a particular space belongs to us or is under our control. The need for individuals to occupy and use places, often exclusively, is protected by laws within societies. Trespassing, assault, theft, and vandalism, all related to the transgression of personal space, are all treated within societies as serious crimes. Even though theft and vandalism seem to apply to inanimate objects, we as individuals feel personally violated when our personal spaces have been transgressed by such acts. The importance of personal space is illustrated even by social, economic, and political status, those with high status occupying the largest spaces in the most desirable locations.[26]

Territoriality is an expression not only of individuality but of group identity as well. Families, communities, and nations exhibit the need to protect the places and territories that they use to define their identities. Similar to individuals, social groups demonstrate their territoriality by posting signs and erecting boundary markers, walls, fences, etc. Fraternities and sororities congregate in houses and explicitly decorate them with symbols and banners to declare their presence and control over a particular space. Furthermore, the spaces that fraternities and sororities establish control over are necessary for the healthy functioning of these social groups. Likewise, retired people often express the need to congregate in retirement communities where they can erect fences and gates. This practice preserves a way of life by keeping children and others away. Illegal social groupings such as gangs also feel the need to protect themselves by establishing control over space; graffiti mark the limits of a gang's territory, contributing to the protection of a gang by warning others to stay out. These examples illustrate that territoriality is related to the concept of segregation, which also involves the control of space, often requiring its reorganization. What group can segregate itself or others without reassigning geographic space?

Once social groups are able to establish control over demarcated spaces and territories, they are then able to enact rules and enforce them to protect and cultivate the group's identity. At higher levels of identity, rules become laws, and more formalized policing agencies are formed. At the national level, in addition to a national police, a military exists to protect the nation's territory from transgression. Protecting a group's territory and protecting a group's identity go hand in hand and are inseparable. For small social groups that see themselves as part of a larger society, political independence is not necessary to exercise control over their social spaces. Only a small degree of autonomy is necessary to express territoriality. On the other hand, nations express a territoriality that requires independent statehood because nations have a strong sense of self-awareness and a desire for self-rule. Nations can achieve self-rule only by having complete sovereign control over a given territory. Nations sharing a territory with other nations inevitably will feel that their rights are impinged upon by the other nations, as these other nations attempt to enact and enforce laws within the common territory to cultivate and protect their identities.

Territoriality seems fundamental to the human condition; consequently, many have argued that it is a biological need, genetically ingrained (Ardrey 1966; Dawkins 1976; Malmberg 1980). On the other hand, territoriality is expressed with considerable variation from individual to individual and social group to social group, suggesting that it is a cultural phenomenon rather than a biological one. Some researchers who believe that territoriality is a cultural phenomenon have noted that hunter-gatherer societies—a social form most closely tied to the land—

demonstrate the weakest forms of territoriality (Alland 1972; Rosenberg 1990). The varying expressions of territoriality and the weak expressions of territoriality demonstrated by hunter-gatherer societies certainly suggest that territoriality is more cultural than biological. Nevertheless, it is noteworthy that social groups demonstrating weak forms of territoriality have been systematically destroyed by social groups expressing strong forms of territoriality.

Of these latter groups, the nation has the strongest form of territoriality. Not surprisingly, we live in an era known as the nation-state era, the name of which indicates that the nation and its form of identity hold primacy over all other social groups and levels of identity. The primacy of nationhood is shown by the earth's surface having been divided into territories nominally defined by nations. Ultimate sovereign authority rests with national governments; larger political organizations such as the United Nations have very little authority without the consent of national governments. Moreover, almost all human beings, regardless of their social groupings, have voluntarily accepted a national identity or have had one forced upon them by national governments. Even though individuals and more localized communities may exercise autonomy vis-à-vis the nation, such autonomy is possible only with the consent of the nation. The nation has the ability to compel individuals and communities, with force if necessary, to conform to the desires and needs of the nation. Individuals and communities may have rights, but these rights can be revoked by national governments. Individuals and communities do not have the same ability in regard to the nation. Therefore, unlike nations, individuals and communities often have to sacrifice their needs to the nation, compromising and frequently altering their identities.

Because we live in the nation-state era, and nations express a strong sense of territoriality, territoriality must be addressed as part of the idea of the nation and be incorporated within the definition of the term. Nevertheless, as noted, territoriality is not exclusively expressed by the nation but by other forms of human identity as well. Territoriality then is multilayered, exactly like the general concept of identity itself. Every person has not only an individual identity but some sense of a familial, community, and national identity, all at the same time. These levels of identity do not act independently but interdependently. The national identity influences and shapes smaller scale identities, including individual ones. At the same time, individual and familial identities shape and influence broader levels of identity, such as the nation. A continual interplay of characteristics exists between the various levels of identity, both within individuals and between individuals and their social groups. A changed characteristic at one level of identity necessarily reverberates through all levels, requiring a reevaluation of identity at all other levels. For example, when a nation goes to war, communities and individual members of the nation will participate in their nation's struggle. The experience of war in return may profoundly change the way in which communities and individuals see themselves, their nation, and other nations. Similarly, individuals and communities may impart their characteristics on other members of their nation. For example, immigrants to the United States change the character of American identity as they share their cultural practices. As a more specific example, Laotian Hmong and Mexicans live side by side in Merced, California. The two groups generally do not get along, but it is interesting to note that when the Loatian children complain about the Mexican children, they do so by speaking English with a Spanish accent (Rodriguez 2003, B11). Moreover, while new immigrants are changing the character of American identity, longer established Americans are trying to shape American identity by insisting that all Americans must speak one language and/or practice one religion—namely, speak English and/or adopt Christian values. Other nations may have few immigrants and be more culturally homogeneous yet certain small groups with unusual ideologies or dogmas may seek to impress their beliefs on their nations. As a characteristic of human identity, territoriality exists at all levels of identity and is part of the interplay between levels of identity. In a manner of speaking, a given nation's sense of territoriality is the product of many personal spaces interacting, and personal spaces are shaped by the nation's sense of territoriality. One of the most interesting examples of this process is found in the answer that Richard Rodriguez gave to Bill Moyers in an interview when asked if he was an American or Hispanic:

> I answered that I am Chinese, and that is because I live in a Chinese city and because I want to be Chinese. Well, why not? Some Chinese-American people in the Richmond and Sunset district of San Francisco sometimes paint their houses (so many qualifiers!) in colors I would once have described as garish: lime greens, rose reds, pumpkin. But I have lived in a Chinese city for so long that my eye has taken on that palette, has come to prefer lime greens and rose reds and all the inventions of this Chinese Mediterranean. I see photographs in magazines or documentary footage of China, especially rural China, and I see what I recognize as home. Isn't that odd? (2003, B11)

Rodriguez's statement is noteworthy because it not only illustrates how identities interact with one another and give rise to new forms of identity, but also that identities remain inextricably intertwined with place and territory as they evolve. Moreover, Rodriguez's references to place and territory show that place and territory are not merely flat, utilitarian concepts with simple linkages to identity but socially constructed and reconstructed concepts with multiple dimensions and varying levels of meanings and attachments.

A Nation's Territory

National territoriality is more than large-scale personal space. Individuals have an intimate knowledge of their personal spaces; they create them and live within them. In contrast, individuals, although belonging to larger social groups, do not know every individual within their large social groups and likewise do not know the larger group territories intimately. In fact, most individuals have never even visited many areas within the territories of their social groupings, especially at the national level. Nevertheless, individuals, as members of nations, have strong emotional attachments to their nation's territory[27] and moreover express a clear sense of the areal extent of their nation's territory. Lacking intimate experience, one gets the sense of the national territory via the interplay of ideas between the various levels of identity. Quite simply, the emergence of a national identity and the sense of a particular national territory come through social interaction. In other words, individuals depend on their social groups to define their broader levels of identity, including the territorialities of these broader levels.

Because individuals develop their broader levels of identity and territorialities through social interaction, individuals' sense of identity and senses of territory can be manipulated; individuals also can be inculcated with particular ideas concerning their identity and territoriality, all because individuals of nations lack personal knowledge of all their fellow members and their nation's supposed territories. State governments as well as individuals and small groups—usually nationalists—can take advantage of social dynamics to inject particular ideas into society with the intent of shaping a national identity with certain cultural characteristics and a specific sense of territoriality. For example, the Ecuadoran government issued a postage stamp with a map of Ecuador showing Ecuador's boundaries extending deep into Peru (Glassner and Fahrer 2004, 89).[28] State governments in particular have the ability to make sure that the histories of certain places and territories are learned, with a prescribed emphasis placed on the value and significance of certain places and territories. State governments also have the ability to organize the cultural landscape in a particular way. The Argentine government, for example, has erected signs with a map of the Malvinas (Falklands) and a slogan that claims that the islands are Argentine, not British (Glassner and Fahrer 2004, 88).[29] State governments also have the ability to promote the use of particular symbols, images, religions, and languages. Just as important to consider, state governments can suppress ideas and beliefs as well as repress and persecute those who promote unwanted ideas that may cause nations to reevaluate themselves. The influence of state governments on the development of national identities is so great that it warrants further elaboration and will be the subject of the next chapter (chapter 3).

Manipulation notwithstanding, identity on its own is a dynamic phenomenon, with much of the dynamism deriving from the interplay between the various levels of identity, from that of the individual to that of the nation. The dynamic aspect of identity means that national identities evolve over time. Conceptions of national territories also evolve over time. In fact, they evolve concurrently because place and territory are components of national identity. Of course, events, politics, and innovations are active in the interplay between the various levels of identity and, therefore, influence the development of national identities. For example, when an innovation like the computer is introduced, people in each region will evaluate it differently; a national consensus will be worked out, and then each regional group will reevaluate it. Innovations do not need to be earth-shattering in their implications. Individually, their impact may be minor, yet cumulatively they are very significant. Subtle yet continual changes in farming practices, industrial technologies, and business methods often have a profound influence on culture over time. As a result of these changes, people's understandings of themselves and their place in the world changes as well. Additionally, new stimuli seldom occur uniformly throughout national territories. Wars, for example, may result in the partial occupation of nations' territories. Such occupations have differing implications for those who experience such occupations and those who do not. Again, national consensuses have to develop concerning the meaning of such occupations; national consensuses in turn cause a reevaluation at the regional and local levels. Historical processes play such profound roles in shaping group identities and explaining the current territorialities of nations that they will receive special emphasis in chapters 4 and 5.

Modern nationalists play a major role in the development of national identities and likewise how nations define and view their territories. For example, at one time people who lived in Prussia considered themselves to be Prussian first, and then German or Polish. Thus a Prussian identity existed and was intimately tied to a territory known as Prussia. However, after the rise of modern nationalism, German nationalists focused on language as the crucial, unifying factor of German identity. In response, Polish nationalists did the same (Herb 1993, 14; Holborn 1969, 294). Prussian identity, as a common identity of those living in Prussia, was eventually shunted aside by what it was to be German or Polish (Davies 1982, 2:131-32). As language became a new determinant of German and Polish national identities—and the national identities of many other Central and East Europeans—the meaning of place and territory evolved as well at the broader levels. Despite the heavy emphasis on language, German and Polish national identity did not evolve according to language alone but according to the new social interactions resulting from the new emphasis placed on language. These new social interactions, however, also carried with them individual and group territorialities that blended together to create national territorialities. Thus, Germany and Poland were not seen as simply synonymous with the spatial distributions of the German and Polish languages respectively or even with Germans and Poles. Indeed, the German and Polish nations delineated national territories for themselves that extended beyond the distribution of German and Polish speakers respectively. To understand why this occurred, it is necessary to realize that language was not the sole determinant in the evolution of identity.[30] The new emphasis on language brought about new social interactions that in turn brought about new territorialities.

The German and Polish cases illustrate that the actual delimitation of groups' senses of territory changes depending on the emphasis placed on other components of identity. For example, as Prussian identity changed, the concept of Prussia changed as well. The Prussian case is a typical example of group identities as they evolved in Central and Eastern Europe. Over the last few centuries, imperial ideologies have been replaced by nationalist ideologies. Imperial ideologies were primarily concerned with religious affiliation; language was generally considered to be an unimportant issue. With the rise of nationalism, language became paramount. Prussian leaders and hence Prussians shifted from being the protectors and propagators of Protestantism to the protectors and propagators of Germanism as defined by language. The shift in identity altered conceptions of place and territory. When language did not matter to Prussians, Prussia was an independent, sovereign unit and, most of all, a bulwark of Protestantism. However, when language became an issue,

Prussians rechanneled their religious fervor and developed the need to act and speak as exemplary Germans and be advocates for all of Germany. As a result, Prussia eventually became a subunit of Germany—a Germany with strong Prussian characteristics.

Despite changing identities for large-scale groups (e.g., nations) and the resulting changes in how place and territory became understood, people who live together in a place tend to develop a common identity through their shared experience of that place. In other words, place and territory can be a defining characteristic of a nation as much as language or religion. In fact, emotional attachments to place can take precedence over other characteristics despite any nationalist rhetoric. For example, many inhabitants of Bosnia see themselves as Bosnian first, then as Croats, Serbs, or Muslims. Religion is not the basis of Bosnian identity. However, as stated, national identity is very complex and easily manipulated by political leaders. By emphasizing certain components of group identity such as language or religion, political leaders are able to redefine a situation to their advantage and fulfill their ambitions. In the case of Bosnia, political leaders in Serbia and Croatia have not accepted a Bosnian identity and thus have tried to prevent the rest of the world from accepting one as well. They have forced the issue of religion in an attempt to delegitimize any sense of Bosnian identity. When a new version of group identity is created, a new group territory is likewise required. Often, of course, and by political design, the new national territory expands beyond the current boundaries of the political state. Political leaders then can claim restitution of national territories through military force. In most cases, political leaders claim historical territories that actually existed (Alexander Murphy 1990). In other cases, they claim "restitution" of fabricated historical territories.

Possession of territories has changed continually in Central Europe and Eastern Europe for many centuries, and, therefore, large-scale group identities have changed as well.[31] Consequently, modern nationalists have had to try to sew together regions that often were isolated from one another (even when in close geographical proximity). The task is monumental because many of the nation's territories were not focused on the modern national core areas. Moreover, many of the territories were divided among and manipulated by outside empires with foreign ideologies. Even under normal circumstances, members living in different regions have different ideas regarding the boundaries of the national territory. The boundaries of the national territory may even be somewhat unclear to its members. Even so, the territory is usually discussed as something whole and inviolable. Varied historical pasts and differing regional perceptions of a nation's members give political leaders the ability to manipulate a nation's sense of identity, including, of course, the nation's sense of place and territory.

The dynamics of social interaction, and the evolution of subjective ideas and conceptions that arise from it, provide a better explanation for actual nations' identities than any attempt to objectively map spatial patterns of language, religion, or any other cultural characteristic. In fact, the emphasis placed on language, religion, and many of the other cultural characteristics that modern nations may have is unwarranted when the evolution of social groups and social groupings is taken into account. When nationalism began to be a potent sociopolitical force a mere few hundred years ago, cultural characteristics were in constant transition across the landscape, providing no obvious means for drawing lines on maps that could identify nations. In the case of language, what became designated as either a language or a dialect had more to do with conceptions that arose in the human mind than with linguistics. The common but mistaken belief that those who speak the same language consider themselves to be one people did not conform to reality. In an attempt to make reality conform to human conceptions, many mutually intelligible forms of communication—which linguists would classify as dialects within a single language—instead were treated as separate and distinct languages; the reverse was done as well. The case of Serbian and Croatian illustrates this situation very well. Serbian and Croatian often were considered to be separate languages until these two peoples attempted to form a single Yugoslav nation. During the attempt to unify, Serbo-Croatian was the designated language, and the varying forms of communication of those involved were classified as dialects of the Serbo-Croatian language. Because the people who spoke the varying forms of communication were grouped together in a single territory, the varying forms of communication began to grow together. Following the breakup of the Yugoslav state, Serbian and Croatian now are considered to be separate languages by the people involved, despite any designation by linguists (Asher 1995, 18). Moreover, conscious efforts have been made by those involved to make Serbian and Croatian separate and distinct languages (Woodward 1996). These actions are being taken to make language conform to the perceived number of nations that exist. In other words, language does not determine national identity; national identity determines language. The case of the Irish language serves as an excellent example of this point as well. The Irish language almost died out completely while the Irish people remained firmly in *place*. It was not a resurgence in the use of the Irish language that led to a rise in Irish national identity but a rise in Irish national consciousness that brought about the revival of the Irish language. Even today, only a small percentage of Irish speak Irish as if it were their mother tongue, yet no one questions the fact that millions more are Irish. In fact, the Irish nation is defined by the territory called Ireland, not the Irish language. No one agrees with this statement more than Irish nationalists, whose primary obsession is to drive foreigners (i.e., British) and Irish traitors out of Northern Ireland.

In addition to language, religion and other cultural characteristics are defined by human conceptions as well, making them not only unreliable as national determinants but also unreliable in delineating nations' territories as they define them. How nations come to understand and define their cultural characteristics has to do with the interplay of all of these characteristics with one another; outside forces often influence this interplay. Until now, language and religion have been treated as constants that shape other national characteristics, including nations' understandings and identifications with particular territories. Languages and religions may be objectively described, but nations' understandings and identifications with languages or religions are not nearly so objective and concrete. Such understandings and identifications are not constants but instead are shaped by understandings and conceptions of other cultural characteristics. Territoriality is a cultural characteristic and is just as likely to shape and define other cultural characteristics as it is to be shaped by the other characteristics. In other words, territoriality is just as likely to shape nations' understandings and definitions of their languages and religions as it is to be shaped by nations' languages and religions. The question then arises as to how nations have come to conceive of and define their territories. This question is addressed again in the next chapters. Before addressing this question, however, we must find a means of locating the places and territories that nations develop strong emotional bonds with and hence come to identify with.

Indicators of a Nation's Sense of Territory

Although nations may express deep emotional attachments to particular places—topophilia—the spatial delimitation of national territories as nations themselves conceptualize them is not a simple matter. Competing regional identities, manipulative political leaders, and fervent nationalists, not to mention wars and the migrations of people, make the task of understanding the spatial extent of nations' "places" very difficult. Nevertheless, some insights can be gained by looking at the spatial distribution of three major indicators: (1) the sites identified by the locations of important institutions and of historical events; (2) the landscapes described in nationally renowned literature, poetry, art, and music; and (3) the historical willingness to use force to hold onto a particular territory—the "tenacity factor."

Site is perhaps the most tangible and easiest to identify. As mentioned earlier, elements in the landscape become symbols and as such serve as "repositories of memories" (Tuan 1974, 145) and concrete evidence and expressions of accomplishments. Seats of government, printing centers,[32] theaters, educational centers (e.g., schools, universities, research institutes), and religious centers (e.g., churches, monasteries, and pilgrimage sites) are the most common examples. Historic sites of battles and birthplaces are just as important, especially if monuments are erected to remind future generations—or even the current one—of who they are. Individual sites, especially those with institutions, not only can hold the cultural artifacts of nations but can house those individuals who preserve, protect, and cultivate these artifacts as well as the less tangible characteristics of nations' identities.[33] Because institutions and historic events are instrumental in defining given nations' identities and who adopts those national identities, then studying the locations of institutions and historic events is not only valuable but necessary in understanding how and where particular national identities emerge and develop.[34] Therefore, locating institutions and historic sites is an important first step in delineating nations' territories as nations themselves conceive of and understand them.

Site identification serves well for describing the built landscape, but landscape description is the most useful for identifying those elements in the natural landscape to which nations become emotionally bonded, and thus fall within nations' senses of territory. Landscape descriptions typically refer to misty mountains, rolling blue rivers, and golden fields of grain. Such references usually are interwoven with strong feelings of reverence and sanctity. Nationalist writers often put more effort into describing nations' territories than the social and cultural characteristics of nations themselves. Many national anthems typically make more references to national territories than to nations themselves. In essence, nations are depicted through descriptions of place and territory; small wonder then that the term *nation* so often is mistakenly used to refer to a place. Thus, by examining literature, poetry, music, and the visual arts, we can highlight and map the important and meaningful elements of the physical landscape for given nations.

The value of poetry, storytelling, music, and the visual arts (especially folk and popular forms of all four) is difficult to overestimate. Nationalism emerged at a time when most people were illiterate. The primary means of transmitting ideas and beliefs was through the oral tradition, supplemented through visual arts. Even in today's world, with its advanced technologies and the concomitant need for high levels of literacy, many significant ideas and beliefs are still transmitted in the informal settings of the pub, the sports field, church, and over the airwaves of radio and television. In fact, most people do not continue with a formal education into adulthood, and the few of us who do usually do not pursue a higher education for more than a small fraction of our adult lives. Therefore, folk and popular forms of communication are still the primary means for most to receive and transmit ideas and beliefs. In other words, the oral tradition is alive and well, continuing to play a vital role in most societies. In order to understand how nations feel about and conceive of their national territories, it is crucial to examine these forms of communication, summarized as landscape description in this work.

The last means of identifying nations' senses of territory is through an examination of the "tenacity factor." The tenacity factor is the measure of nations' willingness and determination to protect or seize a piece of territory. While the first two indicators are a means of identifying significant places, the tenacity factor demonstrates the degree of importance groups ascribe to given places. Although nations use places to define their identity, each place has a varying degree of significance. Therefore, only by examining the political-geographic history of a nation can we determine the significance of place. Specifically, this can be achieved by looking at attempts of national movements or national governments to seize or protect territory through declarations, policies, agreements, military actions, and alliances. In some cases, if nations are unable to maintain or obtain control of territories of minor significance, national identities are redefined to exclude those places. In other cases, territories may be so significant that nations find it very difficult to redefine their identity. In these circumstances, military action may continue even if the costs in human life are great.

Because place and territory vary in degree of significance, it is then possible to categorize them accordingly. For this research, two levels have been chosen: the nation's territories and periphery. The nation's territories include places of national significance, distinguished by maintaining significance over long periods and by being struggled for tenaciously. Political control is crucial to a nation's ability to maintain its sense of identity. The periphery contains places of some national significance, but not to the degree that possession is necessary. In fact, possession may not even be desired. The periphery is important because it ties the nation to the greater world around it, and provides examples of the nation's greatness by illustrating an extended spatial stretch of the nation's involvement in regional, even global, concerns.

The search for all three of the indicators that illustrate nations' senses of territory has to be undertaken on a nation-by-nation basis. Emotional attachments to place are a highly subjective matter; nations' territories are understood and delineated only through the eyes and emotions of nations themselves. In Central and Eastern Europe, many nations have had their sense of identity violated by the continual redistribution of territories. In an attempt to create stability and strengthen claims, many nationalist writers have written a great deal about their nation's territory.

Notes

1. Yi-Fu Tuan defines *topophilia* as "the affective bond between people and place or setting" (Tuan 1974, 4). Tuan has not only written a book about it but has devoted much of his academic career to exploring it.

2. For more information on eugenics, see Stefan Kühl's *The Nazi connection: Eugenics, American racism, and German National Socialism* (2002).

3. In the Spanish case, for example, why did New Spain separate itself from the Spanish Empire when those in control spoke Spanish and were Roman Catholic like those in the motherland? Not insignificant was that the breakaway occurred during, and even as a result of, a heightened period of nationalism. Why, too, did all of these Spanish-speaking Roman Catholics not identify with one another and thus stay together in a single unified New Spanish state? Moreover, why did many Spanish-speaking Roman Catholics form common bonds with the indigenous peoples instead of with one another as part of the rise in national consciousness? (Benedict Anderson 1991, 50-54)

4. The title of the book is *Aristarchus, sive de contemptu linguae Teutonicae* (1617) (Ergang [1931] 1976, 140).

5. Most Ukrainians practice Ukrainian Orthodoxy, but it is not uncommon for Ukrainians in western Ukraine to subscribe to Roman Catholicism as their ancestors converted under the influence of the Poles in earlier times.

6. This information was obtained by the author from Ladis Kristof during a private conversation at the Political Geography Pre-Conference in Tallahassee, Florida, on March 3, 2003. Ladis Kristof is from the area in which Karapchiu is located. He has also written journal articles on frontiers and boundaries (1959).

7. Walker Connor complains that American sociology has promoted the idea that ethnic groups are only minorities within larger societies though ethnic groups can be very large, with majority groups having ethnicity as well (1978, 386).

8. Ted Rogane was born in Germany and sent to Buchenwald concentration camp in July 1944. He became an American citizen in 1953 and proudly flew the German flag on October 6, German American Day. He even noted that he has "turned in the last 20 years into a better German than [he] would be over there [in Germany]" (Mortenson 1992, C6). Interestingly, many Americans would not consider individuals like Ted Rogane to be German because he is Jewish. They do so without recognizing their obvious acceptance of a Nazi definition of what it is to be German. Indeed, it is not uncommon for people to accept extremists' definitions of groups though they reject the extremists who advance such ideas.

9. The Scots, for example, voted for their own parliament in referendum in the mid-1990s. The overwhelming victory for greater self-rule stands in sharp contrast to the failure of a similar referendum in 1979 (Glauber 1997, 17a). Clearly more Scots today think of themselves as a nation than previously. The rise in national consciousness has been attributed to a perceived "indifference and even scorn from England" (Lyall 1997, A3). This perception came about in the 1980s "when many Scots found the Tory Government of Prime Minister Margaret Thatcher cold and unresponsive to Scotland's demands" (Lyall 1997, A3).

10. Interestingly a Pan-African movement of white rulers in Africa also once existed. Apparently the whites who lived as minorities among black Africans saw that they had commonalities and needed to bond together (DuBois 1970, 387).

11. See Hans Kohn's *Pan-Slavism: Its history and ideology* (1960) for more information on the Pan-Slavic movement.

12. See *South Africa's homelands in the age of reform: The case of QwaQwa* (Pickles and Woods 1992, 633-38) for an example of one of these homelands.

13. French and German speakers from places outside of France and Germany are not called French and Germans—definitely not the French and German speakers of Switzerland or the German speakers of Austria. At the same time, those native peoples from France and Germany who do not have French or German as a mother tongue still are considered to be French and German respectively because they are from France and Germany respectively.

14. Walker Connor notes a listing of sixty-six entries of organizations which begin with the word *International* though they should begin with *Interstate* because they are comprised of or deal with states and not nations (1978, 383).

15. While states do represent nations, they only represent those members of a nation that live within the state's boundaries. Members of a nation living outside the state's boundaries are represented by other state governments. Therefore, many nations are not represented by a single state government. Some are even represented by opposing governments.

16. Bruce Feiler illustrates how Jewish identity is tied to the physical environment in his writings:

The desert is one of the most profound places on Earth: It makes one feel small; it makes one feel grateful. And it never forgets. Visiting the region today, one realizes the stories of the Bible have never disappeared; they're just lying beneath the surface, waiting for someone to kick up the dust and lie on top of them. And when I, for one, lay down on them, I realized the Bible was no longer distant. What happened to those characters was happening to me. I was becoming attached to the land. I was reimagining myself. And, yes, I was drawing closer to God. . . . The feeling one gets is awe, coupled with humility: awe at the size of the desert, humility at the help one needs to survive it. The desert is the forge out of which the people of Israel are formed. Staring at it that afternoon, I realized how familiar it seemed, as if I'd been carrying it around with me for years. (2001a, 6-8)

17. For more information on the American cultural landscape, see John Brinckerhoff Jackson's *A sense of place, a sense of time* (1994).

18. No wonder then that schools try to bear the expense of taking children on field trips to museums and historical sites. Even adults eagerly spend their vacations going to historical places of national significance.

19. Richard Randall notes that Ukraine, for example, prepared to change as many as 90 percent of its place-names (2001, xiii).

20. The close, inseparable connection between human beings and the physical world is best illustrated by Simon Schama: "Even the landscapes that we suppose to be most free of our culture may turn out, on closer inspection, to be its product" (1996, 9). He made this statement while discussing the natural, pristine beauty of Yosemite.

21. This information was gained through fieldwork of the author while in Northern Ireland.

22. In *The poetics of space*, however, Gaston Bachelard writes about houses in a way that give them deep psychological meanings similar to the concept of home (1964).

23. Notice that the term *country*, which despite its varied usage always refers to places, is used in the expression instead of the term *nation*, which may be tied to place but often is used as if it is not. We as humans obviously must have strong emotional attachments to place and territory if we are willing to sacrifice our lives for them.

24. Furthermore, homeless people obviously have to occupy space somewhere. Those who do for a while begin to create places by filling them with belongings, thus organizing them to reflect their identity. This is an important step in reentering society. Not surprisingly, homeless people become protective of these places. Unfortunately, having no rights, homeless people often are unable to prevent authorities or others from transgressing and even destroying their places. When their places are transgressed, intense emotional duress follows.

25. Robert Sack defines territoriality as "the attempt by an individual or group to affect, influence, or control people, phenomena, and relationships, by delimiting and asserting control over a geographic area" (1986, 19).

Edward Soja defines territoriality as "a behavioral phenomenon associated with the organization of space into spheres of influence or clearly demarcated territories which are made distinctive and considered at least partially exclusive by their occupants or definers" (1971, 19).

26. The organization of personal space and what it signifies is integral to a phenomenon that Philip Wagner calls *Geltung* (Wagner 1996).

27. "It is characteristic of the symbol-making human species that its members can become passionately attached to places of enormous size, such as a nation-state, of which they have limited direct experience" (Tuan 1977, 18).

28. Because postage stamps are seen by millions of people on a regular basis, governments have decided that they are an appropriate medium for inculcating particular understandings of territorial arrangements into the minds of their citizens. The Ecuadoran example is merely one in a long list of postage stamp examples that Martin Glassner and Chuck Fahrer depict in their book *Political geography* (2004, 89).

29. Signs are a popularly used device in the cultural landscape. In addition to the Argentine case, the Polish government has erected signs stating that the territories taken from Germany after the Second World War are really Polish (Glassner and Fahrer 2004, 88); signs in Japan state that the Sakhalin Islands, now part of Russia, are really Japanese.

30. It is also necessary to move beyond the simpleminded and knee-jerk responses of natural resource procurement and geostrategic explanations to understand why the German and Polish nations claimed lands not inhabited by Germans and Poles respectively.

31. This statement is based on the recognition that boundaries are active, not passive, in regard to human identity. Boundaries simply do not encapsulate and summarize what exists across the landscape even though they are treated as if their function is just that. On the contrary, boundaries shape and alter the flow of trade, people, and ideas. The location of boundaries often determines the languages that people speak and the religions they practice. Likewise, human identities are often altered when boundaries change locations as individuals find themselves in new streams of movement and under the jurisdiction of a new government.

32. Benedict Anderson argues throughout much of his book *Imagined communities* that "print-capitalism" was a major factor in the rise of modern nationalism (Anderson 1991). If this is true, then certainly the locations of printing centers are significant.

33. What would the English language be without Oxford, Cambridge, or London? What would the French language be without the Sorbonne or the government in Paris? What would any language be without its place of cultivation?

34. To ignore geography, particularly the meaning of place and territory, one would have to argue, for example, that the English language would be the same today even if it had developed in a place like Newcastle or even Beijing. One also would have to argue that French would be the same if the Sorbonne were in Marseille or even Calcutta.

3

States as Spatial Entities

We have made Italy, now we need to make Italians.
—Massimo d'Azeligo

In chapter 2, it was noted that the term *nation* is frequently and inappropriately used as a synonym for *country, nation-state,* and *state.* The emphasis, however, in that chapter was on the idea of the nation as a form of group identity. Setting aside the idea of the state and focusing on the concept of the nation is an effective means of beginning the pursuit of understanding a variety of issues from deciphering the character of nations to correctly perceiving the true nature of internal or external conflicts. States, however, should not be left permanently out of discussions of nationhood as if they were inert objects on the world stage. On the contrary, states, like nations, are active entities with their own characters, motivations, and aspirations. They are entities much different than nations, but in this modern era, the *nation-state era,* states are linked to nations like body and soul. They derive their raison d'être and their legitimacy from nations in that they are to serve and protect nations. Thus, to perpetuate their own existences, states bind their identities to nations. They tailor their mechanisms to serve nations, but in doing so they shape and mold nations to fit their own needs as much as they alter themselves to serve nations.

An important linking of nations and states occurs through geography—that is, the shared characteristic of existing in earth space. Chapter 2 emphasized that nations are spatial entities. States are spatial entities too, meaning that place and territory are as much a part of states' existences as they are to nations. When linked together as nation-states, nations and states strive to occupy coterminous earth spaces. Achieving coexistence within coterminous territories is a joint project of nations and states. It is the fundamental means for nations to obtain security and for states to legitimize their existence in the modern era.

The process of cohabiting coterminous territories plays a major role in how nations and states each evolve while in their marriages. As states reshape and remold nations and nations remake states within common geographical space, geographical processes do not merely influence the relationships between nations and states: they shape the fundamental character and nature of nations and states. Geography, that is, earth space, is often treated as nothing more than the stage and scenery upon which and before which international relations play out. In fact, geography, more specifically spatial relationships, spatial flows, and spatial interactions, is the very medium in which world affairs unfold and by which nationhood and statehood develop. Space is integral to the process and not external, as so often treated. Chapter 2 explored how nations, as spatial entities, interweave with particular places and territories as they develop in the context of distinctive spatial relationships. States evolve along similar lines, but more importantly states—as spatial entities— shape the spatialities of nations. The ultimate goal of this chapter is to shed light on the ways in which states actively shape and mold nations through the distinctive spatial relationships that they create.

The synonymous use of the terms *nation* and *state* indicates that it is difficult for many to discern the differences between the two concepts. Deriving their legitimacy from nations, states seem to shrewdly encourage such confusion as they boldly masquerade in front of us as nations on commonly used maps. This chameleon-like practice contributes to the conflation of nation and state as it serves to subliminally inculcate people with the idea that states have fulfilled their raison d'être, to serve nations. The conflation even becomes some sort of confirmation of states' legitimacy. States, however, are much different than nations. Therefore, before examining how states use space and spatial relationships to shape and mold nations, it is important to draw attention to the masquerade of states and discuss that which makes a state a state and emphasize how it is different from a nation.

The State

If nations are a form of shared group identity, then what are states? In short, states are political phenomena with the following attributes: government, organized economy, circulation system, permanent resident population, expectation of permanence, sovereignty, the recognition of other states, and territory (Glassner and Fahrer 2004, 31-32; Storey 2001, 29-40). A more detailed discussion of these state attributes serves as the groundwork for the understanding of how states mold nations.

Government, Organized Economy, and Circulation System

Government is the politico-administrative system of the state that facilitates the functioning of the state. Governments come in many forms, from democratic to authoritarian with myriad hues of monarchic, oligarchic, totalitarian, fascist, and communist regimes in between. No matter what form it takes, government provides organization of the administration system of the state. As part of its managerial role, government ensures an organized economy and circulation system. In terms of economy, government, at the very least, issues money, sets monetary policy, establishes fiscal budgets, enforces economic agreements, levies taxes, and oversees foreign trade. More authoritarian forms of government will, to varying degrees, own the means of economic production and consider workers as employees of the state. Government is so fundamental to statehood that the word *government* is used synonymously with *state*. Thus, when we speak of state action, it can actually mean government action though state action may be appropriate if it includes the other attributes of the state.

In managing the economy, government sets up a functional circulation system of transportation and communication to transport goods and services of the economy, to allow the movement of the people within the state territory as necessary, and to move the military across the state territory to defend the borders of the state.

Permanent Resident Population and Expectation of Permanence

The state also requires a permanent resident population and needs the population to expect that the state is permanent. A permanent resident population is obvious, but it is worth pointing out that people run the state and that the state serves people; therefore, it is essential for the state's territory to be occupied by people. Perhaps the need for the population to expect the state to exist indefinitely is obvious and not necessary to list as a criterion of statehood. However, residents of the state do not always believe in the continued existence of their state. Whether in the aftermath of a war when new states try to establish themselves but are in fledgling conditions, or in situations where small states are threatened with oblivion by much larger states, or in territories annexed by other states but liberation is on the horizon, residents of a state lose their expectation of the state's permanence. Consequently, without confidence in the state's continued existence, the people withhold taxes, refuse military service, and generally disobey laws. When this occurs, this requirement of the state, so obvious and yet so odd that it seems unnecessary to identify, becomes the Achilles' heel of many states.

The lack of expectation of permanence has occurred numerous times and places in recent history. Central and Eastern Europe after both the world wars and in Bosnia-Herzegovina in the 1990s are a few examples. In the aftermath of the First World War, state governments established control over territories only to find their armies pushed out by a neighboring state's army whose government sought to make a claim to the same territory. The Polish-Soviet boundary as it emerged from the ashes of the First World War and became the subject of the Polish-Soviet War of 1919-1920 is one such example. As German forces melted away at the end of the First World War, Polish and Bolshevik armies alternately pushed east and west on several occasions before the boundary between the two countries was finally settled. While armies clashed, "[s]ix worthless currencies and the bureaucrats of three defunct powers were still in circulation, spreading confusion" (Davies 1972, 23). The people in the disputed territories had to decide each time that they found themselves in a new state as the boundaries moved whether they had faith in the permanence of that new state or not. Their choice determined their support of that state and in turn helped determine that state's long-term control of their territory. Poland and the Soviet Union are merely one example of that time. Many other examples exist, such as the territorial disputes between Hungary and its neighboring states of Czechoslovakia, Romania, and Yugoslavia after the First World War. In these cases as well as all the others in Europe at that time, the states that existed as well as the peoples and territories they controlled were partially determined by the faith of the people in those states.

Bosnia-Herzegovina's move toward independence in the early 1990s was threatened by a lack of expectation of permanence on the part of a number of its inhabitants. After the Bosnian state declared its independence in early 1992, many of the state's inhabitants, including Serbs, Croats, and Muslims, gave their loyalty to the new state. However, as the Serb paramilitary units in cooperation with the Yugoslav army took control of Bosnia's territory in an attempt to thwart independence, many Serbs abandoned the Bosnian cause. As the situation worsened,[1] Croats and even some Muslims gave up on an independent Bosnia and turned to other state-building projects (Silber and Little 1997, 291-302). Only after international intervention led by the United States on behalf of the belea-guered Bosnian state did Croats and others rejoin the Bosnian effort (Silber and Little 1997, 309-18).

Sovereignty

Sovereignty differentiates states from other territorial orders (e.g., prov-inces,[2] counties, municipalities),[3] other territorial formations (e.g., colo-nies and protectorates) as well as corporations, trading blocs, and alli-ances. Unlike these other human constructs that do not have sovereignty, states possess total authority over their peoples and their territories, "un-restrained by laws originating outside the area . . . completely free of di-rect external control" (Glassner and Fahrer 2004, 32) or "external inter-ference" (Bartleson 1995; Hinsley 1986; Storey 2001, 35). With sovereignty, states have within their territories a monopoly on power or what Max Weber would call a "monopoly of legitimate violence" or "monopoly of the legitimate use of physical force" (Gellner 1983, 3; Held et al. 1983, 111-112). By reserving force or violence for them-selves, states maintain social order either by employing it or not employ-ing it but never allowing their citizens to unleash it against one another. Though states use force to minimize conflicts between citizens that could endanger states themselves if citizen conflict develops into social disor-der, states are most concerned about direct challenges to their authority and sovereignty. Thus, states most swiftly and harshly employ force against citizens who commit acts of treason, sedition, assassination, and draft dodging.

Sovereignty is frequently used interchangeably or in conjunction with independence because sovereign states have the ability to act inde-pendently. Sovereignty is desired by nations, leading nations to want their own states. Thus, national independence and state sovereignty go hand in hand. History shows that sovereignty is frequently brought about by an internal mustering of forces as many countries had to fight for their independence. The ability to marshal force is critical for a state to protect itself, but the continual use of force, or merely the continual show of force, can be draining on a state's resources and ironically be the down-fall of a state. Over the long run, a state preserves itself by the recognition of other states, in turn giving a state legal right to its sovereignty and the right not to have its sovereignty infringed upon. Conversely, the lack of recognition by other states in the world community endangers a state or an aspiring state. Israel, Kuwait, and Taiwan, for example, have been threatened by states that do not recognize them and, therefore, feel no obligation to respect their sovereignty or any other quality of their statehood. Recognition is so key to self-preservation that aspiring states seek recognition as soon as they are able. Slovenia and Croatia, for example, sought recognition prior to their declarations of statehood in June 1991. Though recognition was slow in coming from already recognized states, it helped Slovenia and Croatia protect their sovereignty when other states placed political and economic sanctions on Yugoslavia for trying to crush their independence movements.[4]

Territory

In simple terms, territory provides states with resources, both natural and human. Beyond this most concrete quality, territory, as delineated earth space, serves as the medium in which all other attributes of states operate and give tangible existences. Without territory, states' other attributes are mostly theoretical, and whatever is able to take real form is largely ineffective. Government administers through laws, but laws, although intended to protect and regulate the behavior of people, are tied to territory (Dijkink and Knippenberg 2001). Polish laws, for example, do not apply to Poles wherever Poles may travel. They apply to Polish territory, meaning that Poles who travel outside of Poland are subject to the laws of other state territories. Similarly, non-Poles are subject to Polish law when they are within Poland's state territory. Thus, territory actualizes law, and governance with police enforcement is highly compartmentalized within bounded earth spaces.

Governments without territory are largely ineffectual until they establish sovereign control over territory. For example, after Soviet and Nazi forces took over Poland in 1939, the Polish government moved to London. It could not enforce its laws without territory. Its agenda was to liberate Poland, but, unable to, it lost its effectiveness and the support of other states (R. J. Crampton 1994, 196). The Western allies withdrew diplomatic recognition in 1945 and then a Communist government took over in Poland in 1947. When the Polish government in London disbanded in 1990, this government without control over territory had long been feckless and mostly forgotten by the world community.

The ineffectiveness of governance without territory is also illustrated by the United Nations. The UN's ability to enforce its resolutions outside its minuscule territory is very limited. Like any governing body without its own territory, it requires the consent of sovereign governments with territories to operate on their territories. It also requires the generosity of sovereign governments with territories to contribute resources to UN projects. Though the UN is clearly not a nation-state nor strives to be one, its lack of territory prevents it from being a state of any kind or from being politically effective.

Territory is not unlimited in spatial extent but delimited by either frontiers or boundaries (Kristof 1959). Frontiers are three-dimensional zones of length, height, and width that are outward looking and part of states that are expanding.[5] Though common in the past, few frontiers exist today as states have come to be enclosed by boundaries. Boundaries are two-dimensional lines of length and height but no width. Boundaries are inward looking and help states keep foreign influences out while enabling states to homogenize their territories, including the people within them. While territories serve as the medium in which the other attributes of the state take real form, boundaries serve as the container of the medium. Thus, boundaries are inextricably intertwined with territory. They exist as differing concepts but not without each another in reality. Together they are powerful forces that help nation-states differentiate themselves from one another.

Territory may seem passive and inert, nothing more than the soil on which we stand, and it is often treated as such, but territory makes governance, an organized economy, and a circulation system possible. It provides the abode for a permanent resident population, makes expectation of permanence reasonable and the recognition by other states feasible; it gives sovereignty its force. The discussion of territory shows that the attributes of the state are interdependent and work in concert as they function. From the anatomy of the state, we turn to the functioning of the state to move closer to an understanding of how the state shapes the nation.

States as Functional Regions

States appear on maps as bright mosaics of randomly colored units with each unit internally monochrome. As such, states appear both distinct from one another and uniform and solid within. This cartographic symbolization—known as the formal, uniform, or homogeneous region—is meant to convey internal homogeneity. Cartographically depicting states in this manner, where states are uniformly colored throughout, conveys and reinforces the message that states possess the same internal homogeneity in earth space as they do in map space. State governments encourage this sort of cartographic practice for defensive reasons.[6] For example, when a "red" state lays claim to some territory of the neighboring "blue" state, without knowing the situation, we are prejudiced into thinking that the red state is the obvious aggressor. Thus we are inclined to oppose its actions because red should not possess blue; only blue should possess blue. For the red state to succeed in a territorial claim against the blue state, the red state must redepict part or all of the blue territory as red.[7] This action helps to mobilize support of the red state's population and the support of other peoples and states for annexation by demonstrating that the targeted territory is rightfully red. Opposition is nullified as the state's actions are legitimized. To use a more concrete example of such a situation, a hypothetical case involving Hungary and Slovakia could be employed. It could be stated that Hungary occupied part of Slovakia. The choice of words carries with it the implication that the Hungarian state took possession of a territory that did not belong to it—that is, red possessing blue. Consequently, anyone hearing such a statement without knowing much about the situation might be inclined to oppose the Hungarian state's action because such actions violate the territorial integrity and internal homogeneity of states. The general cartographic practice of depicting states as homogeneous units gives the Slovak state (i.e., blue) a distinct defensive advantage over the Hungarian state (i.e., red). However, if a more detailed statement were made, one that noted that Hungarians inhabit part of Slovakia—thereby indicating that part of Slovakia (i.e., the blue state) was really Hungarian (i.e., red like the red state of Hungary)—then a different reaction might well result. Thus a statement to the effect that Hungarian troops had occupied territories of Slovakia over which the Hungarian government claimed rightful dominion could well send a different message. Anyone hearing this statement and knowing little about the situation would likely want to know if the Hungarian claims were legitimate before making a judgment.

Though the cartographic depiction of states as homogeneous regions allows states to depict themselves as indivisible wholes and the inhabitants of states who support their states to feel that they stand united, the depiction of states as homogeneous regions is a misrepresentation of states. The seven attributes of the state identified in the previous section are not a uniform and undifferentiated collection. Populations are rarely evenly spaced, and transportation and circulation systems are seldom

symmetrical, uniformly servicing, and unvaryingly efficient. Most notably, state power is also not equally derived from all parts of the state territory though the state government attempts to impose its authority
evenly throughout state territory. Power is usually concentrated in a *core,*
a term used to describe a city or cluster of cities with the greatest political, economic, and cultural influence in the state territory, usually deriving its influence from the largest population cluster of the state territory.
For example, in France it is Paris, and in the United States it is the great
conurbation *megalopolis* that stretches from Washington, D.C. to Boston,
Massachusetts, and includes cities such as Baltimore, Philadelphia, and
New York.

States then are more accurately described as functional regions rather
than homogeneous regions. Functional regions work through a series of
nodes, usually hierarchical in nature. Lines between the nodes indicate
the connections in the network. Enclosed lines on maps denote the earth
spaces that the node network controls. The *core* that political geographers speak of when discussing states is very much the same as the more
generic term *node* used for functional regions. Secondary and tertiary
nodes—that is, cores—are provincial capitals, county seats, and the like
in political geography. The lines between the nodes indicate the circulation system—that is, the communication pathways, transport connections, and general flows of power within the state territory. The core of a
state exerts its power over its state territory through its circulation system. The core's executive, legislative, and judicial decisions spread
through the various pathways of the circulation systems until they encounter every individual within the state territory. Enclosed lines on the
maps represent state boundaries, delimiting the areal extent of state
power (see figure 3.1). This spatial functioning of states applies to all
types of states, from authoritarian to democratic ones. The process is
similar whether power follows through the nodes and connecting pathways from the primary core down to each individual—as with authoritarian states—or from each individual up through the hierarchy to the primary core and out through the network again—as with democratic states.

State territories and their boundaries are often treated passively, as
givens that are separate from political processes. Though territories are
frequently recognized for their natural resources and geostrategic positions, such treatment is still very passive as it focuses on the contents of
the state territory in the way that a vintner may appear to be more interested in the wine than the wine bottle without realizing that the character
of the wine is partly determined by the containers that wine is fermented
and stored within. Such is the case for territories in that their spatial

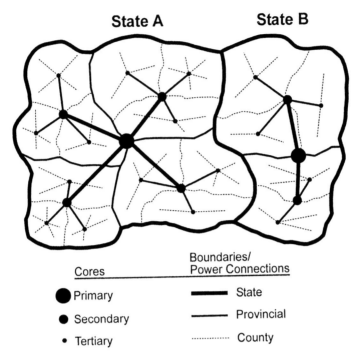

State A   **State B**

Cores

● Primary
● Secondary
• Tertiary

Boundaries/
Power Connections

━━━ State
─── Provincial
·········· County

Figure 3.1 The Functional Regions of States

qualities (e.g., spatial networks) shape their contents in conjunction with their boundaries. Outside the discipline of geography, recognition of the roles that territories and boundaries play in political processes seems only to extend to the concept of gerrymandering. Coined by a journalist, this popular term recognizes that the outcomes of elections are heavily influenced not only by party membership, political issues, and the rhetoric of political candidates, but also by the numbers, sizes, and shapes of voting districts (see figure 3.2). Not only does the political geography of voting districts influence who is elected, but also governmental policy as the result of who is elected. Those elected determine policies that affect every nuance of people's lives ranging from political and economic matters to cultural issues. In Northern Ireland, for example, the Protestant minority was able to use gerrymandering for decades to control the government and governmental policy. Unfortunately, the recognition given to active spatialities of gerrymandering is usually not extended to territories and boundaries in regard to nations and states. However, state territories and their boundaries are not passive givens without effect on the people who live within them but are integral to the functioning of states.

Figure 3.2 Voting Districts
The pattern of voters is the same in the left diagram as it is in the right one. The number of voters in each voting district is also the same: twelve. The boundaries of the districts mark the difference between the two diagrams. The differing district boundaries would lead to differing outcomes in an election if party members vote true to their political parties. In the scenario on the left, political parties "A" and "Z" each would win two seats. However, in the scenario on the right, political party "A" would win three seats and political part "Z" would win only one seat. Clearly the outcome of elections is influenced by the location of voting district boundaries.

States' Territories and Self-Preservation

As already noted, states need territories and preserve themselves by maintaining control over their territories through their spatial networks. Where territories are inhabited by people—that is, most territories—states sustain much of their authority over their territories through people. If people are loyal to a state, then they work with a state to keep their territory under the state's control. Not surprisingly, states demand loyalty of their populations.

The directions of power flow through states' spatial networks are not necessarily significant in the functioning of states when it comes to the issue of loyalty. All states demand loyalty whether democracies or authoritarian regimes. Democracies may allow individuals to determine the criteria for loyalty, but they, like authoritarian regimes, demand loyalty all the same (Held 1989). Indeed, democratic states will demand as much loyalty as authoritarian states because they need to preserve their control over territory as much as authoritarian states.

States obtain loyalty from their populations in part through conformity. In other words, if everyone and everything within the state territory conforms to a set of standards unique in regard to other states, and the state is the sole bearer of those particular standards, then the people of the state pledge their loyalty to that state as their only possible protector. With loyalty of the people, the state government feels secure from within. Conformity fosters loyalty, and loyalty facilitates security. However, few states are endowed with conformity upon their inceptions.[8] When a state has part of its territory and population with characteristics (e.g., measurement standards, educational levels, a language, etc.) that conform more closely to those of a neighboring state, it may perceive a threat and counter it by demanding conformity from that territorial part. If we use the earlier examples of the "red" and "blue" states, the red state may have part of its territory with characteristics that are more blue than red. The red state is likely to perceive that situation as a security threat since the blue state could easily make a territorial claim. To neutralize the threat, or potential threat, the red makes the characteristics of its bluish part conform to its red standards. The idea is that if that territorial part is more red and less blue, then the people of it will be more loyal to the red state and less so to the blue state because the red state will be seen as their natural protector—the protector of red.

Conformity may bring loyalty, but how is conformity achieved? Is it through uniformity, specifically, spatial uniformity—the kind seen on political maps where states are colored in as homogeneous units? As state governments seek to bring about conformity by implementing unique standards, they tend to implement the same standards throughout their territories. If a state creates a highly pervasive set of standards (e.g., those that demand citizens to speak the same language or even the same dialect of a language or practice the same religion or even a single denomination of a religion), then the accompanying demand for compliance to those standards will bring about uniformity with conformity. However, if a state has a loose set of standards, just enough to facilitate transportation and communication across the state territory, regional differences in culture (e.g., linguistic and religious) are likely to persist or develop if they were not present before. Thus, uniformity will not be a subsequent outgrowth of conformity. Some individuals within states and some state governments cannot see the difference between conformity and uniformity and consequently believe that conformity can be achieved only through uniformity.

Unitary and Federal Structures

Pervasive uniform standards and loose conforming standards are usually harnessed to unitary and federal forms of government respectively.[9] In unitary states, the primary core is the source of those standards with the secondary and tertiary cores serving only as distribution points of the state authority concentrated in the primary core. Secondary and tertiary cores have no autonomous power of their own. Unitary states can implement loose conforming standards but the concentration of power in the primary core of the unitary allows, even encourages, the primary core to impose pervasive uniform standards (see figure 3.3).

In federal states, the secondary and tertiary cores also serve as distribution points of state authority, but they also have autonomous power. Working within certain parameters, they can make their own policies for their regions and localities. In some cases, they are the primary authority on certain issues. In the United States, for example, the states (e.g., California, Texas, Florida, etc., generically called provinces) and counties formulate their own policies and practices on a wide range of issues and have virtually sole authority over several areas of governance. Education is one of many of these examples. For education, the fifty states (i.e., provinces) set their expectations and requirements for graduation for elementary and secondary schools. These standards also vary to some degree at yet another lower level in the spatial hierarchy—the individual school districts. The fifty states also operate their own university systems, and commonly charge higher "out-of-state" tuitions to those not from that particular state (i.e., province). The extra out-of-state charges are justified because out-of-state students have not been contributing tax dollars to support the university system. However, despite the rationale, the "in-state/out-of-state" phenomenon that arises in federal systems also has the effect of limiting individuals, coercing them to remain within their states (i.e., provinces). Further curbs on movement are created by requirements for professional certification, necessary for teachers, lawyers, psychologists, accountants, physicians, veterinarians, real estate and insurance agents, and many other professions. Going through the educational system of the state (i.e., province) where certification is desired best ensures professional certification. Thus, the desire to obtain professional certification in one's home state works with the phenomenon of in-state tuition to keep many individuals within their home states (i.e., provinces).

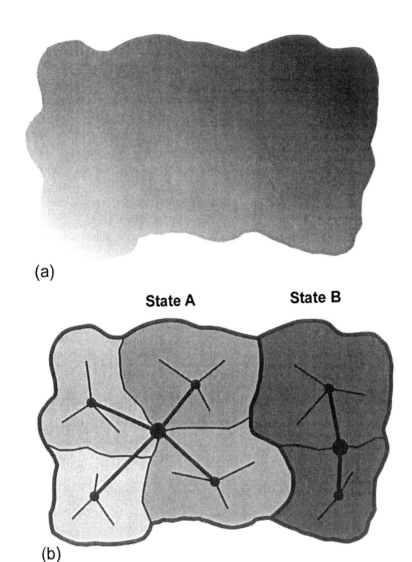

(a)

State A **State B**

(b)

Figure 3.3 Cultural Identity and Functional Regions
(a) illustrates a world of continuous cultural transition with few discernable boundaries; (b) illustrates how states' functional regions can homogenize the cultures within their boundaries. State A represents a federal state where cultural differences persist though they are homogenized within individual provinces. State B represents a unitary state where cultural differences are eliminated, even between provinces.

In unitary states, where "in-state/out-of-state" tuition and varying state (i.e., provincial) certification policies and practices are inconceivable, individuals move throughout the country for services and jobs without worrying about differential costs and standards. Federal states, by allowing spatial autonomy, end up with subnetworks of spatial interaction that present disincentives for individuals to move outside of their states (i.e., provinces). As a result, regional differences in culture are likely to persist, even emerge, in federal states. In some of these subnetworks, people develop their own national identities. In others, they remain very "provincial" (see figure 3.3).

Strong regional differences within states can threaten the state, namely, its territorial integrity if regional independence movements emerge. This is one of many centrifugal forces that can destroy a state. Thus, it is not in the interest of the state to allow too much autonomous decision making because it will allow too much spatial differentiation. For example, if the Canadian government allows the Quebec government to promote the French language and demote English as it has often done, is this such a pervasive action that it will reshape the culture within Quebec to such a degree that it will make the people there not feel Canadian but rather solely Quebecois and thus seek independence? Certainly, that is the goal of the Quebec nationalists, known as Parti Québécois.[10]

It is tempting to conclude that conformity means uniformity, and thus the state needs to implement pervasive policies to bring about total uniformity in order to preserve the state, its territory, and its people. Yet uniformity is not necessarily a centripetal force that precludes the development of a centrifugal force like too much regional autonomy. Uniformity can act as a stronger centrifugal force than diversity. In countries like the Soviet Union and Yugoslavia, the governments, although they frequently gave lip service to diversity, implemented intense policies aimed at bringing about uniformity. Needless to say, those once very diverse countries do not exist anymore. On the other hand, states like Canada and the United Kingdom have become more federally constructed, that is, have given Quebec, Scotland, and Wales more autonomy respectively, and still survive.

States' Functional Regions Shape National Identities

As states integrate their territories by bringing about conformity, or uniformity as the case may be, states' actions profoundly affect the identities of the peoples within their territories. This process is often called "nation-building," a process frequently undertaken by states. Nation-building touches on every aspect of life, including its most mundane elements. As Benedict Anderson puts it, nation-building policies can be "Machiavelian, instilling of nationalist ideology through the mass media, and educational system, administrative regulations, and so forth"—as illustrated by Weber's "monopoly of legitimate violence"—or it can be "genuine, popular nationalism" (1991, 114), accepted and perpetuated by the population of the state.

Though the term *nation-building* may trigger thoughts that are limited to a country's infrastructure, infrastructure is very much a part of a highly constructed world that states create for their populations.[11] The geography (e.g., spatial networks) of states' transportation and communication systems determines which directions individuals can travel and in turn determines who individuals will encounter and what social and business opportunities will be available to them as a result of the locations to which they are encouraged to travel (see figure 3.4). In turn, these spatial networks have a profound effect on the way in which culture develops (see figures 3.5 and 3.6).

In addition to infrastructure, governmental regulations—which fill government archives with endless volumes—touch every aspect of people's lives. Grouped in broad categories such as health, welfare, education, business, transportation, and construction, thousands upon thousands of rules and regulations spew forth endlessly from state governments regulating such ordinary issues as shoe sizes, doorway heights, how many unrelated people may live together in a house, circuit breaker dimensions, sidewalk widths, the height of blades of grass in lawns, and classifications of food. The state determines what foods are "natural," "organic," and "artificial" by criteria that it has developed. The U.S. Supreme Court, not scientists, has decided for itself whether a tomato is a vegetable or a fruit. State governments involve themselves in every aspect of our daily lives, controlling our actions and directing our thoughts in that we are continually confronted with objects, situations, and policies molded by government policies. Individuals can accept or reject them, but a significant part of human existence is reacting vis-à-vis the state.

Many state regulations and definitions are inane, but they cannot be ignored without consequences. With its "monopoly of the legitimate use of physical force," the state has the ability to punish those who do not conform. The denial or suspension of business licenses and professional certifications, the imposition of stiff monetary fines, and incarceration force people into spending an inordinate amount of time and money trying to keep apprised of the never-ending flow of new state rules and regulations. In doing so, people conform in one way or another to the state's demands even if they detest doing so.[12]

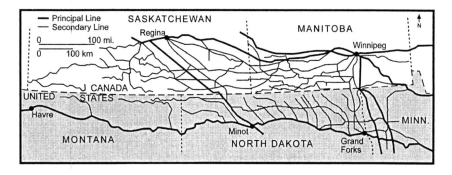

Figure 3.4 The U.S.-Canadian Boundary
This map illustrates how boundaries direct the flow of goods, people, and ideas. Many people living next to one another on either side of a boundary such as this one would likely interact with one another. However, differing transportation systems draw such neighboring peoples away from one another to separate and distinct economic, political, and cultural centers. Even without movement, people on opposing sides of boundaries are subject to differing laws. Source: Jerome D. Fellman, Arthur Getis, and Judith Getis. 2003. *Human Geography: Landscapes of Human Activities.* New York: McGraw-Hill. Figure 12.19, p. 464. Reproduced with permission of The McGraw-Hill Companies.

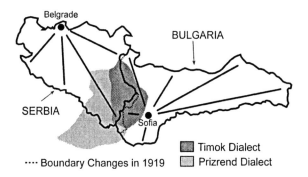

Figure 3.5 The Timok and Prizrend Dialects
This diagram indicates how the functional regions of states alter language and create linguistic differences. After the independent Serbian state and the autonomous Bulgarian province of the Ottoman Empire were created in 1878, the Timok and Prizrend dialects became subject to the differing governmental policies of Belgrade and Sofia. The shift in the political boundaries in 1919 also impacted these dialects.

Figure 3.6 The Duchy of Teschen
This diagram indicates how the Duchy of Teschen was divided between the newly created Czechoslovak and Polish states in 1919. Prior to the division, the people of Teschen had a distinct identity and were known as *Slazacy* (Slonzaks). Following the partition of the duchy and the incorporation of its parts into the Czechoslovak and Polish states, the identity of the *Slazacy* has been subsequently diluted and subsumed within the Czechoslovak and Polish national identities. In contrast to the case of Teschen, the Grand Duchy of Luxembourg emerged as an independent state in the late nineteenth century. Subsequently, Luxembourgian identity has been reinforced and in the last decade or so the Luxembourgish dialect (*Letzeburgesh*) has been increasingly treated as a fully fledged language and the basis of Luxembourgian identity (Gray 2002).

Many people do not realize how much their own identities are altered as they conform to the standards of states, which—along with other cultural characteristics—profoundly shape language. At one level, states determine which languages are allowed to be used in the state—whether for education, law, governance, and commerce, or in the cultural realm.

Even when states do not suppress languages that they do not sanction for these activities, citizens have little incentive to learn languages that they are unable to use in official circumstances. Other times, states vigorously impose certain languages as a means of assimilating minorities. Anglification, Frenchification, Russification, Germanization, and Magyarization are a few examples of language-oriented assimilation programs of European states that promote the use of certain languages to the detriment of other languages. At another level, states set language standards. Thus, not only do states promote certain languages, but they also promote their visions of those languages. Before the rise of modern states, many languages were divided into numerous dialects that varied greatly and employed differing spelling and grammatical standards, even within dialects. States have played a major role in the choosing of dialects, spellings, and grammars in language standardization. At yet another level, states have their own bureaucratic languages that arise from their endless rules and regulations. States' bureaucratic languages can be cryptic and overwhelming, but those who do not try to master at least the rudiments of them suffer the consequences of unsympathetic and imposing systems. In short, states' impositions of certain languages, their versions of these languages, and their infusion of their bureaucratic terminologies and idioms into languages explain why Eric Hobsbawn would write that "[l]anguages multiply with states; not the other way around" (Hobsbawn 1990, 63).

One way to illustrate the impact of states on languages, and thus identity, is to consider the various English-speaking peoples around the world. Their common language is subdivided into differing accents, spelling standards, and word uses. The differences are primarily state-centered, illustrated, for example, by the tendency to classify the differences as American and British, as in American accents, spellings, and meanings, and British accents, spellings, and meanings. American and British categories, like many state-based classifications, exist though variations within each grouping of the English language may be greater than between the groupings. If the variations are greater between the state-based categories, it was very likely the result of state action and thinking. The American and British governments did not concoct the language differences. Nevertheless, the American and British governments created separate networks of spatial interactions, leading those within the United States to develop a different use of the English language than those living in the United Kingdom. These differences manifested themselves most clearly after Noah Webster published *An American Dictionary of the English Language* in 1828. The bureaucratic languages of the two governments widened the language difference along state lines. Thus, when an American hears the acronym *IRA*, he or she is likely to think *Individual Retirement Account* while a Brit is likely to think of the *Irish Republican Army*. *Social Security* is composed of two generic words that are understood in the entire English-speaking world. Yet in the United States, this word combination has a specific social and legal meaning accompanied by a very detailed set of rules and regulations that profoundly affect people's lives. The American understanding of Social Security is something much different than in the rest of the English-speaking world. When Americans hear or see *MP*, they would more likely think *Military Police* while Brits also may think *Member of Parliament*. Governments do not always create words and terms, but their acceptance of particular word choices reinforces language differences between countries. Such is seen, for example, in the varying meanings of words like *guard, conductor, police officer,* and *sheriff.* The British use *guard* when Americans would use *conductor,* while the Irish concept of *guard* is more akin to the American term *police officer.* American county governments have perpetuated the use of *sheriff* among Americans while the word has a much more restricted governmental application in many other English-speaking countries, resulting in less popular usage.

In addition to rules, regulations, and the bureaucratic uses of language, states use education and the news media to shape the identity of their populations.[13] They mandate the specific details of knowledge that young people will learn and then reiterate the information through the news media. The adage that "the victor will write the history" of events is well-known, but the full implications of this adage may not be. At one level—an obvious one—governments portray themselves in a positive light and depict foreign governments negatively, even falsely negative. Governments may also negatively represent preceding governments, legitimize themselves by making false historical connections to earlier governments beloved by the people, or do both simultaneously.

These kinds of practices, where states decide who is good and who is bad, are perhaps known. However, states are involved in the more fundamental issue of who belongs to which group before they are then labeled good or bad. States' boundaries enclose a defined number of human beings, and their functional systems facilitate the interactions that will create and transmit the shared experiences. Thus, states, with their boundaries and spatial networks that integrate their territories within their boundaries, foster the development of differing identities: the "us" and "them" (see figure 3.7).

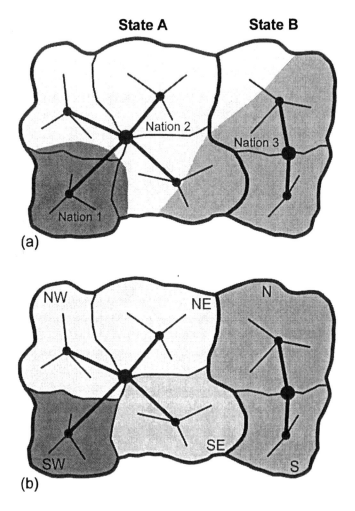

Figure 3.7 National Identity and States' Functional Regions
(a) illustrates the spatial relationships between nations and states before states' mechanisms begin working to homogenize their populations; (b) illustrates the spatial relationships between nations and states after states' mechanisms have homogenized their populations. With State A representing a federal state, Nation 1 has preserved its identity within the southwestern province, but Nation 1's identity has been diluted in neighboring provinces where other nations have come to dominate. Nation 2 has come to dominate in the northeastern and northwestern provinces. The diversity of the southeastern province has led to the emergence of a distinctive provincial identity. State B represents a unitary state where Nation 3 has come to dominate at the expense of Nation 2.

In addition to the above-discussed process whereby states mold their disparate populations of individuals into unified bodies through their spatial networks (i.e., circulation system) that impart rules, regulations, and common bureaucratic languages, states further use their territories to bind their people together through their education[14] and news media systems. Education is territorially based as states require schoolchildren to learn the geography, history, politics, economy, and cultural characteristics of their territory.[15] Schoolchildren may be taught about other countries but the information is always presented separately from their own country's information. Differences between homeland and foreign places are always highlighted and rarely given as much detail. The real world is one in which the natural and human world is frequently in constant transition with few places for obvious boundaries. The state, however, presents a world of clearly marked contrasts through its education system. As Yi-Fu Tuan points out,

> Maps in school atlases and history books show nation-states as sharply bounded units. Small scale maps encourage people to think of their countries as self-sufficient entities. Visible limits to a nation's sovereignty, such as a row of hills or a stretch of river, support the sense of the nation as place. From the air, however, mountains and rivers are merely elements of physical geography, and man-made markers like fences and guard posts are invisible. Aerial photographs are useless in history books. Maps, which also present the vertical view, are another matter. Cartography can clearly be made to serve a political end. In a school atlas the world's nations [*sic*] appear as a mosaic of clashing colors. Pink Canada looms large over butter-tinted United States; there can be no doubt about where one ends and another begins, nor of their sharply contrasting identities. (1977, 178)

In *Imagined Communities*, Benedict Anderson expounds on the process when he discusses how the functional regions of European colonies in Southeast Asia evolved into modern nation-states. He identifies three institutions—the census, the map, and the museum—as underlying this transformation. When discussing the power of the map, Anderson presents his idea of the "map-as-logo":

> Its practice was reasonably innocent—the practice of the imperial states of coloring their colonies on maps with an imperial dye. In London's imperial maps, British colonies were usually pink-red, French purple-blue, Dutch yellow-brown, and so on. Dyed this way, each colony appeared like a detachable piece of a jigsaw puzzle. As this "jigsaw" effect became normal, each "piece" could be wholly detached from its

geographic context. In its final form all explanatory glosses could be summarily removed: lines of longitude and latitude [*sic*], place names, signs for rivers, seas, and mountains, *neighbours*. . . . In this shape, the map entered an infinitely reproducible series, available for transfer to posters, official seals, letterheads, magazine and textbook covers, table-cloths, and hotel walls. Instantly recognizable, everywhere visible, the logo-map penetrated deep into the popular imagination, forming a powerful emblem for the anticolonial nationalisms to be born. (1991, 175)

Anderson goes on to show how museums, with their arranged artifacts and narratives, are designed to show the shared history and unity of both a nation and its state, thereby legitimizing the nation-state by showing its existence through time (1991, 178-84).

In chapter 2, it was stated that individuals within a nation have strong emotional attachments to their national territory though they may have limited personal experience with the national territory, not having traveled and lived in every part of it. It was further stated that the bond is partially developed through the transmission of shared experience brought about by social interaction. The state, in addition to determining the container in which social interaction takes place, injects copious amounts of information on the state territory through its educational system and the news media for its population to socially transmit. This allows individuals to develop topophilia for a large territory, over which individuals have little direct experience. For example, without the existence of the modern state system, a person in New York or Vermont may very well know much more about the neighboring provinces of Ontario and Quebec. Toronto and Montreal are less than a day's drive from New York City and Burlington. However, New Yorkers and Vermonters are more likely to know more about California and Arizona, even Hawaii and Alaska, though they are thousands of miles apart. Despite the distances, California, Arizona, Hawaii, and Alaska are part of the same country while Ontario and Quebec are not and are thus learned about in school and receive more media attention. On television weather maps, for example, Canada appears as an amorphous gray mass without weather. Canada is only mentioned when a nasty Alberta clipper sweeps down from the north and makes life difficult for Americans. Thus, Canada is mentioned only when it is an ominous threat to Americans though the political relationship between the U.S. and Canadian governments is generally positive. On the other side of the border, U.S. weather is hardly mentioned except for the terrible Colorado lows that dampen and ruin Canadians' summer. Mexico and the Caribbean islands are not treated any better in U.S. weather reports. They, too, are ignored until a hurricane strikes. Then images of an impoverished people helplessly struggling against the natural disaster come forth, highlighting the differences between Americans, Mexicans, and the peoples of the Caribbean.

Weather may be a minor issue, but it is a commonality that people can share. Thus, weather information can be used to foster a shared group identity and maintain or create new divisions between peoples. Ireland is a case more interesting than the United States and Canada. Ireland's east-west axis is shorter than its north-south axis, providing a challenge for cartographers because the shorter east-west axis potentially leaves much blank space on a map depicted on a horizontally oriented television screen. Cartographers detest blank space, but shifting the map frame to the east brings Great Britain into the screen and much to be drawn and labeled to fill in the blank space. For many cartographers around the world, bringing Great Britain into the picture is an ideal solution. However, for Irish media, such a solution brings about something less desirable. It shows how close Great Britain is to Ireland, and provides the Irish with details about Great Britain, namely, that with similar climates the Irish and British share something in common. Rather than do this, the Irish media shift the map frame to the west over much empty ocean, leaving Irish weather maps with a lot of blank space.[16] While Great Britain is left out, Northern Ireland is included and given as much detail as the Republic of Ireland. The state boundary between the two political entities is drawn so faintly, when it is drawn, that it is barely discernible. With economic, historical, and cultural information presented in the same manner, one would tend to conclude that Northern Ireland is politically tied to the Republic of Ireland rather than the United Kingdom.

State-Centeredness

Far from being passive, states' territories are not merely pieces of land. They delimit histories, economics, politics, and the very identities of peoples within their boundaries. Their effect is so thorough that their action is seldom realized or questioned but simply taken for granted. As Peter Brown notes,

> It is sometimes said that the last thing that a fish would discover is water. As the basic feature of its environment it is taken for granted. So it appears to be with the twentieth-century men and women and the na-

tion-state. But we not only take the nation-state as a fixed element of our circumstances; we think—or rather assume without reflection—that its existence settles other questions. (1981, ix; also quoted in Peter Taylor 1993, 84)

U.S. history, for example, is written and taught in a series of territorial containers beginning with the thirteen British colonies. History presented in this fashion is not just history written with twenty-twenty hindsight. It is also not written as a self-fulfilled prophecy, for prophecy implies that events could have unfolded differently. Instead, accepting the thirteen colonies as a given puts American history in a spatial container that in turn treats many of the unfolding events of history as givens. Consequently, little attention is given to the fact that the British had more than thirteen colonies in North America prior to the American Revolution. Though the number, extent, and status of British possessions changed continually since the arrival of European settlers in North America, on the eve of the American Revolution, Cape Breton and Newfoundland were also British colonies. Nova Scotia, New Brunswick, Prince Edward Island, the territory of Rupert's Hudson's Bay Land Company, Quebec, and a number of Caribbean islands were also British possessions. Quebec also extended south to the Ohio River and west to the Mississippi River (Bercuson et al. 1992, 117-19; Guibernau 1999, 55; Shepherd 1929, 194). If today's political map is used to delimit history, which is the common practice, little emphasis is placed on the close connections that northern colonies had with one another, such as those of New Hampshire, Cape Breton, Massachusetts, and Newfoundland. Their similar physical geographies, economies, and cultures facilitated these close connections. Likewise, the southern plantation economies of colonies such as South Carolina and Georgia had strong connections with the colonial plantations in the Caribbean for similar reasons. Also overlooked is that representatives from Quebec were invited to the Continental Congress in May 1775 or that among the first military operations of the "American" revolutionaries was the conquering of Montreal and laying siege to Quebec's capital (Bercuson et al. 1992, 139-40). The book *Our Struggle for the Fourteenth Colony* (Justin Smith 1907) best illustrates this goal.[17] Thus, while modern-day Americans treat the establishment of the independence of the thirteen colonies as a complete success, the Founding Fathers themselves would have preferred, and indeed attempted, to found a country of fourteen or more liberated British possessions.

These important nuances of history are overlooked in histories that accept the United States and Canada as givens. Consequently, history is written as the explanation of these givens. Missing are discussions of how territory and territorial conceptions were integral factors of the American Revolution. Thus, little attention is given to those supporting British rule in the thirteen colonies or to those who supported the American Revolution farther to the north. Also, information is scant on how the revolutionaries preached their revolutionary ideas in most of the British possessions in North America and not just in thirteen of the colonies. Absent is the recognition that as revolutionary actions led to thirteen of the colonies becoming independent the political attitudes polarized between the people within the seceding colonies and those deciding to remain British. Subsequently, these attitudes led to migrations, particularly of loyalists in the seceding colonies to those remaining British (Bercuson et al. 1992, 149-55), in turn giving initial rise to two political states in North America: the United States of America and Canada. Frequently omitted is acknowledgment that the solidification of both political states was not certain until the 1860s, that is, after the northern states (i.e., provinces) of the United States succeeded in a war with the southern states, leading the north to impose its values and standards on the south and finally politically integrating the country as a whole. Furthermore, with the north's victory, a legacy has been the depiction of the conflict as a "Civil War," implying that the conflict was an "internal" matter. Yet if the southern states had been successful, two countries would exist where there was one, exemplified by the common southern rejection of the term Civil War and the preferred expressions of either "War between the States" or "The War of Northern Aggression."[18] Also left out of U.S. history books is the reaction to the American Civil War farther north. The people of the British provinces, seeing the power of the northern states and aware of American attempts to annex their territories,[19] responded by politico-territorial integration with one another, that is, through the creation of the Confederation in the proclamation of the Dominion of Canada in 1867, laying the foundation for the country of Canada as seen on the political map today (Bercuson et al. 1992, 419-75).

The unwillingness to accept histories that do not neatly fit into the colored spaces on the map prevents us from acknowledging just how much the "Civil" war questioned and threatened the territorial integrity of the United States and the idea that it was occupied by a single nation.[20] Consequently, the resulting blind spot forces us to focus attention on the issue of slavery as a dividing factor between the North and the South. Yet, though it can be argued that slavery was at the heart of the matter, some solutions to the matter, namely, the attempt of the South to secede, were very much linked to spatial arrangements and alternative territorial conceptions and formulations. The scant attention given to the territorial aspect of the South's solutions is not merely a result of the South's failure to successfully implement its solution. The earlier American Revolution was successful; yet, though the grievances of the colonists are acknowledged, the territorial aspects that worked in conjunction with those grievances are not given due recognition—namely, that it was not only unclear how successful the American Revolution would be, but also what territorial arrangements would be integral to the process, even shape the process. Such is indicated by the current Canadian view of the events, namely, that the American Revolutionaries were rebels and the American Revolution was "The North American Civil War" because it pitted colonists against colonists, resulting in the secession of some colonies but not other ones (Bercuson et al. 1992, 143-45). Though the American Revolution and "Civil" wars—as contemporary Americans see them—had completely different outcomes in terms of territorial independence, succeeding in the former case but not in the latter case, both events are treated as if the territories were clearly understood, unchanging, inevitable, and definitely unrelated to the events themselves. Canada and the United States are accepted as they are today. Despite the mention of the westward expanding frontiers over time, American history and Canadian history are still written as if they took place in a box.

The manner in which U.S. history is typically written is by no means unique. Histories, and for that matter economics, politics, art, and many other subjects, are written according to a state-centeredness reflected on the current political map of the world and its patchwork of colors. Though it may be appropriate at some level, it often is not, and is inappropriate to such a degree that many salient processes are not acknowledged, addressed, or properly analyzed. Many processes do not take place within the clearly delimited boxes of state territories and are overlooked precisely because they do not fit into these boxes. Other processes are misunderstood as they are forced into these boxes. Further misunderstandings arise as well. Accepting the current world map as givens through time leads writers and commentators to refer to countries when they did not exist. For example, it is common to read statements about Germany, Italy, or France as far back as the eighth or ninth centuries and even earlier or to encounter generalized statements about centuries-old and millennia-old characteristics and behaviors of these countries. Quite simply, these countries are not that old, and a majority of the countries on today's world map are less than one hundred years old. Moreover, many countries, such as Italy and Germany, which only came into exis-

tence in 1861[21] and 1871 respectively, did not encompass the same territory, people, or economic or transportation systems in history that they
do today. Yet these countries are commonly written about as if they had.
Consequently, discussions of history, economics, politics, and culture
that accept any country that appears on today's map as given and eternal
inadequately explain or simply misrepresent the causes and characters of
what is discussed. Moreover, the use of contemporary political maps to
depict historical situations presents contradictory and even false information. For example, it is not uncommon to read information about the Second World War illustrated by maps showing today's political boundaries.
Consequently, though the author may speak of locations in Germany, the
locations appear in the boundaries of Poland on a current map because
those places are no longer in Germany. In addition to the impressions of
location conveyed by such maps, distances, directions, and generally the
world in which people of the time lived in and their perceptions of it are
also misrepresented. All such erroneous information shows that it is necessary to think outside the box—that is, the colored boxes on maps—to
understand many processes (Alexander Murphy 1991a; 1991b). What
exists today is partially the product of evolving spatial relationships.

Despite the pitfalls and inadequacies of state-centeredness, state-
centered thinking is pervasive and difficult to avoid. John Agnew argues
that state-centered thinking is a "territorial trap" that is difficult to break
out of because its underlying assumptions[22]—which accept states as givens—are "circular and cumulative," interacting with one another and
"mutually reinforcing" (72). The territorial trap has ensnared most social
science research, especially international relations theory. One of the
consequences of the territorial trap is that it leads us to conceptually
frame our writings according to the state: we collect and organize our
data at the state level. The very word *statistic* means "science of the
state" (Ayto 1990, 500), and state-centeredness is further reinforced by
the collection and calculation of statistical data without the realization
that such activities are rooted in the state. Additionally, choropleth maps
emerged from the plotting of statistical data on maps, further impressing
state-centeredness on the human mind. While the typical political map
suggests differences between states by its assignment of differing colors,
the choropleth map assigns numerical values to its colors. Thus, for myriad issues from incomes to literacy rates and health conditions, individuals are continually presented with color palettes that illustrate quantita-
tive differences between their state and other states.

State-centeredness is so omnipresent that attempts to think in other
ways are undermined by information and data formatted according to the

state (Alexander Murphy 1993, 103-5). Alexander B. Murphy puts it best when he observes that

Even explicit attempts to consider other regional forms rarely escape the bonds of state-centered thinking; the large-scale regions we identify are almost invariably based on collections of states that are thought to share certain characteristics, and small-scale regions are usually limited to economic, political, or cultural units that exist within, and are subordinate to individual states.

States are implicated in most large-scale data gathering activities, resulting in a flow of information that reinforces the ideological stranglehold of the state in our conceptual compartmentalizations of the world. Even direct challenges to state sovereignty do not entirely escape its influence. Suprastate organizations such as the European Community [now European Union], while overtly premised on ideals that transcend individual states, are in many ways still tied to state interests. Thus, considerable decision-making power within the European Community [Union] is vested in the ministers of member states, and state governments are charged with the implementation and enforcement of community directives and regulations.

For all the effort to direct attention away from the state as an all-pervasive force in modern society, however, the literature attacking state-centered thinking from below has not extricated itself from a reliance on state-derived regional conceptions. The tendency is to select states or to analyze differences from place to place within individual states. (1993, 104)

State-centeredness may be nearly impossible for many social scientists to break out of, but for most members of states' populations, it has become a very acceptable way of thinking. Many people find state-based histories, geographies, economics, politics, cultures, and data unproblematic and comfortable. They readily accept the map-as-logo, as Benedict Anderson puts it (see earlier quote, pages 88-89), and proudly display the diagrams of their states on posters, billboards, business signs and cards, as well as wear them on T-shirts, sweatshirts, shorts, and caps. They readily fly their states' flags and sing their states' anthems. In times of crisis, they rush to the defense of their states, often suffering great personal sacrifice and even loss of life. These kinds of behaviors are very much akin to Michael Billig's idea of "banal nationalism" (1995).

People are also state-centered because their financial well-being is invested in their states. In John Micklethwait and Adrian Woolridge's book, *A Future Perfect*, in which they address the issues of globalization and note the arguments that globalization is undermining the idea of the nation-state, the authors make the following observation: "In 1900, government spending in today's industrial countries accounted for less than one tenth of national income. In the United States, it accounted for less than 3 percent. Today, in the same countries, it accounts for an average of one half" (2000, 150-51). They argue that state government spending is unlikely to decline significantly for three reasons. First, the middle class benefits greatly from state spending, on everything from health care to education. Second, public-sector workers make up a substantial proportion of the electorate. Third, the large and growing ranks of retired people depend greatly on states' social security and, therefore, are unlikely to vote for or support any radical changes in states' spending (2000, 151-52). If Micklethwait and Woolridge are correct, then state-centeredness is not only burned into our minds, but also firmly rooted in modern economics. With our economic well-being tied to states, we work to maintain states as they are though these efforts may be pursued unconsciously.

States and their mechanisms are very powerful forces that shape the actions, behaviors, and identities of people and in such a pervasive manner that the people hardly notice. States' actions are frequently so forceful that states develop antagonistic relationships with their populations. Such relationships make for interesting studies, but more often the relationship between states and peoples is consensual (Foucault 1980, 131; Gramsci 1971, 12; Storey 2001, 44-45) as partly suggested by the previous examples. Indeed, in this era of modern nationalism, nation and state have developed a symbiotic relationship with each another.

The Curious Relationship of States and Nations

States in the broadest sense of word are very old human constructs that trace themselves back to the earliest human civilizations. As noted earlier, states require permanent resident populations, but populations of a specific character are not required. Thus, states have existed in many forms, each with its own raison d'être. City-states—perhaps the earliest form of the state—are small, frequently containing populations with similar cultural characteristics. The classical Greek city-states, for example, all were inhabited by Greeks with none claiming to be truly and exclusively the rightful Greek state. In contrast, empires are enormous, but like city-states they do not derive their legitimacy from the idea that they are the sole representatives of single, homogeneous groups of people. However, whereas a people of commonality may stretch across multiple

city-states, a single empire will stretch across peoples of varying characteristics. Found in the Roman Empire, for example, were hundreds of
different languages and dozens of religions. Even twentieth-century empires like Russia and China were culturally very heterogeneous. Both
city-states and empires contrast with nation-states in that ideally single
peoples (i.e., the nations) occupy nation-states with each state serving as
the true representative of its people. Thus, the raison d'être of states is
now to serve nations.

The nation-state is a relatively new human construct, assuming its
character of today only beginning with the Enlightenment of late eighteenth century and tracing its protocharacteristics as far back as the
Treaty of Westphalia in 1648. The historical development of the nation
and the nation-state will be discussed in greater detail in chapters 4 and
5. Suffice it to note at this point that with the rise of nationalism at the
end of the eighteenth century, states have found their legitimacies in nations. Nations satisfy states' requirement of a permanent resident population. In return, nations' need for a genuine political self-government is
realized in state sovereignty and state government. The needs of nations
and states are mutually fulfilling in other ways as well when they are
linked. An important nexus for nation and state is territory, which is integral to both of their existences. Nations partially derive their identities
through particular territories, and states, with their sovereignty over territory, allow nations to protect and cultivate their identities.

Spatial Disjunctions

Though nations can exercise sovereignty over their territories through
states, the spatial extents of a nation's territories often are not the same as
the spatial extents of the state's territories. Disjunctions occur as nations
occupy lands beyond states' borders, and states commonly find multiple
nations within their borders (see figure 2.1). The nation-state ideal, in
which every nation possesses its own state and every state is occupied by
a single nation, is hardly the norm in the world. With as many as five
thousand nations in the world and only approximately two hundred
states, hardly a correlation between nations and states exists. Walker
Connor noted in a 1971 survey that less than 10 percent of the 132 of the
then existing states could justifiably be described as nation-states though
almost all the countries of the world are treated as nation-states (1978,
382). Moreover, countries like Hungary and Albania are considered true
nation-states because their populations are almost 100 percent Hungarian

and Albanian respectively though sizeable populations of Hungarians and Albanians live outside of the Hungarian and Albanian states. More than thirty years after Walker Connor's survey, the number of states on the world's map has increased to almost two hundred, but it is unlikely that still any more than 10 percent conform to the nation-state ideal. For example, multinational states like the Soviet Union and Yugoslavia broke up into fifteen and six republics respectively. Slovenia conforms to the nation-state ideal and now Croatia does too, thanks to the expulsions and accompanying humans rights violations of Croatia's Serb minority. Otherwise, the successors of the Soviet Union and Yugoslavia no more conform to the nation-state ideal than their predecessors. Thus, where two countries that did not conform to the nation-state ideal existed, nineteen now exist in their places.

Wars between states, oppression, and national conflict often result from the spatial disjunctions between nations and states. Many of the world's most intense and prolonged conflicts revolve around nations' attempts to control territories they perceive to be rightfully theirs. The list is long,[23] but it is worth noting a few: Northern Ireland—where Irish nationalists and Unionists/Loyalists have differing conceptions of what relationship Northern Ireland should have with the Republic of Ireland and the United Kingdom; the former Yugoslavia—where nations dispute one another's claims to territory; the Israeli-Palestinian conflict—where two groups assert their claims to a similar homeland; India-Pakistan—where Indians and Pakistanis both claim rights to Kashmir and Jammu; Taiwan—where some Taiwanese prefer independence and others unification with mainland China under Taiwanese leadership, in conflict with mainland Chinese who see Taiwan as a renegade province of China; and Tibet—annexed by China in the 1950s, the Chinese government harshly suppressing the Tibetan people. These examples can be classified as conflicts that involve two or more states, though some would argue that they are internal conflicts. Clear examples of internal conflicts rising from spatial disjunctions between nations and states are perhaps more numerous: the Basque region of Spain, Kosovo of Serbia and Montenegro, Chechnya of Russia, Abkhazia and South Ossetia of Georgia, Nagorno-Karabakh of Azerbaijan, Kurdish areas, most notably in Turkey and Iraq though tensions also exist in Kurdish areas of Iran and Syria, and lastly East Timor of Indonesia and Eritrea of Ethiopia before both gained independence from their respective countries. These are some of the conflicts that have captured the world's attention in recent decades though many others exist. A. J. Christopher estimates that a potential of ten to twenty new states may emerge from these and other conflicts (1999).

States' Attempts to Create Nation-States

To bring the spatial distributions of nations and states into coterminous coincidence, states will act both externally and internally—using their "monopoly of legitimate violence" when they deem necessary. Externally, states will attempt to annex lands beyond their borders where members of their nations reside, often justifying their actions because neighboring states are oppressing their members who live there as minorities. If this option is not possible, states will try to influence the politics of neighboring states on behalf of their minorities. Internally, states will seek to inculcate their populations with the state idea (i.e., raison d'être). Because the state idea usually is to serve a single nation, states are likely to perceive minorities as threats, particularly if they are members of other states' titular nations, meaning that other states may advance territorial claims on behalf of their minorities. To nullify a real or potential threat to their territories, states, as they solidify their control over their territories through their functional networks, will tend to homogenize their populations (see figure 3.7). In doing so they will assimilate, expel, or exterminate any minorities who do not conform to certain expectations and requirements (Gellner 1983, 2). The term *ethnic cleansing* emerged to describe this process as it occurred during the breakup of Yugoslavia in the 1990s though the processes to which it refers are much older.[24]

As states attempt to eliminate the spatial disjunctions between their territories and the distributions of nations, states' actions add to the complexity of human identity. At one level states create their own layer of identity known as citizenship (Schwarzmantel 2003). Unfortunately, citizenship is often confused and conflated with national identity though they are differing forms of identity. In addition to bestowing citizenship, states—with their spatial networks—actively involve themselves in determining tribal identity, ethnicity, and race though these forms of identity are not necessarily state based like citizenship and can exist independently of states. Similarly, states also shape national identity.

Citizens and Nations

Citizenship is what states bestow on their populations. In bestowing citizenship, states usually impart to their citizens their state names. For example, the French and Nigerian states impart the words *French* and *Nigerian* to their citizens respectively. Thanks to the phenomenon of citizenship, French and Nigerians exist. However, it is quite possible that nations with those names already exist. For example, a French nation exists side by side with a state-based French identity, and their co-existence is very much a product of the modern nation-state era in which nations and states are linked together and mutually evolving. Further-more, because the raison d'être of states derives from nations, it is not happenstance that nations' names and state identities use the same words. Indeed, states deliberately choose the same names as part of their process of binding themselves to nations.

The coincidence of nations' names and names for state-based identi-ties makes it appear that only one identity exists where there are two. Indeed, membership is overlapping but not totally coincident and, there-fore, it is important to distinguish between two identities though they may have the same name. For example, a person may be French not only because he or she is a member of the French nation but because he or she is from France and thus has citizenship[25] within France. In such cases, a person has two identities but with the same name. It may seem inconse-quential to distinguish between being French for national reasons and being French on citizenship grounds if one is French regardless. How-ever, though the majority of the population in France may be French on both counts, not everyone is. Basques, for example, may be called French because they have French citizenship and are from France but they may consider themselves as members of the Basque nation. There-fore, such individuals are both French and Basques. Referring to them as only French or only Basques when they have both identities fails to rec-ognize the complexity of identity and may fail to adequately explain situations in research and news reporting. French identity deriving from citizenship is not insignificant because those with it share a common identity by living in a functional region (i.e., France) where they are con-joined with other peoples in the identical circulation and educational sys-tems that use the same bureaucratic language. The influence of citizen-ship can be seen in its influence on the Basque nation as a whole. Though Basques in France may share a common national identity with Basques in Spain, they are divided by citizenship in that Basques in Spain have Spanish citizenship, meaning that Basques in Spain are also Spaniards. The spatial division of Basques across two states means that not all Basques have the same combinations of identity, best described by Guntram Herb and David Kaplan's term *nested identities* (1999). Unity may be compromised, and that is why nationalists want to bring their people into the same state so that everyone is influenced by the same state actions.

State-Nations

Nations do not always exist side by side with state-based identities of the same name. In the aforementioned Nigerian case, no Nigerian nation stands alongside a Nigerian state identity. Nigerians exist but only as citizens of the Nigerian state, though the popular practice of conflating nation and state leads many to assume that a Nigerian nation exists. The Nigerian situation is by no means rare but rather very common. Throughout much of Africa, Southwest Asia (i.e., the Middle East), Central and Southeast Asia, and the Americas, the peoples of countries exist because they are citizens of states and not because they are nations—at least that is how their identities began though many have developed corresponding national identities. Not coincidentally, many of the countries in these regions were formerly European colonies. When the European empires drew boundaries for their colonies on the map, they did so with the intent of claiming nàtural resources and not on behalf of supposed nations that lived within the drawn boundaries. With decolonization in the mid-twentieth century, these colonies became states, and the people of them were soon called nations though little attempt was made to re-draw the boundaries according to the nation-state ideal.[26]

It may be tempting to call these states and their same-named peoples "artificial" because they were created by European colonialist powers. However, the antonym for artificial—which means created by human beings—is natural, which means from nature or some deity (e.g., God). Therefore, all states—being human constructs—are artificial. Not only is the artificial/natural dichotomy inaccurate in classifying states, but it also brings with it very biased cultural and ideological baggage that convolutes a clear understanding of nations and states. The origins of the artificial/natural dichotomy will be discussed further in chapters 4 and 5. Suffice it to say that less biased terminology should be applied. James Anderson has coined the term *state-nation* to refer to situations in which a state predates the nation and employs the commonly used *nation-state* for the opposite occurrence (1988, 21). More commonly, the terms *civic nation* or even *territorial nation* have been coined to describe the former situation and *ethnic nation* to depict the latter situation[27] (Anthony Smith 1986b, 129-73; Anthony Smith 1991). Though state-nation is less frequently used in scholarly literature, it poignantly illustrates the power of states in shaping human identity in the very construction of the term, which places *state* antecedent to *nation*.

Interestingly, state-nation and civic nation have been applied to Western Europe as well as to the former European colonial areas already mentioned. The French in particular are used as the model of the civic nation. Thus, the French, a clearly recognized nation, developed by the very processes that are working today in countries like Nigeria, though no Nigerian nation exists. The real difference then between the French and Nigerians is the effect of time. The French have been molded by the mechanisms of the French state much longer than Nigerians have by their state. Thus, it is not accurate or fair to refer to the French nation as natural and the Nigerian nation as artificial when both are the product of similar forces. The Nigerian nation may one day be just as cohesive as the French nation if the Nigerian state survives long enough.

The survival of a state is crucial for its corresponding nation. The American Civil War, for example, illustrates that American national identity was not fully cohesive fourscore and seven years after an emerging national identity led to the American Revolution. The United States survived and implemented more state mechanisms to homogenize its people to the degree that they would identify with the state with a corresponding national identity. Today, American national identity is very cohesive (Associated Press 2002)—just as much as French nationhood, which has developed over roughly the same period. Similar processes have worked in other states though the states eventually failed. A Yugoslav nation and a Soviet nation developed in Yugoslavia and the Soviet Union respectively, with numerous individuals within Yugoslavia identifying themselves as Yugoslavs in censuses.[28] Unfortunately, many academics and nationalists of competing nations dismissed such state projects as artificial and labeled Yugoslavs as nothing more than the products of state manipulation and mixed marriages. Yugoslav and Soviet national identity failed not because they were not real but because the Yugoslav and Soviet states failed before the corresponding identities became cohesive and widely accepted. Despite the failure of the Yugoslav and Soviet states, the new states that emerged immediately began nation-building projects of their own. Among others, Bosnian, Macedonian, and Moldovan national identities already are present, though many also dismiss them as artificial. They are a testament to the pervasive forces of states in that they show that states can mold people together into nations, which could be identified as state-nations—note the quotation at the opening of the chapter.

States and Other Forms of Identity

Nationhood and citizenship are not the only nuances of human group identity. Tribal, racial, and ethnic identities—among others—are also very important layers of human identity. These identities are not necessarily political in that they are not tied specifically to statehood. However, they have often become political as many nations derive their identities from particular tribes, races, and ethnic groups. Some nations are comprised of a single tribe, race, or ethnic group. *Ethnic nation*, for example, is a term used to describe a national identity derived from a single ethnicity. Because states derive their legitimacy from nations, they too politicize these other forms of identity by crafting their citizenship laws according to specific tribal identities, races, and ethnicities. Thus, the interplay between nations and states ensnares tribal, racial, and ethnic identities, not only politicizing these identities, but also transforming their characters and creating new ones (Jenkins 1994).

Koen Wellens' article on the Premi of China is an illustrative study on how state action alters ethnic identity (1998). In the 1950s and 1960s, the Chinese government undertook a classification program that led to the official recognition of fifty-five *minzu* (i.e., ethnic groups or nationalities), though perhaps a thousand sought recognition. Among the groups were the Premi. Traditionally, the Chinese used the term *Xifan* when referring to the Premi, though the Xifan were a much larger group of which the Premi were the southernmost branch (22). After the new classification, the Premi of Yunnan province were labeled *Pumi* and the Premi of Sichuan province were designated *Zangzu*. Pumi was simply a Chinese word for Premi framed within the "limitations of the syllabic Chinese language" (20). On the other hand, Zangzu means *Tibetan* (18), a term for an already existing group that was much larger. Interestingly, no political motive underlay the differing classifications. State bureaucrats simply applied language and religion to classify groups, but because two groups of bureaucrats were sent to two provinces, each group came to its own conclusions when examining language and religion. The differing outcomes show that language and religion are not as clear-cut and concrete as often thought. In this case, state action and political manipulation were limited to merely the naming of a group. Nonetheless, classification systems have more profound effects in that they determine which groups will exist, how many will exist, and who will be in those groups. The Chinese classification project was limited to ethnic groups but is likely to have long-term implications for the development of national consciousness among the people classified.

While it remains to be seen what state action will do to the evolution of identity in China, other examples—which have worked over longer periods—show the effects of state action. Earlier, Benedict Anderson's ideas of the roles of maps and museums and their influence in shaping national identity were noted. Anderson also notes the census. His examples, which he draws from Charles Hirschman's work on British census taking in colonial Southeast Asia (1986, 1987), show how states reshape forms of identity or, as Anderson puts it, "continuously agglomerated, disaggregated, recombined, intermixed, and reordered" identities in their Southeast Asian colonies (1991, 164). Drawing on the work of Hirschman, Anderson notes how British census categories slowly became less religious and more racial with some races receiving their names from islands (e.g., Javanese) and then after independence combined into state names like *Malaysian, Chinese,* and *Indian* while maintaining their racial undertones (1991, 164-65).

In chapter 2, the former apartheid government of South Africa was noted for its manipulation of tribal identity. It is noteworthy here to identify some of the effects of the South African government's manipulations. As one example, the South African government created a province known as Transkei. The government ended hostilities between numerous tribes who suddenly found themselves within this new territorial unit. A modern transportation system worked in conjunction with a modern economy to end traditional subsistence farming and encourage people to migrate to the newly growing cities. A new educational system used a standardized *isiXhosa* language, which eliminated dialectical difference. All these actions of the South African state encouraged intermarriage and led people of the province to think of themselves as Transkeians (Hammond-Tooke 1970).

The cases of China, Southeast Asia, and South Africa depict state action as nothing more than the mindless and often overpowering deeds of thoughtless bureaucracy. Often state action is just that, but other times it has a specific political agenda. States act very deliberately when they perceive certain identities to be threats. Not understanding the nuances of multilayered and nested identity, nor even understanding that identity is multilayered and nested, state leaders and bureaucracies are quick to label individuals with particular cultural characteristics as threats or the enemy. For example, Saddam Hussein, the former leader of Iraq, saw Kurds and Shiite Muslims within Iraq as potential enemies and thus persecuted them. Persecution led to disloyalty and the typical situation in which states create self-fulfilling prophecies in making an enemy out of people that it distrusts. Instead, Saddam Hussein could have been more all-embracing and promoted a more multicultural Iraqi identity that embraced and earned the loyalty of the people that he persecuted. Ironically, Hussein's opponents used similar simpleminded ideas of identity to vilify Hussein. Presidents George Bush and his son George W. Bush would argue that Hussein was so despicable that he would kill even his own people by pointing to Saddam Hussein's treatment of the Kurds, implying that Hussein was killing fellow Iraqis. Such an argument is partially true in that it recognizes only the state-based identity of Iraqi citizenship but not the multilayered and nested identities of Iraqis. Whether this argument was crafted out of ignorance or not, it served the political agenda of American presidents. Interestingly, both the Iraqi (i.e., the Hussein) and American governments selectively used information to define who is and is not an Iraqi.

Discerning the Various Levels of Identity

States' active roles in reshaping tribal, racial, and ethnic identities along with both states' and nations' tendencies to draw on these forms of identities to formulate criteria for citizenship and nationhood further confuse the lines between nations and state-based identities (i.e., citizenship). Identities are further confused when political agendas lead states to oversimplify identity in general and then subsequently perceive certain cultural characteristics as threatening. These confusions often result in the failure to recognize the complexity of shared group identities and the consequent failure to adequately explain actual situations in research and news reporting. Yet the differences between these forms of identity are significant though individual names may be overlapping and have multiple meanings.

The Hungarians of Romania, for example, are written about without considering what makes them Hungarian or that they have multilayered identities. These people are labeled Hungarians for their ethnicity—namely, that they speak the Hungarian language, eat Hungarian food, wear Hungarian clothes, and have Hungarian views and values. What is overlooked is that these people are also Romanians in the sense of citizenship—that is, that they live within the Romanian nation-state, meaning that their identity has been shaped by the Romanian state. Hungarian and Romanian nationalists commonly ignore this layer of this group's identity. Hungarian nationalists despise the effects of Romanian state policy on ethnic Hungarians in Romania but will not acknowledge the profundity of these effects because they want these people within the Hungarian fold. Romanian nationalists do not see how much their state has shaped the ethnic Hungarians to be like them because they focus on the cultural differences that persist. Thus, they call these people Hungarians to emphasize the differences. Ironically, the Romanian government, seeing ethnic Hungarians within its state's boundaries as members of the Hungarian nation, perceived the ethnic Hungarians as a threat and treated them accordingly. In response, many Hungarians—who simply may have been an ambivalent ethnic group while receptive to Romanian nationhood—became politicized through persecution and subsequently adopted Hungarian nationhood.

While intense labeling goes on, seldom are individuals concerned asked directly to which nation they belong. The thoughtless tendency to label these people Hungarian for their ethnicity or Romanian for their citizenship is an injustice. The complexity of multilayered and nested identity is further compounded by the complexity of nationhood. Ethnicity and citizenship are usually bestowed upon individuals. Ethnicity is based on a set of cultural characteristics, frequently with nebulous parameters, often of little consequence to those within an ethnic group who are indifferent or ambivalent toward such labeling placed upon them. Citizenship is imparted to individuals largely by states and by virtue of where individuals live, though they may freely move to other states. In contrast to ethnicity and citizenship, nationhood exhibits great self-awareness and a conscious, self-directed decision to be part of a group known as a nation regardless of what state one lives within. Though outside forces such as the state may influence the decision of individuals, national identity is still an inner-generated loyalty toward a specific group of people. Therefore, because nationhood is a personal choice it is not fair to label everyone within Romania as Romanians because they are from Romania with Romanian citizenship or label a specific subset exclusively Hungarian because they are ethnically Hungarian. Because nationhood is a personal choice, the only way to ascertain nationhood of the ethnic Hungarians in Romania is to ask them. Those who see themselves as a separate and distinct people who need a government and thus state of their own are likely to say that they are members of the Hungarian nation. Those who note that their cultural characteristics are not of the majority but are willing to share the same political fate as the others within Romania are likely to classify themselves as members of the Romanian nation.

What is important to remember is that each person has a number of identities. In the case just discussed, where three identities were highlighted, a person can be Hungarian, Romanian, and Romanian in terms of ethnicity, nationhood, and citizenship or Hungarian, Hungarian, and Romanian for the same categories. As mentioned, it is important to note the differences in the types of identities that an individual has. Hungarian nationalists and the Romanian state are in great disagreement over the number of Hungarians who live in Romania, which range from one to three million. Their varying estimates derive from their tendencies to measure one layer of identity while treating individuals as if they had only one layer of identity.

The Bosnian case is just as illustrative but also tragic. Serb and Croat nationalists perceived a world in which Serbs had to be Eastern Orthodox Christians, Croats had to be Roman Catholics, and Muslims had to be Muslims. They saw these categories of identity as exclusive and unprob-lematic and denied the legitimacy of Bosnian, Yugoslav, or any other form of multilayered and nested identity. Unfortunately, as they worked to make their perceptions the only operating reality in Bosnia-Herzegovina by the end of the 1990s, international diplomats like Lord Owen accepted these simplistic conceptions of identity.[29] Unfortunately, they were like people who reject Nazism but accept the Nazi definition that Jews cannot be Germans. Despite such conceptions, there were Serbs, Croats, and Muslims who not only saw themselves as Serbs, Croats, and Muslims, but also Bosnians, Yugoslavs, and members of other groups as well.

Nations' Influence on States

So far in this chapter, it appears that the relationship between nations and states is unidirectional with nations as recipients—even victims—of states' actions. Though states' actions can be overwhelming, nations are not helpless victims in the nation-state relationship. State bureaucracies are after all composed of people, and this allows people to direct states' powers. Sometimes these people are benevolent as they operate states' mechanisms, and other times those who take control of state power are from a single segment of society who desire to employ the state's mechanisms to impose their values and culture on the entire population of the state.[30] Thus, the relationship between states and nations is multi-directional, or circular, as nations influence states while states influence nations. It is sometimes difficult to detect whether an idea emanates from the nation or the state in the symbiotic relationship between nation and state.

The United States provides examples of both of these aforemen-tioned situations. The U.S. Census Bureau is an example of a benevolent state agency in that it created a list of five racial categories on its 1990 census questionnaire. Many Americans, however, found that these categories did not adequately represent who they were. In response, the U.S. Census Bureau created sixty-three racial categories for the 2000 census. This single example illustrates how the state attempts to accommodate its multicultural population. At the same time, segments of the American population have changed or tried to change state policy with the intent of using the state's mechanisms to redefine American identity. Those who venerate particular symbolism and see Americans as properly Christian and English speaking have perhaps done the most to change state (read U.S.) law. The Founding Fathers did not see the need to create a pledge or pass legislation protecting state symbols. Yet, in 1942, those desiring a pledge successfully lobbied the U.S. Congress to officially recognize the Pledge of Allegiance.[31] Certain segments of American society also desire to ban flag burning, though thus far the state (i.e., the Supreme Court) views flag burning as a constitutionally protected form of free speech. Therefore, those desiring to ban flag burning seek to change the Constitution. The U.S. Constitution does not specify that Americans should subscribe to a specific religion. Yet in recent history, those wanting Americans to be more Christian have inserted Christian statements into state language and practices. For example, individuals sponsored legislation so that "under God" was inserted in 1954 (Baer 1992a; Baer 1992b) and "In God We Trust" was printed on paper money beginning in 1957 (United States Department of Treasury: Fact Sheets). The U.S. Constitution does not specify that Americans should speak a particular language. Yet in the 1980s and 1990s, almost two hundred years after the Constitution was written, many Americans have tried to make English the official language of the United States (Gallegos 1994; Tatalovich 1995). Though the English-only movement has not succeeded in changing federal law, it has changed many local and state (read provincial) laws to mandate the use of English under certain circumstances. All these changes in the state's (read U.S. government's) treatments and expectations of its population are aimed at creating greater uniformity within the population. Interestingly, it is not the state that is seeking to homogenize its population so much as it is segments of the population directing the state's mechanisms to homogenize the entire population according to its conception of nationhood.

Earlier it was noted that Irish weather maps, and indeed many kinds of Irish maps, include Northern Ireland and understate the political boundary between the Republic of Ireland and Northern Ireland. What is the source of this kind of cartographic depiction? Is it the Irish state or is it a segment of Irish society directing the mechanisms of the state? Even in seemingly more clear-cut cases such as the state requirement that all

Irish schoolchildren learn the Irish language, the source of such requirements may not appear to be what it is. Again, is it the Irish state or is it a segment of Irish society directing the mechanisms of the state? Drawing the line between the two is not easy if one is continually influencing the actions of the other. It may be a chicken-and-egg sort of question.

Though nations and states bind themselves to one another, the evolving relationship between nation and state can reinforce this bond or can tear it apart. In Yugoslavia, for example, each successive census contained new identity categories. As one example, the category "Muslim in an ethnic sense" did not appear until 1961 and the category "Muslim in a national sense" first materialized in 1971 (Burg and Berbaum, 1989, 538). The Yugoslav state added and changed categories such as these in response to the evolving identities in Yugoslavia—much in the same way that the U.S. government has responded to demands and pressures of its citizens. In earlier times, Muslims had identified themselves as Croat, Serb, or some other designation. However, as Croat and Serb identities increasingly derived from Roman Catholicism and Eastern Orthodox Christianity respectively, the Muslims found themselves without an identity category. Thus, the Yugoslav state created the "Muslim" category for them because it was the common denominator of those who did not identity with the other census categories. The Yugoslav state was responding to the evolution of identity; however, identity became increasingly polarized as it was fueled by conflicting nationalisms within the state. Thus, the Yugoslav state aided in the development of identities that had increasing problems coexisting within the same state, though it simultaneously tried to suppress such nationalistic feelings while promoting a Yugoslav identity. Serb nationalists receive considerable blame for the disintegration of the Yugoslav state. They are accused of taking control of the state mechanisms and using them to Serbianize the Yugoslav population. They are accused of doing this since the inception of the state in 1918 (Lampe 1996, 125-28; Macartney and Palmer 1962, 221-22; Singleton 1985, 143-44), most clearly seen in that the Serb capital— Belgrade—became the new state's capital and the Serbian king became the Yugoslav king. Croat and other nationalisms, rising in tandem or in response to Serb nationalism, exacerbated the tensions. Though Josip Tito suppressed nationalism during his reign between 1945 and 1981, diverging nationalisms continued to develop and foment, expressing themselves again after his death, undermining the Yugoslav state again and finally destroying it in the 1990s.

Nationalism and Patriotism

Nations require states, and states satisfy their needs for a permanent resident population by linking themselves with nations. Nations and states bind together as their respective nationalist projects and state-building projects evolve. When states do not have nations, they will create them—known as state-nations. In such cases, nationalist projects and state-building tend to be synonymous. For ethnic nations—which develop from ethnic groups that predate corresponding states—nationalist projects and state-building also tend to fuse together. Ethnic nationalism is a bottom-up process, and state-building is a top-down process. They may develop in opposing directions, but they frequently become entangled in each other. Ethnic nations possess a certain degree of cultural homogeneity but lack statehood while states have the political mechanisms but lack a set of cultural criteria to homogenize their populations. With states frequently ambivalent about any particular set of common criteria for its population (concerned solely with loyalty of the population to the state), ethnic nationalism frequently commandeers state nationalism and steers it toward its goals. In the aforementioned Yugoslav case, Serb ethnic nationalism commandeered the Yugoslav state and attempted to define Yugoslav identity in its own image. Such cases are not unusual. In the Soviet Union, the state attempted to create a Soviet nation. Lacking any sense of what the cultural characteristics of the Soviet nation would be, the Soviet nation was defined by the dominant group, the Russians, who in turn conceived of a Soviet national identity identical to Russian national identity (Wixman 1980, 26-35).

Though ethnic and state nationalism have complementary needs that frequently lead to their fusing together, their other goals may conflict and lead to difficulties. While states seek to preserve their territorial integrities, ethnic nationalisms may have goals that threaten states' territorial integrities both internally and externally. A state with more than one ethnic nation may find that the dominant ethnic nation crafts policies that alienate other groups within the state territory. Such was the case in Yugoslavia and the Soviet Union. Such could also be the case in the United States if any one ethnic group takes control of the state mechanisms and forces its identity on the other groups. Though the Christian and English-only agendas have not become fully institutionalized, each success has agitated non-Christian and non-English-speaking Americans who otherwise have readily accepted and supported American identity. Externally, if ethnic nations have ethnic brethren living outside their states, they may seek to incorporate the lands of their ethnic brethren into the state. Ethnic nationalism's irredentist claims and practices can lead states into conflict with neighboring states that can ultimately undermine states' primary goal of preserving their territorial integrities.

Though nations and states complement each other, they foster differing loyalties: nationalism and patriotism respectively. Nationalism is a loyalty to one's people, and patriotism—originating from the Greek *patriōtēs,* meaning *fatherland*—is a loyalty to one's state as it is manifested in its territory. Thus, patriotism is more closely tied to the state and citizenship. For state-nations like Americans, little difference exists between the two concepts of nationalism and patriotism, most likely because no spatial disjunctions exist for nation and state in that the United States is almost exclusively inhabited by Americans and Americans claim no additional territory as their own. With the American identity fully framed by state nationalism, loyalty to the people and loyalty to the state are more or less the same. The tendency for Americans to use the word *patriotism* to describe their feelings rather than *nationalism* may stem from the mid-twentieth century when extreme forms of nationalism proved to be destructive; for example, the "N" in Nazi refers to national. Thus, Americans began to see patriotism and nationalism as differing sides of the same coin whereby patriotism was a positive expression and nationalism a negative one[32] (Fyfe 1940).

While state nations frequently find few differences between nationalism and patriotism because they developed within the territories of their states, ethnic nations find themselves in completely differing situations. Ethnic nations typically derive their identities from ethnic groups whose ethnogenesis predates statehood. Obtaining their own state territories is then the last step for ethnic groups who evolve into nations—that is, ethnic nations. They may take control of existing states or carve their own states out of already existing states. In the former case, they often find national minorities that they must contend with. In the latter case, they most probably will meet resistance in creating their own states. Frequently, they will not succeed in establishing state boundaries that fully enclose the nation, resulting in a very unsatisfactory situation.

In these situations, where nations' territories are not coterminous with their states' territories, it becomes clear that nationalism and patriotism are not synonymous as feelings of nationalism and patriotism lead to conflicting feelings and fail to be mutually reinforcing. In such cases, though states may represent nations and even press claims to their nations' territories that lie beyond states' territories, states have their own interests—especially concerning self-preservation. Thus, states of ethnic nations will act in their own best interests rather in their nations' best interests when the two interests are contrary. Take the case of the Irish state—that is, the Republic of Ireland—vis-à-vis Northern Ireland and the desire of Irish nationalists. When Irish nationalists established an Irish state in the 1920s, they were unable to extend their new state's boundaries over six counties in the north—which remained in the United Kingdom as Northern Ireland. Irish nationalists would still like to extend the Irish state's boundaries to include Northern Ireland to bring the entire Irish nation on the island of Ireland into a single Irish nation-state. The Irish state is sympathetic to the Irish nationalist cause and would extend the boundaries of its state accordingly. Yet the Irish state is primarily concerned with self-preservation and will not take any action that would threaten its well-being. Most obviously, since the Irish state's army is no match for the British army, the Irish state will not attempt to satisfy the Irish nationalist cause through military action. Such an action could destroy the Irish state. Hence, Irish nationalists formed their own guerilla force—the Irish Republican Army (IRA)—to carry out their cause. The Irish state is not necessarily unsympathetic to the Irish nationalist cause and also not necessarily unwilling to use its apparatus, more specifically its diplomatic arm, to aid the Irish nationalists. It has also not been unwilling to allowing Irish nationalists to use the Irish state's territory to store arms, recruit, train, and seek refuge from the British military in Northern Ireland. This support, however, may only be extended as long as it does not provoke some form of retaliation from the British that would harm the Irish state, in which case, the Irish state may see it in its best interests to withdraw support from the Irish nationalists and even press the Irish nationalists to negotiate a compromise unpalatable to the Irish nationalists—which it has done. In such a case, patriotism and nationalism are in conflict as those who continue to pursue the nationalist cause become increasingly unpatriotic as they do so.

Ireland is only one example where spatial disjunction between nation and state puts patriotism and nationalism at odds. The war in Bosnia-Herzegovina in the 1990s is another example. Bosnian Serb nationalists benefited greatly from the Yugoslav state—which was run primarily by Serbs—in their national cause. However, after the Yugoslav state began to suffer greatly from political and economic sanctions placed on it by the international community for aiding the Bosnian Serb cause, the Yugoslav government pressed the Bosnian Serb nationalists into accepting a peace settlement that the Bosnian Serb nationalists found unacceptable (Silber and Little 1997, 335-44).

States' Roles in Shaping Nations' Sense of Territories

In examining the territorial relationship between nations and states, usually only the spatial distributions of nations are considered relative to states' boundaries. Hence, illustrations such as figure 2.1 are used to illustrate where nations are distributed relative to states. These illustrations, however, tend to treat national and state territories as fixed and immutable, coincidently coexisting in earth space, while emphasis is placed on the control of them. Nations' territories, however, are as fluid and changing as human identity itself. As states have enormous influence in shaping nations' identities, they likewise have enormous influence in determining the places and territories that nations bond to. States' functional regions direct the movement of people within and across particular territories. The shared contact of people within the spatial networks of states' functional regions encourages people to simultaneously bond with one another and with the places they become intimately involved with. States' rules, regulations, media, and educational systems reinforce the shared experiences of places and in turn help them to develop into national places of significance. Thus, states' spatial networks act as conduits for the development of nationhood and one of its attributes, national sense of territory—or national topophilia.

Where states' boundaries are stable through time, spatial disjunctions between nations' territories and states' territories are unlikely to develop as national consciousness develops within states' territories. Such is the case with many state-nations. However, in cases where states' boundaries shift often, nations may lose contact and control of places and territories they hold dear. Though spatial disjunctions develop between states' territories and nations' territories, memories of the places that have shaped nations' identities can remain strong. Accordingly, irredentist feelings emerge. Such is the case for many ethnic nations. The shifting boundaries of Central and Eastern Europe are a clear indication of these situations (see figure 3.8). Irredentist feelings will emerge where shifting boundaries leave significant places and territories outside nations' current states. States can use their mechanisms to remold nations' topophilia within existing state territories, and irredentist feelings will fade. However, when nationalists use their states' mechanisms to cultivate the psychological attachments to places and pass them on from generation to generation, the spatial disjunctions remain and irredentist feelings intensify.

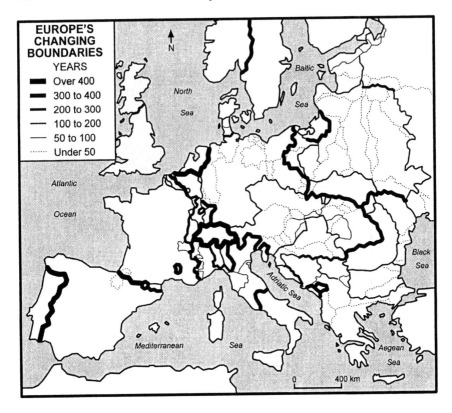

Figure 3.8 Map Showing the Permanence of European Boundaries
(Pounds 1963, 29).

The process of identifying the individual places that are significant to nations as they were discussed in chapter 2 is aided by the identification of past states, their territorial configurations, and the location of their boundaries. Indeed, a sort of historical dialogue between the micro-scale places and the macro-scale state territories that have existed through time informs us of nations' territories as they define them. Therefore, the identification and mapping of historical state boundaries contributes to the understanding of which places and territories define nations' identities. Illustrations depicting spatial distributions of nations and states become more explanatory when they include a third layer—that of past state boundaries that continue to represent nations' senses of territories (see figure 3.9).

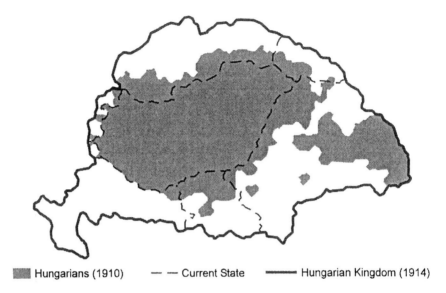

Hungarians (1910) — — Current State ════ Hungarian Kingdom (1914)

Figure 3.9 Nations, States, and Past States
In this diagram, the spatial disjunctions between the spatial distribution of Hungarians and the modern Hungarian state are clear. The additional delineation of the Hungarian Kingdom's boundaries as they once were helps to explain the contemporary disjunctions between the Hungarian nation and state. Furthermore, the consideration of the historic kingdom's boundaries helps to explain why places and territories beyond the modern Hungarian state's boundaries are significant to the Hungarian nation.

Unfortunately, national conflict is frequently attributed to the simple spatial disjunctions between nations and states. This view inadequately explains numerous actual conflicts as nations frequently attempt to extend their states' boundaries into territories not inhabited by their members. To compensate for the insufficient explanations of such behavior, concepts of "geostrategy" and "resources" are then employed with the assumption that human greed drives people to want more. Because every place and territory is located next to some other place and territory, and because every place and territory has some resources, they become safe explanations for would-be pundits. Unfortunately, these explanations stem from views that places and territories are just commodities and fail to appreciate the full meanings of places and territories in regard to their roles in human identity. Similarly, such utilitarian views fail to recognize the territorial aspect of ethnic cleansing and thus treat the phenomenon as mere hatred of one people for another simply because they are different. These views, however, fail to explain for example why the majority of Roman Catholics and Protestants live peacefully together in the world though they are in conflict in Northern Ireland. They also inadequately explain, for example, why most Jews and Muslims coexist without conflict in most places except in Israel, especially the West Bank. Only the ability to see that territories are more than mere commodities, valued only for their strategic locations and resources, explains national conflict more clearly. Thus, the Northern Ireland and Israeli-Palestinian conflicts are really about nations attempting to exert control over places and territories they use to define their identities. Religious belief is bound up in these conflicts, not as determinants but as corollaries. Territory then is very much at the root of ethnic cleansing though it is often suggested but improperly addressed in explanations of national conflict.

National conflict then is not merely the result of the spatial disjunctions between nations and states but more precisely the spatial disjunctions between current and past states where past states enclosed the significant places of nations that current states do not. When nations claim territories inhabited by their fellow members, political leaders and the international community in general show understanding and sympathy, even support. However, when nations attempt to exert control over territories not inhabited by their members, they are treated as aggressors. This is the result of the modern nation-state era in which nations and states ideally are supposed to be coterminous. This sort of thinking, which determines support or opposition in national conflicts, presents a dilemma for nations who have strong emotional attachments to territories not inhabited by their members. The nation-state ideal suggests that nations should give up such territories or their claims to them, depending on the circumstances. However, nations do not easily relinquish territories that help to define them. Many find it more palatable to conform to the nation-state ideal by ethnically cleansing their territories. Indeed, ethnic cleansing is the product of the nation-state ideal combined with sense of territory. Though ethnic cleansing is often treated as merely one group acting on its hatred of another group, ethnic cleansing actually refers to the "cleansing of territory" of other groups to conform to the nation-state ideal and thus legitimize a nation's claim to territory.

Ethnic cleansing was mentioned earlier as a project of states. In this section, it seems to be a project of nations. In reality, it is a joint project of both nations and states, and it is often difficult to discern which one initiates any given ethnic cleansing project. It may seem that the ethnic cleansing idea begins with nations who then employ their states' mechanisms to carry out such projects. However, because states influence the development of national identities, states can mold nations in such ways that nations will launch ethnic cleansing projects.

The close linking of nations and states not only makes it difficult to determine where the concept of ethnic cleansing originates, but it also makes it difficult to determine the origins of many ideas and actions involving nations and states. In many ways it is understandable why nation and state are so easily confused. A major goal of this chapter has been to distinguish between the two concepts by highlighting the spatial disjunctions between nations and states. However, an interesting question arises as to why so many spatial disjunctions exist between nations and states around the world if nations and states are so inextricably intertwined. The answer lies in their historical development—the subject of the next two chapters.

Notes

1. Every military defeat suffered by the Croat and Muslim supporters of Bosnia drove a wedge deeper between the two groups. According to Silber and Little, the news of the defeat of Srebrenica in 1993 led the Croats to turn on the Muslims and launch a drive to join the Croatian areas of Bosnia-Herzegovina with Croatia (1997, 296).

2. The fifty states of the United States more appropriately fit the notion of *province*, a subunit of a state, because they do not possess sovereignty, which is possessed by the United States as a whole and wielded by the federal government in Washington, D.C. Applying the term *state* to New York, California, Texas, etc., is confusing for a number of reasons. To avoid this confusion, some academics, as well as the United Nations, capitalize *State* when they refer to one that is sovereign and leave *state* lowercase when they write of one that really conforms to the idea of a province (Glassner and Fahrer 2004, 33); others take the same approach but apply it oppositely (Pounds 1963, 1). These approaches only work well in written form and not orally.

3. Other names used in their place include department, oblast, kray, okrug, opština, prefecture, division, parish, governate, commune, circonscription, republic, region, wilaya, and district (Glassner and Fahrer 2004, 33).

4. When U.S. Secretary of State James Baker passed through Belgrade just four days before Slovenia and Croatia planned to declare independence from Yugoslavia, representatives from both republics met with Baker in the hopes of receiving recognition (Silber and Little 1997, 150-51). The United States, however, and member countries of the European Community withheld recognition for fear that it would promote bloodshed if the Yugoslav govern-

ment were to forcibly oppose the independence movements. Recognition would have also required the United States and other states to condemn and possibly come to the aid of Slovenia and Croatia. Slovenia achieved independence, nevertheless, and with little bloodshed. The Croatian situation was much the opposite. The German government, feeling morally obligated to recognize Croatia, pushed the other members of the European Community to recognize Croatia's independence and statehood by the end of 1991 (Silber and Little 1997, 150-51). Eventually, other countries followed suit. Recognition obligated the other states of the world to support the sovereignty of Croatia. It also forced them to do something about the bloodshed on the grounds that such action would impinge upon the sovereignty of Yugoslavia, whose government was perpetrating the bloodshed in an attempt to preserve its sovereignty over Croatia.

5. Examples include the U.S. western frontier as it expanded to the Pacific Ocean, the Russian frontier as it expanded across Siberia, and the Austro-Hungarian Military Frontier as it was designed to help the Austro-Hungarian Empire expand into Southeastern Europe at the expense of the Ottoman Empire.

6. The cartographic practice of making clear distinctions between "us" and "them" leads to many negative circumstances. An interesting work on the subject is Michael Shapiro's *Violent cartographies: Mapping cultures of war* (1997).

7. In 1990, for example, Saddam Hussein spoke of Kuwait as the "nineteenth province" of Iraq. In terms of geographic visualization, he was arguing that Kuwait should be the same color as Iraq, not a separate and distinct color entity. As it turned out, Saddam Hussein convinced enough of Iraq's population but not enough of the world community that his version of the world political map was appropriate. Despite Saddam Hussein's failure, cartographic depiction is very integral to state control over territory, especially the legitimization of such control.

8. The history that explains why few states are endowed with conformity will be discussed in chapters 4 and 5.

9. For more information on federal states, see Graham Smith's *Federalism: The multiethnic challenge* (1995).

10. This sentiment is best illustrated by the following referendum in 1980 when the Parti Québecois was the party in power in Quebec's government: "The government of Quebec has made public its proposal to negotiate a new agreement with the rest of Canada based on the equality of nations; This agreement would enable Quebec to acquire the exclusive power to make its own laws, levy its taxes and establish relations abroad—in other words, sovereignty—and, at the same time to maintain with Canada an economic association including a common currency; No change in political status resulting from these negotiations will be effected without approval by the people through another referendum; ON THESE TERMS DO YOU GIVE THE GOVERNMENT OF QUEBEC THE MANDATE TO NEGOTIATE THE PROPOSED AGREEMENT BETWEEN QUEBEC AND CANADA? _____ Yes _____ No." (The Parti Québecois http://www.uni.ca/pq.html)

11. Michael Mann uses the term *infrastructural power* and argues that it is a more potent force today than *despotic power* (1984).

12. Those who do not wish to conform frequently expend more energy avoiding the long arm of the state's mechanisms, to the extent of changing personal identity and moving residences. Ironically, such people's identities are shaped by the state as much as or more than if they conformed to the state's demands.

13. Antonio Gramsi (1971) and Michael Foucault (1980) argue that states use education and media to subjugate their populations though both also argue that individuals frequently consent to the subjugation.

14. See *Foucault's challenge: Discourse, knowledge, and power in education*, edited by Popkewitz and Brennan (1998).

15. In a federal state, provinces may require that additional material be learned about the province, reinforcing provincial identities.

16. It could be argued that the blank space to the west of Ireland is not really blank because Ireland's weather comes from the west (i.e., via the westerly winds). However, the west coast of the United States is subject to a similar situation in that it too experiences weather that comes in from an ocean to the west. Indeed, television stations in California, Oregon, and Washington will shift their map frames so that these states are on the edge of the television frame, leaving the open ocean to fill most of the screen. However, in contrast to the Irish situation, the maps are recentered to show the weather in the rest of the United States though the weather in the east is very unlikely to have an effect on the west coast. Perhaps there is more political intent or state-centered thinking behind American weather maps. Nevertheless, it is interesting how the framing and reframing of weather maps of Ireland—and also more general maps of Ireland—by Irish sources frequently result in the elimination of Great Britain. It may be done easily, and it certainly is in most cases. Once, while I was in the small Irish town of Doolin, just north of the Cliffs of Moher, I noticed an interesting map of Europe hanging behind the bar in a pub. In place of Great Britain was an enlarged island of Ireland. The map had a humorous intent but it also underscored a sentiment.

17. Though the American Revolutionaries were unable to convince Quebec's leaders to join the Revolution, the revolutionaries were able to conquer about half the land area of Quebec, which in a few decades turned into Ohio, Indiana, Illinois, Michigan, and Wisconsin. A remaining piece went to Minnesota when it was created. The teaching of American history does not emphasize that these states were carved out of Quebec.

18. When I was an undergrad, I spent a summer living on a farm in Germany. One day the teenage boy of the family showed me a book of facts that he had. As we were flipping through it, we came across a list of U.S. presidents. I quickly noticed that a 16a and 16b were listed for Abraham Lincoln and Jefferson Davis respectively. The format was unfamiliar to me as an American. Though simple, it suggested two countries where I had been taught that one always existed. I had an immediate negative reaction to what I had been taught.

19. The attempts made during the American Revolution have already been noted. Other attempts were made during the War of 1812, and British North America was very much a part of American visions of Manifest Destiny in the 1840s and 1850s. The desire to annex territories to the north remained strong in the 1860s, and the purchase of Alaska in 1867 is an example of that desire. Obviously, the purchase of Alaska cannot be left out of American history but the story of the purchase has been shortened in such a way that it underscores the notion that the United States is a given. While it is acknowledged today that Secretary Seward's desire to purchase Alaska was not well received, and thus called "Seward's Folly," the full story is not frequently given. It is only noted that people considered Alaska to be a worthless "national icehouse." With modern-day Americans valuing Alaska greatly, this shortened version of history actually vindicates Seward and treats him as a visionary while it depicts his opponents as shortsighted. However, the shortened history fails to mention that Americans considered Seward's desire to purchase Alaska as a folly because they preferred that efforts should have been directed at annexing the British provinces to the north and that the purchase of Alaska would have drained U.S. strength to the degree that the United States would not have been able to annex the British provinces (Offices of the Historian and of Public Communication 1991, 119). Interestingly, Congress consented to the purchase of Alaska in the same year that the British provinces banded together to form Canada, clearly sending a signal to the United States that they would not consent to annexation and that they were mobilizing to prevent such a move.

20. The continual recitation of the Pledge of Allegiance with its "one Nation, indivisible" and then after 1954 "one Nation under God, indivisible" contributes to and reinforces the unwillingness to think outside the colored boxes on the world map.

21. Though the Italian state was founded in 1861, Venetia (containing the city of Venice) was not acquired until 1866. Rome and the Papal States did not become a part of Italy until 1871. Trentino (South Tyrol) was not obtained until the end of the First World War. To bring about unification, Piedmont had to relinquish Savoy and Nice to France in 1860 (Ergang 1954, 156-58, 375).

22. The geographical assumptions that Agnew identifies are "states as fixed units of sovereign space, the domestic/foreign polarity, and states as 'containers' of societies" (1994, 53).

23. For a more detailed account of territorial conflicts, namely boundary conflicts, see Malcolm Anderson's *Frontiers: Territory and state formation in the modern world* (1996).

24. See William Wood's article *Geographic aspects of genocide: A comparison of Bosnia and Rwanda* (2001) for a more detailed and geographically sensitive treatment of ethnic cleansing. See Cathie Carmichael's *Ethnic cleansing in the Balkans* for a broader treatment of the phenomenon. See Andrew Bell-Fialkoff's book entitled *Ethnic cleansing* (1996) for other examples of ethnic cleansing.

25. It could be said that the person has French nationality because the term *citizenship* is often used synonymously with the term *nationality,* but the term *nationality* is avoided in this text because it is also often used interchangeably with *nation* and *ethnic group.*

26. In a broader sense the breakup of the Soviet Union could be considered part of the decolonization process though it did not occur until the 1990s. Kazakhstan, Uzbekistan, Turkmenistan, Kyrgyzstan, and Tajikistan were all Soviet creations but remained as territorial realities on the map with corresponding national identities developing within them.

27. Jan Penrose notably points out that the territorial nation/ethnic nation dichotomy suggests that "territory is not significant to 'ethnic' nationalism" (Penrose 2002, 290-91). For those of us who see territory as integral to nationhood no matter what strain, it is perhaps wise to take Penrose's point and not use such muddled terminology.

28. In 1981, 5 percent of the population identified itself as "Yugoslavs." Though this number may appear to be low, other studies have shown that a majority of the population in many instances identified with the term Yugoslav and only a small percent lacked any sense of Yugoslav identity (David MacKenzie 1977, 453; Rot and Havelka 1973, 113-18; Wachtel 1998, 1, 249).

29. In his book *Balkan odyssey* (1995), Lord Owen acknowledges again and again the complexity of identity in Bosnia-Herzegovina, yet continually put forth proposals for the division of Bosnia-Herzegovina into cantons designated for one of the three groups simply defined.

30. Much research on states has been directed at distinguishing between the segments of society who govern and those who are governed and examining how certain groups come to power and then maintain their power. Such research has produced a number of theories from pluralism to elitism and Marxism (Storey 2001, 40-44). John Breuilly is concerned with this issue of who governs in his book *Nationalism and the state* (1994, 1-2) as he states that "To focus upon culture, ideology, identity, class or modernisation is to neglect the fundamental point that nationalism is, above and beyond all else, about politics and that politics is about power. Power, in the modern world, is principally about control of the state. The central task is to relate nationalism to the objectives of obtaining and using state power. We need to understand why nationalism has played a major role in the pursuit of those objectives. To understand that we need to examine closely how nationalism operates as politics and what it is about modern politics that makes nationalism so important. Only then should we go on to consider the contributions of culture, ideology, class, and much else."

31. Francis Bellamy wrote the Pledge of Allegiance in 1892. Interestingly, he was a Christian Socialist (Baer 1992a; Baer 1992b).

32. The sentiment was echoed by the French leader Charles de Gaulle when he said that "Patriotism is when love of your own people comes first; nationalism, when hate for people other than your own comes first."

4

The Birth of Modern European Nations and States

I tend to live in the past because most of my life is there.
                                                        —*Herb Caen*

The previous chapter highlighted the symbiotic relationship between nations and states by examining how states mold nations while nations alter states to meet their needs. With such power over each other, it would seem that nations and states should be conterminous by now. Yet numerous spatial disjunctions between nations and states exist around the world and are the source of much conflict. It is tempting to argue that the spatial disjunctions result from aggressive nations and states seizing opportunities to take lands and their resources away from the weaker and more vulnerable nations and states. However, though history has witnessed its share of conflict over natural resources, the reliance on this single issue as an explanation papers over more salient explanations for the spatial disjunctions between nations and states. Most notably, nations and states are relatively recent human constructs, born out of earlier human conceptions of sociopolitical organization and territorial formations, yet not completely free of them. Indeed, many carry with them the legacy of their past incarnations. Some are even an aggregate of premodern elements recast in the mold of the modern nation and the modern state. They leave the impression that new nations and states are artificial and that "real" nations and states are much older than they really are. These lingering red-herring elements from the past aside, it is difficult to pinpoint the origin of modern nations and states. Both have been continually evolving while they drag the past with them. It is tempting to follow a single strand of a current characteristic of a nation or state into the deep recesses of time and argue that a nation or a state began with that single strand. While the other strands of the nation or state were not present earlier in history, the very strand that is followed was part of different tapestries of social and political organization in earlier times. It is misleading to date nations and states by their single oldest characteristic. Nations and states are both very complex and contextual. Thus, any single date that is chosen as the line that separates the time before their existences and the time after they came into being will inevitably be an oversimplification.

The difficulty in dating nations has given rise to several schools of thought. Anthony Smith has identified four paradigms in regard to the age of nations: modernism, perennialism, primordialism, and ethnosymbolism (2001, 43-61; see also Smith 1994). Modernism argues that nations came into existence only after the French Revolution in 1789. Modernism breaks down into at least five subsets, each of which focuses on the differing causes that led to the emergence of nations after the French Revolution. These subsets are socioeconomic, sociocultural, political, ideological, and constructionist. Perennialism takes the position that *nationalism* is a recent concept but asserts that most nations are old while accepting that some nations are newer. It does not accept that nations are natural "givens" but argues that nations are old because they possess many historical continuities. Primordialism insists that nations have existed since the beginning of time and are natural, organic, even biological entities. Finally, ethnosymbolism contends that many memories and cultural practices are subjective, even fabricated, but recognizes the influence that old identities have on the development of modern national identities.[1]

So many social, economic, political, and technological changes have occurred over the last few hundred years that it is difficult to imagine how earlier people could have conceived of their identities in the same way people today identify themselves through the term *nation*. To admit the profound changes that humanity has experienced over time yet to insist that human social groupings have remained unchanged is to engage in "nation-centered thinking," which is akin to the state-centered thinking described in chapter 3. State-centered thinking accepts states as givens, mere containers that exist outside of and are inert, not interacting with social, economic, political, and technological interactions and evolutions. Nation-centered thinking likewise does not question the existence of nations and simply describes their conditions and experiences over time.

Nation-centered thinking is not employed in this book because it is believed that the changes associated with history have led to continually changing human perceptions and the frequent reorganization of human social groupings. Even in cases where particular groups can be traced back several hundred or even a thousand years in history, it should be acknowledged that earlier members of such groups conceived of themselves and their world in manners so different from today that their senses of identity could hardly be called nationhood—though the names of these groups may have persisted over long periods of time. As the characteristics associated with nationhood are traced back in history, they seriously break down as we pass the French Revolution in 1789. Thus, to be concerned with the idea of nation is to be concerned with the ideas of the Enlightenment and Romantic periods of the seventeenth through the nineteenth centuries. These are the times when identity expressed in terms of nationhood as we understand it today clearly came into being.

To draw a single line at 1789 is to ignore the warnings above and consequently results in a line that is misleading. Thus, a thin line is drawn in 1789 because it marks the time when all the threads representing the various characteristics of nationhood came together to form the tapestry of nationhood. Because many of these threads can be traced back earlier in time, another thin line is drawn where these threads first began to be pulled from their earlier tapestries of identity and began to be rewoven into a new tapestry that would be recognized as nationhood beginning in 1789. A number of threads of nationhood—depending on how they are defined—can be traced back millennia. However, it is not until about the early sixteenth century that many of them exist, and that they begin to be rewoven. Thus, instead of one thick line drawn in history, two thin lines are drawn to mark a time span from the early sixteenth century to the French Revolution, denoting the incubation period for modern nations.

To limit ourselves to a single time span is also an oversimplification. States have greatly influenced nations; therefore, the evolution of the modern state should also be considered. Modern states trace their origins back to the Treaty of Westphalia in 1648. Indeed, our modern state system is frequently called the Westphalian system, and it too became recognizable by today's standards around the time of the French Revolution. It is tempting to ignore the evolution of states because their evolutionary periods overlap those of nations. However, state evolution did not merely parallel the evolution of nations. States and nations progressed together, fueling each other's evolutionary developments with their synergies. Thus, fuller dimension is given to the understanding of national evolution by remaining sensitive to state evolution.

By today's standards, nations and states were fully recognizable phenomena after the French Revolution. However, they did not stop evolving. As new social and scientific ideas developed in conjunction with more experiences of warfare, nationhood and statehood continued to change, taking on characteristics that were not present or as fully developed after the French Revolution. These characteristics deserve attention as well, but they will be the subject of the next chapter.

Several hundred years is a large body of history to consider, even when limited to the evolution of nations and states. The intent of this chapter, however, is not to consider every nuance of the history of nations and states in early times. Instead, it confines itself to the gestation period of the national idea with the goal of examining how territory became an integral component of nationhood while acknowledging the role states played in weaving territory into nationhood. Doing so will provide a foundation for understanding how nations and states continued to evolve, particularly in regard to their territorial components, after their birth in the late seventeenth century.

Medieval Views and Relationships

Today, we walk down corridors and acknowledge one another with a smile or nod and then go into the privacy of our offices to send a venomous e-mail message to the person that we just acknowledged in the hallway. Computers are certainly changing the relationship between human beings. The harsh words that we write in electronic messages but will not say to another person's face give new meaning to the word *flaming*. While computers alter interpersonal relations, they are also transforming national and international politics. They allow us to penetrate the boundaries of authoritarian states, expose their human rights' violations, and prevent them from acting with the same impunity of the past. Computers also allow states and businesses to track the movements and actions of individuals to a degree never seen before. The computer age also allows thieves to hack into our personal information and steal our identities without breaking a window or forcing a door.

The attention that computers receive today was focused on television only a decade or so ago. Television was accused of destroying the very fabric of family life as it removed family members from the forum of the dining room table and set them down in front of the television set. Here the daily verbal exchange of personal experiences and ideas was traded for the simultaneously enlightening and mind-numbing barrage of information streaming in from the outside world. Television, for example, may have played a crucial role in shaping American opinion of the Vietnam War as the war's daily events were broadcast almost immediately into people's living rooms. The experience was much different, even shocking, compared to the earlier news-reels of World War II and the Korean conflict which appeared edited and censored, long after actual events, and in more restricted forums such as movie theaters.

Not long before the advent of television and then in conjunction with it, automobiles worked their effects on the human mind and society. They spread families over greater distances in widely scattered suburbs, no longer to live together in the same neighborhoods or the same apartment buildings. In the United States in particular, automobiles allowed the middle class to flee the inner cities, leaving them to decay. They also allowed racial segrega-tion to intensify as they allowed racial groups to build their communities far-ther apart than before.

Computers, television, and automobiles have had a profound effect on individuals and social identities in the last hundred years, but other techno-logical and social innovations have had deeper effects over the last several hundred years. A millennium ago, Europeans had yet to discover or invent the printing press, gunpowder, a quality telescope, or many other technolo-gies. Capitalism had not yet emerged as an economic system (Wood 2002). Europeans believed that evil caused disease and that the earth was the center of the universe. Time, languages, and the legitimacy of rule were understood much differently than today (Benedict Anderson 1991, 9-36). Time was thought of cyclically—the passing of the days, weeks, months, and seasons, combined with birth, maturation, and death. It did not include the modern notion that individual events interact with one another in a cause-and-effect relationship to produce change. Progress was an unknown concept (Agnew 1994, 60; Duncan 1998, 94-109). Medieval Christians did not see them-selves linked to biblical times through a horizontal and measurable timeline. They saw the biblical world and their world as linked vertically to God, who served as the locus of time, but these worlds were not linked directly to each other by either time or events. Events could be laid out sequentially, but it was an ordinal system, which meant that the distances between events were not measured. Thus, medieval Christians saw themselves wedged between Jesus' crucifixion and his Second Coming with immeasurable time in be-tween. No matter how many years, decades, or centuries would pass, they saw biblical time, their time, and the end of times as existing side by side in what Benedict Anderson calls *simultaneity* (1991, 24). Subsequently, me-dieval Christians identified with one another but did not see themselves as a cohesive community bound together in a contextual history. They saw them-selves even less as members of broad "national" communities bound together in a contextual history. The study of history was viewed as meaningless because it was not seen as explaining current situations or as a means of creating a better future. George Santayana's statement that "Those who cannot remember the past are condemned to repeat it" would ring nonsensical to medieval Christians who lived in cyclical time marked by the continual repetition of days and seasons, birth and death. The intimate experience with cyclical time and the concern with salvation meant that medieval Christians knew more about Biblical history than their own (Duncan 1998, 107). By the nineteenth century, our modern sense of horizontal and progressive time had developed, and emerging national identities of this era likewise required national histories set in historical context to solidify. However, the lack of concern that medieval Christians had with chronicling their own histories left a dearth of information about their time that would present problems for future nationalists, particularly Romantic nationalists of the nineteenth century, who felt the need to write their nations' histories.

Along similar lines of thinking, medieval Europeans saw languages as belonging to one of two categories, sacred and profane, whereby sacred languages were the religious languages—in the Roman Catholic world of Western Central Europe it was Latin—and profane languages were the vernaculars of the peasants. People took no pride in their vernacular languages because they were not pathways to salvation as were the sacred languages. However, most did not learn the sacred languages because they required higher learning. Instead, they placed their trust in a clergy who knew these languages of the sacred texts. Similarly, the masses obeyed their rulers, who they believed had a special connection to God and, therefore, had a divine right to rule. The clergy's specialized knowledge of the sacred languages was used to foster such a belief.

Medieval European views meant that medieval society was structured much differently than today and that Europe's political geography was likewise organized along different lines. The ruling classes saw themselves as separate and distinct from the masses they ruled, and they did everything they could to exaggerate their differences in order to justify their rule (Gellner 1983, 10). One way they widened the chasm between themselves and the masses was through education, a privilege that they reserved for themselves. The notation in chapter 2 that few educated Germans actually spoke German is an example of how the ruling classes used language to erect social barriers. By refusing to learn the various vernaculars Germans used and instead employing Latin, the German ruling classes not only made communication between the classes strenuous, but they became fluent in the sacred language and thereby placed themselves closer to God, in turn earning the awe of the masses and justifying their rule. The ruling classes also exercised despotic power. Law to them was not something for themselves to obey but rather a means to keep their subjects in line. The separation between the ruling and the ruled meant that little vertical social mobility existed. Horizontal movement was the norm as members of the ruling classes readily found their spouses in the ruling families of other countries (see figure 4.1). Indeed, the royal houses of Europe were intertwined with siblings and cousins ruling at the same time in many countries and any one of them ruling multiple territories.[2] Thus, to argue that nations are very old because the term *nation* has been used for a long time is misleading. For example, the term "the German nation" was used in the Middle Ages by the ruling classes to refer to themselves and not the people they ruled—the ones who actually spoke German but probably did not realize they collectively did so. While the term "German nation" vertically excluded the German masses, its horizontal boundaries were less clear since those who employed it for themselves were intermarried with many of the other ruling dynasties of Europe.

It was not until the early nineteenth century that Ralph Waldo Emerson would write that Americans would be the "'first nation of men'—the first nation of individuals rather than of kings or classes" (quoted in Prestowitz 2003, 36). Interestingly, Americans like to think of themselves as a young nation. This belief is not rooted in fact but in a mythology that glorifies the virtues of youth and vitality and the subsequent desire to be eternally young. If you cannot be young, at least pretend to be. Americans are really one of the world's older nations by modern conception, but Americans' insistence on their youthfulness perpetuates the notion that *nation* is an old concept. It is true that the word *nation* is old—having derived from Latin—and as an old word it contributes to the belief that nations are old. However, the idea that nations are culturally homogeneous social groups vertically aligned so that they comprise both rich and poor is a modern concept advocated by Americans and accepted today by many other peoples. Few today would think of a nation as only those who rule a country. Therefore, though the word *nation* has existed for centuries, nations as we understand them today did not. Unfortunately, the application of the word *nation* to differing social formations over time has also contributed to the assumption that nations are very old because the long use of the word leads to the presumption that its associated definition is likewise just as old. To have prevented today's assumptions, it would have been better to have coined different words for the differing social constructions, underscoring that the modern idea of nation is only about two hundred years old and that Americans are really an older nation, not a younger one.

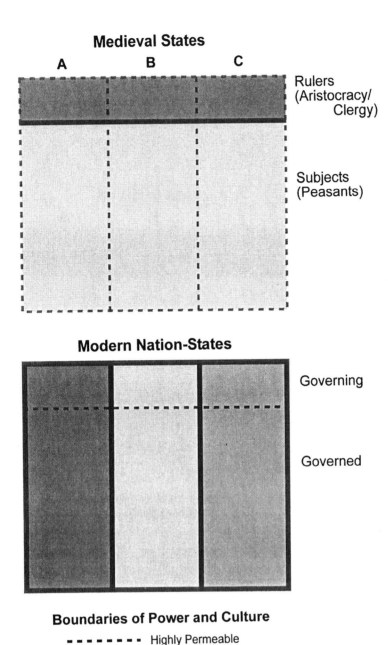

Figure 4.1 Medieval and Modern States
This diagram illustrates the horizontal nature of medieval states and the vertical character of modern states.

Medieval society stands in sharp contrast to the modern nation-state era. Today, legitimacy of rule is derived from membership in the citizenry. Therefore, modern leaders do not exaggerate their differences with the citizenry but instead go to great lengths to demonstrate that they are cut from the same cloth. Appearing on talk shows, playing sports, riding horses, and appearing at local shopping malls and grocery stores wearing leisure clothing and speaking in the vernacular is a way of showing one's worthiness to lead. Modern leaders also do not enjoy despotic power. On the contrary, they are expected to conform to the law in every detail; any slip is a disqualification for leadership, and any indiscretion in office brings impeachment, censure, or some other reprimand or condemnation. In contrast to the past, leaders also willingly submit the details of their life to be scrutinized and allow themselves to be publicly interrogated. For example, Janet Reno, the attorney general in the Clinton administration, commented during her confirmation process that she always paid sticker price for automobiles because she would one day seek public office and would not want to be accused of undue influence in negotiating the price of a car—influence which, incidentally, she did not have when she bought many of her cars. The attempts of modern-day leaders to demonstrate that no barriers exist between themselves and the general citizenry indicate that modern states have vertical social mobility (see figure 4.1). It is inconceivable in our modern state system that leaders be recruited from other countries (Gellner 1983, 14-18) and that entire groups of countries have leaders so closely related as siblings and cousins. Inconceivable also is the lack of interest that medieval leaders had in the traditions and practices—often including the laws—of the countries that they ruled. Absent now too is a medieval equivalent of a leader simultaneously serving in the roles of president, provincial governor, and county administrator, not only in one country but in multiple countries.

The different and unfamiliar social structures of medieval times went hand in hand with a different and unfamiliar political geography as well. Today we look at a political map and assume that each country represents a people by a similar name and that the culture is the same from border to border and from leader to the most common citizen. Though these assumptions may be problematic, they reflect today's ideal of the world's political geography. In contrast, states in medieval society were personal possessions that were bartered and traded, and frequently fought over, but were generally passed on as inheritance. Boundaries were not set around peoples but determined by leaders' abilities to extend their power over earth space. In both the medieval mind and practice, the boundaries of political power were most easily set along physiographic features such as rivers, mountain ridges, coastlines, and the edges of forests and swamps. These kinds of practices extend back to the earliest days of human history and perhaps before. Without modern technologies, namely, mapping and transportation technologies, leaders—and even the people they ruled—had different conceptions of their territories. Today's maps, which present a vertical, "bird's-eye" view of territories, are recent tools in human history. Though they are the basis of our mental maps today, premodern humans had a horizontal rather than vertical view of their lands. From such a perspective, physiographic features served as landmarks to demarcate the extent of political control rather than abstract lines on maps that could be identified on the earth's surface with sophisticated surveying equipment.

In addition to using physiographic features, many medieval leaders in Europe even used the same physiographic features that their predecessors, the Romans, had relied on for many of their political boundaries. For example, when Charlemagne's empire was divided in 843 among Charlemagne's three grandsons (Charles, Lothar, and Louis) (Greer and Lewis 1997, 208), it was along the Roman administrative divisions, each separated by broad belts of uninhabited forests and marsh, from which the term *march* derives (Pounds 1951, 147-48). The lands of Charles, Lothar, and Louis became known as *Francia, Lotharinga* (Lorraine), and *Germania* respectively. As population clusters grew and expanded toward one another, people cleared forests and marshes between their communities and came to view the rivers as boundaries. Before long, it was thought that Charlemagne's empire had been divided along the Meuse and Rhine Rivers with *Francia* lying to the west of the Meuse, *Lortharinga* located between the Meuse and the Rhine, and *Germania* extending east of the Rhine. That the rivers could not have served as boundaries in numerous localities did not seem to matter. As the middle kingdom of *Lotharinga* weakened and disintegrated, leaders of the two other kingdoms began to absorb territories of the middle kingdom from both west and east. While *Francia* and *Germania* struggled politically and militarily against each other to control the lands of *Lotharinga, Francia*'s leaders legitimized their claims in Roman terminology. *Lotharinga* was also known as *Francia orientale* (or eastern France), and it together with *Francia* had comprised the Roman province of *Gallia,* which extended east to the Rhine (Pounds 1951, 149), suggesting that both were part of a larger naturally integrated politico-geographic unit. Thus, France's leaders saw the rightful boundaries of France as falling along historical imperial Roman boundaries defined by rivers rather than by the edge of settlement of the French people. Indeed, the idea of a modern French nation defined by a single language and culture did not emerge until the late nineteenth century. In the Middle Ages when France and Germany began developing into modern states, no distinct French and German nations existed as understood today as cultural characteristics were in continual transition across geographical space. Illustrating this point is the name *France* itself, which derives from the Franks, a Germanic people closely related to the Germanic peoples in *Lotharinga* and *Germania*. Thus, France and Germany did not arise because separate and distinct French and German peoples existed, and France's and Germany's boundaries were not drawn to enclose each respective people, for each people did not exist when these states began to develop. Instead, France and Germany were created first by medieval rulers who carved out territories for themselves along physiographic features and then by modern states that culturally homogenized the people within their boundaries drawn by medieval rulers along physiographic features.

Though political maps of Europe before the year 1800 contained political entities with names that are used by states today, these medieval states did not possess political or cultural homogeneity. Furthermore, the horizontal nature of medieval power, which revolved around such practices as intermarriage and vassalage, meant that medieval states were parts of complicated spheres of overlapping political power. One poignant example is that of twelfth-century "England" and "France." Within them, the County of Brittany and the Duchy of Aquitaine counted among the many territorial possessions of King Henry II (1154-1189) of England. However, Henry ruled them as a dutiful vassal of the French king, Louis VII (1120-1180), with whom he fought bitterly in his role as king of England (see figure 4.2). Familial relations explain how the king of England became a vassal for the king of France. Henry II of England and Louis VII of France were cousins. However, Henry was Louis's vassal concerning Brittany and Aquitaine because Henry married Louis's ex-wife, Eleanor of Aquitaine (Barber 1964, 48-50; Warren 1973, 43-45). In other words, Henry assumed sovereignty over Aquitaine as Eleanor's husband though the territory remained in Louis's kingdom as Eleanor held title to the duchy via her connection to her ex-husband Louis. Moreover, Eleanor was Louis's niece as well as his former wife. Typical of medieval politics, Henry and Louis were then related in many different ways. Though the two fought as kings, the two reinforced their familial connections when they arranged for Henry's son to marry Louis's daughter. It was not unusual for awkward situations to arise with these complex political-territorial relationships. For example, when Count Raymond of Toulouse attempted to separate the County of Toulouse from the Duchy of Aquitaine, Henry—the duke of Aquitaine as well as the king of England—naturally resisted the move (Warren 1973, 82-88). He sought sup-

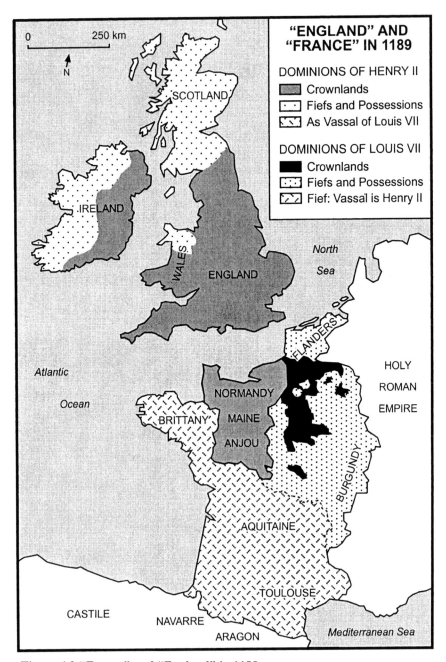

Figure 4.2 "France" and "England" in 1189
The map illustrates the complex and overlapping character of medieval political-territorial power.

port from King Louis VII, in whose name Henry held title to Aquitaine. On the one hand, Louis supported Henry in his cause because the loss of the County of Toulouse to the Duchy of Aquitaine would have also been a loss to Louis's kingdom. On the other hand, Count Raymond of Toulouse was also Louis's brother-in-law. If Henry succeeded in stripping Raymond of his position, Louis's sister and her children would have been dispossessed as well. Moreover, if Henry were successful in his campaign, his power would have potentially eclipsed Louis's. Certainly, as king of France, Louis did not want one of his vassals to become more powerful than he was. The situation was certainly a dilemma for Louis in many ways. He decided to give tacit support to Henry's military campaign against Raymond but went to take up temporary residence with Raymond in the city of Toulouse. Louis's actions then presented a dilemma for Henry. A direct assault on Raymond in Toulouse ran the risk of harming or capturing his king, to whom he was loyal concerning Aquitaine. To avoid such a consequence, Henry had to turn to the less desired strategy 'of attacking Raymond's forces elsewhere in the county.

The complex system of political-territorial relationships in the Middle Ages meant that the laws in the numerous territories of the more powerful monarchs seldom conformed to a common standard. Moreover, monarchs had little desire and made little effort to bring them into alignment. Thus, great disparities existed in culture over great distances, but otherwise culture changed so slowly over space that the hardly perceptible differences over short distances left few clear and distinct cultural boundaries (see figure 3.3a).

To understand medieval Europe's political geography, it is important not to conflate the concepts of *land* and *state* though they may overlap and even be conterminous in earth space. Though such conflation should not be done with contemporary states and lands, even greater misunderstandings result from confusing these concepts when considering the medieval world. When we think of a land, we tend to think of a fixed physical landscape with particular physical and human characteristics. We are inclined to think of a state as a land with a government and political boundaries. States rise and fall and readily move their political boundaries. However, if *land* and *state* are conflated in the human mind, then it is difficult to accept that political boundaries move because it suggests that the land is moving too. Thus, we tend to reject language that speaks of moving states and project today's boundaries into the past while carrying with these projections the assumptions of cultural and political homogeneity that become increasingly untrue as we go further and further back in time. For example, to be German, Italian, or Irish no more referred to single homogeneous groups than do the terms *European, Asian,* or *African* today; and Germany, Italy, and Ireland were about as unified as Europe, Asia, and Africa today. Nevertheless, these assumptions of unity are reinforced by writers and editors when they—for brevity and in the name of clarity—shorten statements such as "in the territories that would eventually become Germany, Italy, and Ireland" to simply "in Germany, Italy, and Ireland." By employing state-centered thinking as described in chapter 3, histories are written with the assumption that events took place within the current boundaries of states. The assumptions are further reinforced by anachronistic maps containing information on the past with today's political boundaries.

Unfortunately, the limitations of cartographic depiction encourage the conflation of lands and states and assumptions about the cultural and political homogeneity of lands and states. On a map of Europe, for example, it is difficult to depict the hundreds of tiny medieval states with their complex political connections. Lines showing boundaries would be blurred, and place-names written large enough to be legible would crowd and overlap one another and cover over the states. Even so, any attempt to depict the political-territorial relationships would only apply to brief moments in time as boundaries shifted constantly in earlier times. In addition, territories coming under individual rulers were not always conterminous. Though it would be cartographically possible to shade territories falling under the same ruler with the same shade, such cartographic depiction would overstate the political homogeneity of these territories. Though under the same ruler, such territories were not subject to the same laws. Moreover, they had differing connections with other territories. For example, it is difficult to depict on a map the earlier example of Brittany and Aquitaine in the twelfth century as they were both simultaneously part of the Kingdoms of England and France but in differing ways. The modern nation-state era does not present so many problems for cartographic depiction. It is now inconceivable, for example, that California, Texas, and New York would be part of the United States but also simultaneously part of other countries, in turn involving them in differing international military, political, and economic alliance systems that would frequently be at odds with one another. Despite the greater political complexity of medieval Europe, cartographic complications are avoided by omitting many state boundaries. Lands such as Ireland, the Italian peninsula, and the Low Countries ("The Netherlands") each receive a single color or pattern. Unfortunately, such practices leave the visual impression that these lands are unified political states with culturally homogeneous populations when they are not. Such practices also result in maps that encourage readers to conflate the ideas of *land* and *state*.

It is important to distinguish, for example, between England, France, and Germany as lands and states because they existed as lands but not as states in medieval times as we understand the concept of state today. As states, England, France, and Germany began as possessions of individual families who routinely intermarried, states much smaller than those states today. France as a state, for example, began in the tenth century with the possessions of Hugh Capet, who ruled a fifty-mile stretch around Paris (Greer and Lewis 1997, 210, 220). Interestingly, when an author writes about the history of France in the tenth century, is he or she writing about what happened in this small territory or what happened in the land that we now consider France, though it meant little to the people of the time? It would take another four hundred years before the Capet family and their successors would extend their territorial possessions so that they would resemble the French state seen on today's political map. It would take even longer to create a cultural and political homogeneity similar to that of today.

Not recognizing the differences between the lands and states of England and France would lead one to reject the fact that the English kingdom in the twelfth century extended almost to Paris, south to the Pyrenees Mountains, and east along the Mediterranean Sea to the Rhône River (see figure 4.2). It would be tempting to include as part of this rejection the belief that the English had unduly taken most of France. To do so, one would have to ignore that the English kings were Normans—and then Plantagenets from farther south in Anjou, who rarely could speak English but instead spoke French and some of whom spent little time in the England we know on the map today.[3] One would also have to ignore that many of their military campaigns on the continent were to put down the rebellions in their ancestral homelands of the people who were most culturally like them and that they enjoyed the support of the people on their island possessions who were most culturally different from them. In rejecting the territorial extent of England (as a political entity) in the twelfth century, one would have to reject the influence of Norman and Plantagenet culture and its political systems on those of the English as they intermingled in the spatial networks of a single kingdom that included them both (Matthew 1983, 97-100). Furthermore, the inclination to see the English as having marauded around France in an attempt to gain more possessions is to overlook that the wars were not English against French but wars of Normans and then Plantagenets against the Capetians and their allies with both sides having similar cultural characteristics and having intermarried. In this premodern era, the wars were not nationalistic but dynastic with families struggling against one another and internally to extend their control over territory regardless of who lived there. The complicated structure of medieval politics and political geography is illustrated by the fact that the king of England held many of his possessions on the continent (e.g., Brittany and Aquitaine) as a vassal of the French king, though the two were often hostile to each other. In time, these wars would evolve from family feuds into something more nationalistic; however, nationalism was not the cause of wars but rather a by-product as the dynasties polarized and calcified over time with the rise of the modern state. Not understanding the political geography of the medieval period and its underlying principles and processes is misunderstanding history and earlier senses of identity.

The Sixteenth and Seventeenth Centuries

Medieval social identities and political geographies were very different and even incomprehensible by today's standards. Slowly evolving, they nevertheless changed little over the thousand years or so of their existence compared to the pace of change after the Middle Ages. Beginning in the sixteenth and seventeenth centuries, social and political as well as technological, scientific, and economic developments rapidly increased, transformed medieval society, and sent it down a pathway toward the modern nation and state.

Social and Political Developments

European medieval politics were marked by personal and familial sovereignty legitimized by a Christian belief in rule by divine right. Christian universality also allowed leaders the right to expand their territories in the name of spreading the faith and sanctioned attempts to consolidate Christian territories to build a unified Christian state on earth. Though centuries of intermarriage, intrigue, and war failed to bring about a politically unified Europe, these medieval practices came closest to their fruition with the reign of Charles V, Holy Roman Emperor (1519-1556). From all four of his grandparents, Charles inherited a number of territories: Austria, Burgundy, the Low Countries ("The Netherlands"), Castile, Navarre and Aragon, which included the southern Italian peninsula (known at the time as Naples), Sicily, and Sardinia, and all the Spanish possessions in North and South America. In 1519, he was elected Holy Roman Emperor. In 1526, Charles's younger brother Ferdinand inherited the Kingdoms of Bohemia and Hungary. With his aunt Catherine of Aragon married to Henry VIII of England, Charles was betrothed to their daughter Mary, meaning that he was first in line to inherit England and all of its possessions. With the vast resources of these lands, Charles and his Habsburg dynasty were poised to overwhelm and take France—the last serious obstacle to his personal power, then swallow up the remaining smaller Christian principalities, and finally unite the Christian realm into a single state (see figure 4.3).

Figure 4.3 Dynastic Empire of Charles V in Europe, 1526
Charles V also ruled the Spanish possessions in the Americas.

Unfortunately, unbeknown to Charles, Charles's advent came too late. The tides of history were already changing as the medieval views of the world were evolving into something new. Beginning within his own empire, cracks began to appear with the rise of religious reformers, most notably Martin Luther (1483-1546). Luther set out to reform the entire Roman Catholic Church, but his strong beliefs did not win everyone over. Instead, Luther's beliefs and activities split the Church. Consequently, with a new Protestant and Roman Catholic division, Protestants and Roman Catholics would not jointly accept a single divine right monarch, for they saw each other as heretics. As a devout Roman Catholic, Charles attempted to suppress the new Protestant ideas. This attempt drained his resources and diverted his attention away from challenging the Valois dynasty in France. Around the same time, Henry VIII of England desired to divorce his wife, Catherine of Aragon. The pope most likely would have granted an annulment—he certainly had for Henry's sister on weaker grounds (Read 1969, 63). However, Henry's wife Catherine was Charles's aunt. On behalf of his aunt, and since he would lose the inheritance of the English throne if Henry successfully divorced Catherine, Charles used his great power to pressure the pope into denying Henry's request for an annulment (Greer and Lewis 1997, 377). Ironically, Charles's attempts to keep Henry VIII a good Roman Catholic pushed Henry into accepting many of the new Protestant ideas, ultimately breaking with the Roman Catholic Church and helping the Protestant Reformation to become successful. With Henry's divorce of his wife, their daughter Mary lost her inheritance of the English throne, and Charles decided to marry Isabella, the daughter of the king of Portugal, potentially adding another kingdom to his realm, though losing England. Charles, however, protected his cousin Mary in England as best he could. After Henry's death, Mary inherited the throne after all and attempted to return England and her possessions to the Roman Catholic fold—earning her the title "Bloody Mary" to Protestant historians for her heavy-handedness. Charles attempted to add England to his realm once more by negotiating a marriage between his own son Philip and Mary. The move was intended to outmaneuver King Henri II of France, who had added Scotland to the Valois dynasty after betrothing his son to Mary, Queen of Scots (Starkey 2001, 124-28). Charles's endeavor failed, as did Mary's attempt to secure the ascendancy of Roman Catholicism in England, and Charles was unable to quash the Protestant Reformation in his own realm. Exhausted, Charles abdicated in 1556. With his passing, Western and Central Europe watched its final and closest effort to unite Latin Christianity into a single state wither away. Europeans may not have realized what was happening for at least another century.

Martin Luther, though a religious reformer, advocated many ideas that would transform social relations and identity to such a degree that they not only undermined Charles V's attempts to unite Christians into one political state, but also would thwart any such attempts in the future and even make the notion of such a project inconceivable. Some of Luther's most profound ideas in this regard involved language and legitimacy of rule. Luther believed that individuals could relate directly to God rather than through the clergy, one of the strata of the ruling classes. The clergy, however, served as the mediator because clergy knew the sacred language of Latin, which common people could not speak or write and which would be very difficult for them to learn under the political and economic environment of the time. Luther, however, avoided this problem by arguing that individuals could commune with God by reading the Bible in the vernacular. Luther's ideas on language took away an important justification for those who ruled: in time people would no longer believe that the rulers would have to be obeyed because their knowledge of the sacred language gave them special access to God. In espousing such beliefs, Luther effectively demoted sacred languages and elevated vernaculars to the same level. Eventually, people would see all languages as equal with none having special access to the divine. In time, people would take pride in their vernacular languages, and many would see them as fundamental characteristics of their identities. Devout Protestants would facilitate this process as they translated the Bible into vernacular languages, not only in their Protestant realm but also in the Roman Catholic realm and wherever their missionaries traveled. Many modern standard national languages trace their origins back to Protestant translations of the Bible.

Luther had profoundly new ideas on the legitimacy of rule as well. Rather than seeing all religious and political authority flowing from God through the pope and then the ruling classes, Luther saw each individual monarch as *summus episcopus* ("head bishop") (Garraty and Gay 1972, 535). The concept of *summus episcopus* meant that monarchs had the right to determine ecclesiastical appointments, have final say in biblical interpretation, and enforce uniform faith and liturgy within their individual realms as they desired. The concept and practice contributed to the eventual destruction of the politically complex medieval Christian world in which familial dynasties and their subjects were tied together by the overarching political and religious authority of the Roman Catholic Church. No longer to be kept on a common pathway of development, Christians would disperse down differing pathways of cultural development defined by the territorial states where they lived. Many political leaders found *summus episcopus* attractive not only for the reasons mentioned, but also because it meant that they could dissolve monasteries, confiscate their land, and accumulate church monies that previously flowed to Rome. These activities further contributed to the reformulation of complex, political-territorial relations into the discrete units characteristic of modern nation-states.

As Protestantism—namely, Lutheranism—grew more popular with the conversion of many ruling families, bloody conflicts ensued between Lutheran and Roman Catholic states as their leaders would not accept each other's beliefs. Unable to overwhelm each other, they concluded a truce within the Holy Roman Empire in what is known as the Religious Peace of Augsburg in 1555 (Garraty and Gay 1972, 536-37; Greer and Lewis 1997, 369). It allowed each ruler to choose the religion—either Roman Catholicism or Lutheranism—for his territory, embodied in the Latin phrase *cuius regio, eius religio* ("He who rules a territory determines the religion"). The practice formally institutionalized the process whereby the people would be religiously homogenized according to the territories in which they lived. In the Protestant territories, vernacular language became part of this homogenizing process.

The uneasy truce between Protestant and Roman Catholic leaders continued to witness conflict and eventually exploded into war in 1618, lasting until 1648, in what is known as the Thirty Years' War. Much bloodshed ensued, but neither side could overwhelm and defeat the other. Admitting stalemate, the leaders ended their hostilities with the Treaty of Westphalia (1648). The treaty reaffirmed many of the principles laid down in the earlier Augsburg treaty (1555), perhaps most notably *cuius regio, eius religio* (Alexander Murphy 1996, 84). This time Calvinism was added to the list of choices, providing for greater religious diversity among territories but still promoting homogeneity within them as leaders forced conversion or drove religious minorities out of their territories (Garrety and Gay 1972, 590).

The Treaty of Westphalia also laid down the rudiments of modern international practices such as the establishment of formal—not familial—diplomatic ties, alliances, and rules for war and peace. It incorporated many of the ideas of Hugo Grotius concerning "just war," which argued that war could be prosecuted only to maintain legitimate rights: "defense, the obtaining of that which belongs to us or is our due, and inflicting punishment" (Grotius 1925, 171; also quoted in Alexander Murphy 1990, 535). The Treaty of Westphalia is significant because it sharply curtailed and would eventually end the practice of the ruling classes engaging in war to carry out family feuds and instead began forcing them to justify their actions on behalf of their states rather than their familial interests. In other words, it ushered in the era of the modern state and state-centered thinking. The political map of Europe also moved a step closer to that of nation-states as the Netherlands and the Swiss Confederation became independent states and the boundaries of the Holy Roman Empire shrank down to something more akin to a modern German state (see figure 4.4). Though the characteristics of nations and states became more recognizable in 1648 than they ever had before, these characteristics had to develop more fully over the coming centuries before modern nations and states actually emerged. The process was slow since many medieval views and practices continued for a long time, some into the twentieth century. For example, monarchs continued to see themselves as having a divine right to rule and to see themselves as living above the law. They would also continue to operate within a horizontal stratum: intermarrying and seeing themselves as a people different than the ones they ruled. The political map of Europe continued to reflect the complicated structure of medieval political relations for some time. For example, though the boundaries of the Holy Roman Empire receded to something more akin to a nation-state, Prussian and Habsburg territories straddled its boundaries with sizeable portions of their territories outside the empire (see figure 4.4). Also, the kings of France, Denmark, Sweden, and Spain ruled territories within the Holy Roman Empire though the greater part of their territories lay elsewhere. The idea of nation, as defined by common language and culture, had not developed yet either, as illustrated in the following passage about the Habsburg lands:

> Historians have traditionally laid much stress on the different characteristics of the inhabitants of the Habsburg lands, on their diverse racial origins and their different languages which accentuated differences. In the seventeenth century, belonging to the same country and acceptance of the same laws were much more important than any feeling of racial or linguistic solidarity. Germans, Slavs or Magyars were much more conscious of being Tyroleans, Austrians, Styrians, Bohemians, Moravians or Hungarians. . . . In rural areas the language spoken by the lord had some influence on the region's linguistic destiny, but sometimes the lord adopted the language of his vassals. On the whole the rural areas tended to preserve their local idiom, but in the seventeenth century the linguistic map was not firmly fixed, and changes from one group to another were more common than has subsequently been believed. Above all, the mental attitudes of the time, with each group protected by its privileges, did not conceive of linguistic unity as essential for a state, nor did they conceive of undying racial enmities underlying differences in language. Hungary gives the most striking example of this variety, with its Croats, Magyars, highlanders of Upper Hungary, speaking Slovak dialects related to Czech (literary Czech having

been adopted by the upper classes) and the Transylvanians including German and Magyar elements. Latin remained the language of government, a
common means of expression, standing above all these linguistic groups.[4]
(Cooper 1970, 4: 508-9)

As this quotation indicates, identity was not expressed as national identity is
conceived of today. Certainly, national identity has a place component as
identity had during the seventeenth century, but the territorial component of
identity in the seventeenth century was likewise not bound up in the same

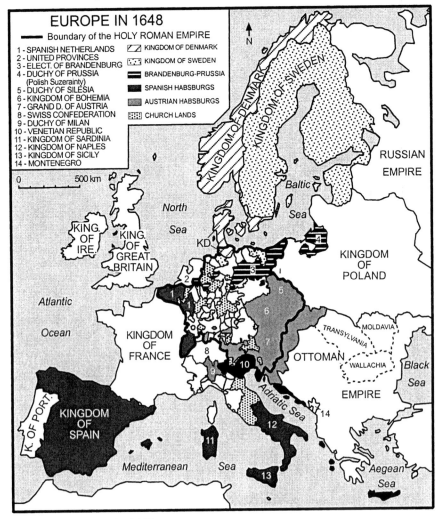

Figure 4.4 Europe in 1648

way with notions of common language and culture as are contemporary notions of nationhood. Nevertheless, the Treaty of Westphalia in 1648 marked a significant milestone in the development of modern nations and states, though they did not simply appear with the treaty. At the same time, the Treaty of Westphalia did not initiate the process of creating modern nations and states on its own but in conjunction with a number of economic, technological, and scientific developments.

Economic, Technological, and Scientific Developments

The changing group dynamics and social views of the sixteenth and seventeenth centuries were able to evolve in the direction of modern nations and states only with economic, technological, and scientific developments. Many of these had to operate for decades before having social effects. Capitalism, the printing press, military weapons such as the longbow, crossbow, and gunpowder, and scientific discoveries made with such inventions as the telescope made possible the ideas of modern nations and states.

The Age of Discovery blossomed after the Portuguese charted their way around Africa and Columbus brought the Americas to the attention of Europeans. Before long, vast quantities of goods from explorations began to flow into Europe, particularly Western Europe. The wealth fostered the growth of a middle class of bankers and merchants. Large percentages of Europe's population remained agricultural, but the barriers of the isolated manorial estates began to erode as the increasing flow of goods and services led to greater urbanization and the mixing of people and social classes within countries. Capitalism also challenged the idiosyncratic political geographies of the Middle Ages. Capital and goods flow best when standards and laws are uniform. Thus capitalist forces pressured the monarchies to standardize their realms. However, distrust and competition between monarchs resulted in different standardization in the emerging modern states. At the same time, capitalism also encouraged individualism and secularization, which in turn eventually encouraged members of societies to question the privileged positions of their monarchs and instead to see them as no more than fellow citizens of their nations.

In the year 2000, the *Biography* series of Arts and Entertainment (A&E) television produced a documentary about the one hundred most influential people of the last millennium. Academics and others concluded that the number-one-ranked person was Johann Gutenberg (*Biography of the Millennium* 1999). Gutenberg is known for his moveable type printing press, which he invented in 1436. However, it was not until the 1450s that commercial production of books began (Steinberg 1966), following the appearance of the now famous Gutenberg Bible. Astoundingly, by the early 1500s, more than twenty million books had been produced and had begun changing societal perceptions and behaviors (Benedict Anderson 1991, 33; Febvre and Martin [1958] 1997, 186). The printing press greatly aided Martin Luther and his revolutionary ideas in surviving the wrath of the Church and the Church's supporting political leaders as it quickly and widely disseminated his writings, in turn gathering Luther supporters from both the masses and political leaders who were to protect him during crucial moments. Prior to the printing press, someone like Luther would have been easily suppressed and quickly disposed of without many knowing what the person advocated. In addition, Luther's belief that everyone should read the Bible in one's own vernacular language was made feasible only with the printing press as the previous methods of producing Bibles—or any written materials—were laborious and slow, taking decades if not centuries to produce the necessary quantities of Bibles for the general population.

Innovations in warfare greatly transformed society as well. During most of the Middle Ages, monarchs depended on mounted knights as their military forces. In compensation for the services of their specialized training, knights received land. So much land had to be parceled out to these vassals that monarchs ruled only small portions of their kingdoms directly. The collective resources of any monarch's vassals usually far outweighed the resources of the monarch. Thus, monarchs were generally at the mercy of their vassals, though they held supreme titles. However, the inventions of the crossbow and the longbow in the fourteenth and fifteenth centuries began to change power relations (Greer and Lewis 1997, 319). The crossbow and the longbow did not require extensive specialized training. Additionally, crossbows and longbows could penetrate the armor of knights. The highly specialized martial skills of the knights became less valuable as the monarchs could arm their peasant populations with these new weapons without needing to grant them land in return. The monarchs paid their new armies of foot soldiers by levying taxes. As aristocrats and nobles lost power, many transformed themselves into servants of monarchs' domains, helping the royal domains to become centralized states as they collected taxes and ran the emerging state bureaucracies. The invention of the printing press only fueled the growth of the state bureaucracies. These innovations were slow in transforming society but allowed many monarchs to successfully strengthen their powers within their domains by the early sixteenth century, the time when Martin Luther expressed his ideas of *summus episcopus* and such ideas likewise seemed feasible. Before long, monarchs would claim absolute power within their respective realms. Concurrently, as the use of gunpowder in military weaponry increased from the sixteenth century onwards, modern militaries developed further as commoners were recruited from across a kingdom's territories to train and work together in unison. This process, fostered simultaneously by growing state mechanisms, contributed to the formation of nations since modern militaries would help to mix people of a territory and blend their cultural characteristics into national characteristics.

An important element of medieval Christianity was the belief that the world was geocentric rather than heliocentric. It was not an original idea, for it had developed among the ancient Greeks. Nicolaus Copernicus (1473-1543) questioned this belief in the sixteenth century and argued that the universe was heliocentric. However, he could provide no proof, only reasoning. It would take several more decades before Johannes Kepler (1571-1630) and Galileo Galilei (1564-1642) provided more convincing proof. Kepler provided the precise mathematics of actual planetary movements equated to a heliocentric universe. Galileo constructed a telescope that allowed him and others to peer more deeply into the night sky and see the details that confirmed a heliocentric universe. Isaac Newton's ideas of gravity completed the scientific explanation and proof of a heliocentric universe. Though these scientists seemed only to uncover the facts of reality, the ideas had great social implications. Christians had spent centuries intertwining their biblical beliefs with the Greek view of a geocentrically constructed universe. Consequently, Christians had come to see the Earth as the center of God's universe, humans as God's crown of creation, and God as very active in running the mechanics of this universe. For many, the new heliocentric universe marginalized God and humanity. In time, monarchs would find their privileged positions questioned.

It is important to note that the social, political, economic, technological, and scientific developments that contributed to the rise of modern nations and states were not sequential (though laid out linearly in this text) but generally coincident within a broad time frame and mutually reinforcing. For example, capitalism encouraged technological innovation and secularization, which both in turn contributed to the erosion of medieval social barriers and identities. The printing press disseminated Martin Luther's ideas, facilitated capitalism and the development of modern state bureaucracies, and generally laid the groundwork for public education. Luther's ideas promoted individualism and a work ethic that fueled capitalism (Weber 1978; 2002; Green 1973). Technological innovation and modern science spurred capitalism and continually challenged the privileged position of the ruling classes. Though the synergies of all these innovations, discoveries, and new views fostered the social homogenization within territories that would contribute to the rise of modern nations and states, it would require another century and the added effects of other factors before their synergy would produce modern nations and states. Ingredients by themselves or poured together into a bowl are not the same as the final product resulting from a thorough mixing and either cooking or fermentation time.

The Enlightenment

Newton's ideas, published in *Principia (Mathematical Principles of Natural Philosophy)* in 1687, captured the imagination of intellectuals who thought that Newton had ushered in an age of "light," from which the term *Enlightenment* originates. The period would last until 1789, the beginning of the French Revolution. During this period, the factors noted previously worked to change social identities and political systems to finally create modern nations and states in Western Europe. In particular, the new scientific discoveries that led to the realization of a heliocentric universe brought into question the principle of rule by divine right. With the heliocentric universe operating under the force of gravity, not by God's hand, God was no longer seen as necessary to the functioning of the solar system. With rulers deriving their legitimacy from the belief that they were agents of God—that is, helping God run the universe—removing God from the equation likewise removed the fundamental argument of divine right rule.

The long-reigning dynastic-imperialist philosophy allowed rulers to claim any territories that they wished because they would be governing in the name of God. Spreading the word and expanding the empire were synonymous. Tribal, racial, and ethnic identities were not relevant in determining boundaries, and nationalism was yet unknown. The primary concern of rulers was religious adherence because the legitimacy of rulers was tied to specific faiths—explaining the earlier Thirty Years' War between Roman Catholics and Protestants, who saw each other as heretics at first and then later as differing faiths. Consequently, any concern that rulers had about tribal, racial, and ethnic groups was limited in large degree to religious affiliation. Those with the same affiliation perhaps would be more receptive to the ruler's authority than those with other beliefs. The religious issue notwithstanding, rulers would leave subjects with differing tribal, racial, and ethnic characteristics in peace as long as these peoples recognized the authority of their ruler. Indeed, most empires were multitribal, multiracial, and/or multiethnic (Benedict Anderson 1991, 19, 83), and rulers did little to homogenize the populations of their empires before the rise of modern nationalism.[5]

The new Enlightenment ideas meant that a new legitimacy of governance obviously had to be found, and the new scientific philosophy provided an answer. The new science of the Enlightenment placed great emphasis on mathematical and mechanical laws, the ideas of which led to the belief that all things were bound by universal laws and truths, including social behaviors and interactions. Subsequently, the concept of natural law emerged—the idea that human law was derived from *reason.* The Romans had developed the idea of natural law but it became very popular again during the Enlightenment with people from both periods considering it to be the highest form of law (Greer and Lewis 1997, 120, 448). Upon the Roman idea of natural law, Enlightenment thinkers developed other concepts such as natural rights (e.g., life, liberty, and property). With *reason* chosen as the basis of law and rights, it may seem odd that such laws were labeled *natural* when reason is something found in the human mind rather than in nature. However, the heavy scientific emphasis of the Enlightenment led thinkers to conclude that if physical laws of nature such as gravity governed human beings, then there must exist laws of nature that govern the entire human experience, including thought and action. Just as gravity acts in a predictable rational manner, then so can the human mind in what can be described as reason. Similarly, just as humans can act against nature's physical laws and suffer consequences, humans also can act against the natural law of reason and likewise suffer consequences. The positive side of the idea of natural law is that individuals are seen as having been endowed by nature with basic universal human rights and that those rights must be protected. The negative side of natural law is that some human behaviors are seen as unnatural and, therefore, condemnable. Likewise, some human behaviors that are seen as natural are not only seen as justifiable but mandatory, thus needing to be imposed on everyone everywhere in the spirit of universalism.

In social terms, the new Enlightenment idea that equality existed between all individuals likewise provided no basis for systems of preference or favoritism[6] as seen in medieval society whereby the ruling classes stood above the law. Therefore, the governance and functioning of states should not be based on the medieval practice of particularism and exceptionalism but instead on the practice of protecting the rights of individuals. This new idea that the individual was the basic building block of society was expressed first in England by figures like John Locke (1632-1704) and John Milton (1608-1674). Locke, for example, believed

the [individual's] liberty, dignity, and happiness remain the basic elements
of national life, and that the government of a nation is a moral trust dependent upon the free consent of the governed. (Kohn 1955, 18)

The new social ideas of the Enlightenment, with their emphasis on the
rights of the individual, implied a restructuring of the politico-territorial order. If sovereignty by divine right was rejected, then certainly the territorial
ordering of divine right monarchs had to be rejected as well. Indeed, the
large, sprawling territories of empires could not adequately serve individuals,
or protect their rights. With administrative centers at great distances from
many inhabitants, administrators were separated from those that they served,
making it impossible to provide for the needs of individuals. To serve individuals, states need to have small territories. Small states facilitate the participation of individuals in government because the ratio between the governing and governed is much smaller than in large states. This situation
existed even in the classical Greek city-states, which, by virtue of their small
sizes, maximized the participation of individuals (that is, free males) in their
own governance. Enlightenment thinkers were well aware of the classical
Greeks. They admired them greatly and emulated much of their thinking.[7]

Although Enlightenment thinking implied a spatial reordering of the
world's states to create a political map of many small states, a movement to
bring this about did not materialize. Such a movement would have had difficulty because the existing territorial order had a weighty inertia. Imperial
leaders could easily be disposed of, but the newly emerged state bureaucracies were much more difficult to eliminate. Though they can change to serve
new needs, they strongly resist being abolished. Interestingly, though technological innovations made modern state mechanisms possible and monarchs
gave them life by using them to break the independent attitudes and actions
of their vassals, modern state bureaucracies assumed lives of their own. In
time, they no longer needed their monarchs and thus never came to their aid
when monarchies were swept aside. More adaptable than monarchies to the
changing social environment, state bureaucracies dovetailed so well into the
Enlightenment that they became one of its basic features, even fostering the
idea of nation. Designed to serve monarchies, their homogenizing effects
preserved the monarchs' territorial order long after the monarchs were van-
quished or powerless.

Although Enlightenment thinkers were intrigued by every little detail of
classical Greek culture—to the point of blatant imitation—Enlightenment
thinkers could not bring themselves to start a movement to replicate the classical Greek city-state. The existing politico-territorial order of the eighteenth

century had too much meaning for them to question it. Indeed, even though Enlightenment philosophy implied small states, it did not provide a logical means of areally delineating small states. In other words, if individuals were the basic building block of society with all having the same rights regardless of cultural characteristics, then where should boundaries be drawn? No particular answer was implied, for Enlightenment philosophy saw all individuals as having the same rights no matter in which state they lived. Cultural differences were seen as irrelevant because basic human rights transcended culture (Hobsbawn 1990, 19-20). Thus, beyond the argument that small states most empowered individuals, the lack of particular criteria for determining where boundaries should be drawn precluded Enlightenment thinkers from ever challenging the existing imperial-territorial order, or their own acceptance of it. Additionally, the small medieval political entities were known for their idiosyncratic laws and capricious leaders, neither of which ensured the rights of individuals. Thus, Enlightenment thinkers could hardly oppose the homogenizing effects of the large state bureaucracies which could be employed to bring about universal standards. Rather than advocating the creation of small states, Enlightenment thinkers accepted the existing states and their territories and focused their energies on bringing about democratic reforms within them and ensuring that universal standards translated into universal rights.[8] Thus the Kingdoms of France, Great Britain, Portugal, Spain, Denmark, and Sweden were pushed from their pedestal of dynastic-imperialism to a pathway that made them evolve into nation-states without any call to change their political boundaries (see figure 4.5).[9]

In one sense, the questioning of the imperial-territorial order was hindered even more as Enlightenment philosophy evolved. When Locke's ideas spread to France, they influenced people such as François-Marie Arouet Voltaire (1694-1778) and Jean-Jacques Rousseau (1712-1778).[10] Rousseau, however, did not place as much emphasis on the individual as did Locke. In fact, as Hans Kohn points out,

> with the old dynastic and religious authority in the state breaking down [Rousseau] saw the necessity of establishing the collective personality of the nation as the new center and justification of society and social order. ... [He believed that] the whole people must be united in the closest possible feeling of affinity, of common destiny and common responsibility. ... [Furthermore] the true political community could be based only on the virtue of its citizens and their ardent love of the fatherland. Public education had to implant those feelings in the hearts of all children. (Kohn 1955, 20-21)

Figure 4.5 Europe in 1795

This new emphasis on the whole people rather than the individual certainly ran against the idea of creating small states. The new thinking implied a redrawing of boundaries based on the distribution of peoples. But what defined a people? National consciousness had not fully emerged as it was still in its infancy. The only mechanisms in place that could cultivate a common identity among a group were the imperial state bureaucracies. However, the imperial state bureaucracies had not been deliberately cultivating common national identities among subjects, only a sense of common loyalty to the state. Because common loyalties were defined by the imperial-territorial order, the new national identities were likewise defined by the imperial-territorial order. Indeed, "the people," as Rousseau defined them, were determined by "their ardent love of the fatherland" (see block quote above), not by common cultural characteristics like language and religion. The fatherland, however, was defined by the existing territorial structure. Therefore, membership in nations also was determined in large degree by the map of imperial states (see figure 4.5).

Though Rousseau placed more emphasis on peoples rather than individuals, he accepted the Enlightenment premise that individuals' rights were essential. However, individual rights could best be protected through group membership because collective groups could provide security to individuals. Therefore, peoples were not seen as individuals bound together by common cultural characteristics but rather as individuals bound together for collective security. As such, common culture was not the basis of group identity. States then existed to provide security; therefore, it was important that the individuals within states develop an "ardent love of the fatherland" in order for states to fulfill their missions of providing security. It meant that Rousseau was concerned about drawing boundaries that would maximize states' abilities to provide security rather than enclosing people with the same cultural characteristics within the same state. In determining security, Rousseau was then primarily concerned about the size of population relative to natural resources, as he notes in his statement that "The ideal [state] is achieved when the land can support its population, and when the population is of a size to absorb all the products of the land" (quoted in Pounds 1954, 53). Accompanying the idea of achieving security through optimal size was the idea that security also could be achieved by the optimal location of states' boundaries. Physiographic features such as rivers and mountain ridges were seen as the most easily defendable. Today, natural resources tend to be seen as necessary for a people's well-being but unrelated to determining the existence of groups, the actual members of groups, the number of countries, and locations of their boundaries. However, Rousseau's emphasis on natural resources and boundary location entangled human identity so thoroughly with the natural world that he and those who built on his ideas believed that nature determined the number, sizes, and appropriate territories of nations:

The lie of the mountains, seas and rivers which serve as the frontiers for the various nations who people it (i.e. Europe), seems to have fixed for ever their number and their size. We may fairly say that the political order of the continent is, in some sense, the work of nature. (quoted in Pounds 1954, 53; also quoted in Sahlins 1990, 1436)

Interestingly, physiographic features had been used for centuries for political boundaries. Thus, many of Europe's states in the late eighteenth century were seen as already being in equilibrium with their environments in terms of their sizes and with their boundaries drawn along mountains and rivers, or they would not have existed at all. Aggressive wars were seen as attempts by the leaders of some states to breach optimally located boundaries and destroy the optimal size of targeted states. Conversely, defensive wars were seen as attempts to restore the optimal sizes of states and their ideally located boundaries. So, despite the radical reforms brought about by the French Revolution in 1789, no significant calls were made to change the French state's boundaries. Territorially, the French Republic was exactly the same as the French Empire (see figure 4.5), and membership in the French nation was defined by the French Republic's boundaries. The other nations and states of Western Europe were to be defined similarly. The ideas of the French Revolution radically changed the way in which Europeans viewed and described their existing political geography but were not radical enough to lead people to question their political geography.

Over time, as states cultivated the loyalties of their peoples, they likewise promoted characteristics that were later associated with nationhood. For example, modern state bureaucracies adopted vernacular languages for administrative purposes, not for nationalistic reasons—nationalism had not yet developed until the Enlightenment. The era's new thinking had demoted Latin from its favored status as a sacred language and encouraged the use of vernacular languages in its place. It began with Martin Luther's ideas and culminated in the heliocentric universe. In addition, the development of capitalism and the invention of the printing press had also encouraged the use of vernacular languages. Capitalists grew from a burgeoning middle class that did not know the sacred languages, and their economic orientation had a secular flavor. As their commerce benefited by the printing press, they encouraged printing houses—which were already engaged in printing Bibles in vernacular languages as Martin Luther had advocated—to also churn out commercial materials in the vernacular. Thus, the initial adoption of vernacular languages was purely an administrative choice on the part of state bureaucracies (Benedict Anderson 1991, 42-43, 77-79), and the catalysts for this administrative choice had been new religious ideas, science, technological innovation, and economics. However, the bureaucratic use of vernacular languages created for those living in states a common bond that supplanted the previous bond of loyalty that people had to their divine right monarchs. This common bond held people together, but the membership of groups was determined by states as they framed and promoted vernacular languages within their territories. Thus, people were not only bonded eventually through their newly standardized vernacular languages, but also through their states. For example, it was the territory of the Kingdom of France via its state bureaucracy that determined who would become a French speaker, though later the causal effects would be perceived in reverse, in that the French language would be thought of as a determinant of French nationhood and not vice versa as it was.

The French Revolution in 1789 commonly marks the end of the Enlightenment. However, a number of ideas and practices that emerged after 1789 are the direct results of the Enlightenment and should be considered with the Enlightenment. One of the most notable of these ideas is the choropleth map, which assigns different colors or patterns to territories according to numerical values assigned to such territories. The numerical values are derived from statistics, a science that had originated just prior to the French Revolution. Significantly, *statistics*—which means "science of the state"—had only emerged with the full development of the modern state at the end of the Enlightenment. It was not until the 1820s that the Enlightenment science of statistics would be applied to maps and mapping (Jeremy Crampton 2003, 137-38; Robinson 1982, 156-70). Not coincidentally, the practice was first employed in France—an early hearth of the Enlightenment—by academics and bureaucrats interested in the well-being of their country's citizens. They called their endeavor "moral statistics," and they began mapping education levels, crime, poverty, and even "improvident marriages."[11] The aim was to identify areas within France that needed social improvement. Though choropleth maps highlighted regional differences within states, their intent was to identify such differences so that the French state bureaucracy could redirect wealth and resources to eliminate these differences. Thus, choropleth maps helped states to homogenize their populations. In doing so, choropleth mapping would also contribute to state-centered thinking, as noted in chapter 3. Because states set differing standards for homogenization, choropleth maps fostered the "us" and "them" mentality so characteristic of nationalism.

Romanticism, Idealism, and Other New Philosophies

Enlightenment ideas spread eastward across Europe and influenced thinking but were modified heavily and even rejected to a large degree. What emerged was a new series of philosophies, first Romanticism, then idealism, and then even newer variations of thinking inspired by them. Each followed quickly on the heels of its predecessor with some individuals changing with the times and serving at varying points as representatives of many of the new philosophies. Some of the many key figures were Johann Gottfried Herder (1744-1803), Johann Gottlieb Fichte (1762-1814), and Georg Wilhelm Friedrich Hegel (1770-1831) (Beiser 1992; 1993; 1996; Kohn 1967b; Richards 2002). The point here is not to provide a typology of the different philosophies and their proponents, highlighting their subtle differences, but rather to underscore how evolving ideas led to new conceptions of identity and the political organization of earth space.

One of the major shifts in thinking was initiated by Herder. He rejected the sterile nature of the Enlightenment view with its emphasis on rational scientific thinking and the rights of the individual. Instead, he focused on the irrational and creative force of the people as a collective, *das Volk* (Kohn 1967b, 274; Wilson 1973, 829). Herder believed that

> humanity was something man could achieve only as a member of a nation and that nations could arrive at humanity only if they remained true to their national characters, or souls. Each nation, then, by developing its language, art, literature, religion, customs, and laws—all of which were expressions of the national soul—would be working not only for its own strength and unity, but for the well-being of civilization as a whole. Each nation had a special "mission" to perform in the progress of man toward humanity—the cultivation of one's own characteristics. (Wilson 1973, 823-24)

Much earlier, Martin Luther sowed the seeds for a new view on languages by arguing that individuals could pray and commune with God in their own vernacular languages; therefore, the Bible should be translated into vernacular languages. Luther's arguments and efforts helped to break down the sacred/profane categorization of languages: profane (i.e., vernacular) languages were placed on equal footing with sacred languages. Beginning in the Romantic period, Herder took the process a step further and elevated vernacular languages even higher by arguing that they were a defining characteristic of nationhood. According to Herder,

> every language has its definite national character, and therefore nature obliges us to learn only our native tongue, which is the most appropriate to our character, and which is most commensurate with our way of thought. (Kohn 1967a, 432-33)

In essence, Herder argued that language is a "currency of thought" and each vernacular language embodies a nation's cultures, beliefs, and values, molding their thinking and behavior in a way not completely translatable into other languages:

> [Herder] argued that languages originated not from the instructions of God—as was the presumption of conventional theology—but from men imitating natural sounds of particular regions: "the entire, many voiced, divine nature is the language teacher and muse," he wrote. Different languages would be indicative of different locations and historic traditions. What to our ears may be even more startling, coming as it did from a clergyman, Herder's insistence that language and human reason developed simultaneously and naturally, so that "the first, most primitive use of reason could not occur without language." "Man," Herder thus concluded, "is, in his distinctive features, a creation of the group, of society: the development of a language is thus natural, essential, and necessary for him." The conception of a natural evolution of language and reason would later provide a leading motif for the likes of Fichte, Schelling, and Hegel, the architects of German idealism. (Richards 2002, 341-42)

Interestingly, the new emphasis placed on language developed not merely from Luther's ideas as they gained momentum over time, but also from the efforts of Enlightenment scholars. The scientific emphasis of the Enlightenment led scholars to examine the linguistic relationships within and among languages. One man in particular, Sir William Jones, is noteworthy for a number of accomplishments (Cannon and Brine 1995; Murray 1998). Interested in "Oriental" literature, he translated and made available to Europeans a number of classic works written in Persian and Arabic. In 1783, he went to India, within a few months founded the Bengal Asiatic Society, and began translating Sanskrit works. The results of his efforts were revolutionary:

> The discovery of the Sanskrit language and literature was a crucial event in the development of our historical consciousness, and in the evolution of all cultural sciences. In its importance and influence it may be compared to the great intellectual revolution brought about through the Copernican system in the field of natural sciences. The Copernican hypothesis reversed the conception of the cosmic order. The earth was no longer in the center of the universe; it became a "star among stars." The geocentric conception of the physical world was discarded. In the same sense the acquaintance with Sanskrit literature made an end to that conception of human culture which saw its real and only center of the world in classical antiquity. Henceforward the Greco-Roman world could only be regarded as a small sector of the universe of human culture. (Cassirer 1967, 17)

Perhaps even more significant, Jones announced at a society meeting in 1786 that he believed Sanskrit had such a close relationship with Latin and Greek that the languages sprang from a common source (McCrum, Cran, and MacNeil 1987, 51). Much of Jones's work came at the tail end of the Enlightenment and the beginning of the Romantic period, as he died in 1794, and his discoveries helped to chart the course for Romanticism and the other newer philosophies to come.[12] For example, Georg Wilhelm Friedrich Hegel "called the discovery of the common origin of Greek and Sanskrit the discovery of a new world" (Cassirer 1967, 17). With the inspiration of Jones, Jakob Grimm (of the Brothers Grimm) went on to find concrete evidence of these common origins. "'Grimm's Law' established beyond question that the German *vater* (and English *father*) has the same root as Sanskrit/Latin *pitar/pater*" (McCrum, Cran, and MacNeil 1987, 52). Romantics were obviously excited about language, and it was Jones's linguistic scholarship that led many during the Romantic period to examine the relationships within and between languages. From the Romantic period onward, linguists began constructing family trees of languages similar to genealogical trees. Until the Romantic period, individuals within Europe were aware that similarities existed among the languages they spoke. However, the similarities were not analyzed or classified. People in one village frequently considered the language spoken in a neighboring village to be a completely different language because pronunciation and a few words were different, though linguistics since the Romantic period came to classify what was spoken in the two such villages as the same language and probably even the same dialect. Therefore, though Romantics and their successors argued that language was the "currency of thought" that bound people together into a single nation, such ideas were unknown to many people themselves and played little role in determining how individuals bonded together in larger groups. In actuality, it was the academics' and scholars' new interest and effort in classifying languages coupled with Romantic philosophers' promotion of language as a basis of identity that encouraged individuals to identify with others that spoke the same language. The efforts of Romantics were successful largely because they coincided with the newly emergent modern states. Modern bureaucracies with their homogenizing mechanisms made use of linguistic research to bring about language standardization within their state territories. With the concurrent rise of universal education, language standardization soon touched everyone's life within individual states, meaning that each state subsequently, if inadvertently, promoted language as a unifying characteristic for their nations as they imposed language standardization on their citizens.

Fused together with the new emphasis on language was a new regard for nature. Nature was seen as being unique from place to place and perceived as a molding force in the development of languages and nations. As Herder wrote, nature

> has sketched with the mountain ranges she formed and with the rivers she made flow for them the rough but definite outline of the entire history of man. . . . One height created a nation of hunters, thus supporting and necessitating a savage state; another, more spread out and mild, provided a field for shepherd peoples and supplied them with tame animals; another made agriculture easy and essential; and still another began with navigation and fishing and finally to trade. . . . In many regions the customs and ways of life have continued for millennia; in others they have changed, . . . but always in harmony with the terrain from which the change came. . . . Oceans, mountain chains, and rivers are the most natural boundaries not only of lands, but also of peoples, customs, languages, and empires; and even in the greatest revolutions of human affairs they have been the guiding lines and the limits of world history. (Wilson 1973, 821-22; Ergang 1966, 37-38)

Indeed, it should be remembered that though the Industrial Revolution may have been under way, livelihood was still intimately tied to the land and to such a degree that it was seen as having played a major role in the creation of the peoples that existed. For example, the word *pole* in Polish translates as *field*, meaning that Poles were seen as the people of the field (i.e., farmers); Hungarians were viewed as separate and distinct because they were nomads who lived on the Pannonian Plain, which provided them with their livelihood; the name *Vlach* (also *Wallach*, the forerunner to the terms *Wallachian* and *Romanian*) was synonymous with shepherd because it likewise explained how the Vlachs originated and were dependent on the Carpathian uplands and other mountainous areas in the region that provided them with their way of life.

The belief that nature and/or God determined the number and location of peoples and countries existed during the Enlightenment and before, but it passed from the dispassionate analysis of Enlightenment science to Romantic thinking, which infused the belief with an intense emotional zeal. While Enlightenment thinkers believed that physiographic boundaries provided security and each physical environment provided particular natural resources that helped to determine economy and way of life, Romantics—as indicated by Herder's statement—saw the connection between humans and the environment as being much deeper and more profound. Romantics saw the connection between individual nations and their particular environments as mandated by nature and/or God and sacred. In the United States, for example, Americans in the early nineteenth century saw westward expansion to the Pacific Ocean not merely as something beneficial to Americans, but rather a God-given mandate in what became known as Manifest Destiny. It, like many ideas concerning boundaries, did not argue that boundaries should be drawn around a people with common cultural characteristics—as emphasized by Romantics themselves—but that boundaries should be drawn for a people along physiographic features according to nature's and/or God's will regardless of who else lived there: witness the eradication of Native Americans. Similarly, Irish nationalists came to argue that nature and/or God created an island called Ireland and, therefore, nature and/or God intended for one people (i.e., the Irish) to live there under the governance of a single Irish state. In many ways, this belief is expressed in Article 2 of the Constitution of the Republic of Ireland, written in 1937, as it states that "The national territory consists of the whole island of Ireland, its islands and the territorial seas" (quoted in Pringle 1985, 4). This claim is made despite the fact that the Loyalists/Unionists of Northern Ireland, having long been the majority in Northern Ireland, remain *loyal* to the United Kingdom and prefer to maintain the *union* of Northern Ireland and Great Britain—as indicated by their names. Nevertheless, various threads of Irish nationalism maintain that anyone not Irish living anywhere on the island is somehow unnaturally there.[13] As another example, the view that the Atlantic, the Pyrenees, the Alps, and the Rhine River were France's natural boundaries are reflected in the writings of such individuals as Buache de la Neuville, who wrote in 1791 that France's boundaries should be fixed according to "the natural division of the Globe formed at its origin by the Creator" (quoted in Sahlins 1990, 1443). By the middle of the nineteenth century, the concept of natural boundaries provided the French public with "a lesson of sacred union" (Gaston Zeller, quoted in Sahlins 1990, 1448) and a sense of historical continuity—a critical element of Romantic thinking.

The Americans, Irish, and French were by no means unique in developing Romantic notions of natural boundaries; many other nations developed similar views. Most importantly, despite the heavy emphasis that Romantic thinking placed on language as a national characteristic, the continually changing language landscape provided few obvious linguistic boundaries that could be used as political boundaries. On the other hand, the concept of natural boundaries provided clear demarcations and thus provided states and emerging nationalists idealized locations for their political boundaries, as noted, for example, in Herder's statement. When these idealized natural boundaries were realized, states then employed their mechanisms—as identified in chapter 3—to also make natural boundaries into sharp linguistic boundaries. Thus, though it is commonly remembered that Romanticism and its successors emphasized language as a national characteristic, it has been frequently forgotten that the concept of natural boundaries played an instrumental role in determining where particular languages developed as they were used to determine political boundaries and in turn determined the limits of states' homogenizing effects on languages.

German Romantic songs and anthems are interesting to note as examples because Romanticism is seen as having primarily emerged among German intellectuals with German Romantics often noted for explicitly stating that the German nation was defined by language. A closer examination of renowned works shows that despite the heavy emphasis on language, German Romantics frequently used physiographic boundaries to delimit linguistic boundaries and thus identify what they thought was Germany's rightful boundaries. *Lied der Deutschen (Song of the Germans)* or *Deutschland-slied*—also commonly known as *Deutschland über alles (Germany above all)* by its first line—is a prime example. The very first stanza, which provides the only detailed physiographic description of Germany, indicates that Germany should extend "From the Maas to the Memel, From the Etsch to the Belt" (Alexander 1999-2002, 13; Herb 2004, 162). Originally written in 1841, this piece grew in significance as it became the German national anthem in 1922. Since this song was used by the Nazis, the Allies prohibited the anthem in 1945. In 1952, the Federal Republic of Germany adopted the third stanza as its anthem. The first stanza was controversial for its first line and because many of the physiographic features identified lay beyond the new boundaries of the German states (i.e., either East or West Germany) and the lands of German speech. The Maas flows deep into the Netherlands, the Memel is found in Lithuania, the Etsch (more commonly known as the Adige) flows in northern Italy and into the Adriatic at a point far south of Venice, and the Belt(s) are waterways well inside Denmark. By the mid-twentieth century the combination of forgetting that earlier Romantics used physiographic features to identify the extent of German speech and the proud use of this song by the Nazis led many to conclude—in conjunction with its commonly used title—that the song indicated territorial aggressiveness. Nevertheless, the idea that the German language and Germany were framed by physiographic features is affirmed in the research of such individuals as Richard Böckh (1869). He argued that if the boundaries of the watershed of the Rhône and Rhine systems were used as the boundaries to separate the German and French states, then a minimal and almost equal number of German and French speakers would live as minorities in each other's countries (see also Pounds 1954, 60).[14]

The Romantic understanding and use of the term *natural political boundary* is not a casual one and should caution us not to use the term casually either. Indeed, the term *natural* is applied to those things that are made by nature and/or God (depending on one's belief system), and its antonym— *artificial*—refers to those things created by humans. Unfortunately, the term *natural political boundaries* is frequently applied to those boundaries that follow physiographic features without realizing the implications of using *natural* in conjunction with *political boundaries* and without realizing that those fervent Romantic nationalists who speak of *natural political boundaries* are doing much more than simply talking about political boundaries that follow physiographic features. They are enlisting nature and/or God on their side of the argument and are as frequently as fervent and uncompromising as any zealot who believes that God is with them and against those who disagree with them. Therefore, though it is tempting to refer to the many political boundaries that follow physiographic features as natural political boundaries, such applications misuse the term *natural* and dramatically understate the arguments of Romantic nationalists when they use the term *natural political boundaries*.[15]

As Romantics spoke and wrote of the natural and thus the unique characteristics of national identity, they rejected the Enlightenment idea of universalism. Herder, for example, advocated a view of nature and history as organic processes: "an endless creative process in which attention should be centered not on the general and common but on the individual and unique" (Kohn 1955, 31). This view had developed after medieval cyclical views of time evolved into views of progressive and organic time by the Romantic period. Later, Hegel believed that the only way to truly understand any subject was through the study of its historical development, known thereafter as *historicism* (Greer and Lewis 1997, 474). History then was more than a random collection of events; it was guided by a unifying Reason or *Zeitgeist* (spirit of the time) with every aspect of human life interrelated in a cultural *whole*. From Hegel's ideas came the pursuit of the *historical method* in scholarly inquiry. Included within Hegel's view of history was his idea of *dialectic,* the notion that events were driven by the forces of opposing ideas: a reigning *thesis* opposed by a challenging *antithesis*. In their struggle, neither successfully destroys the other but instead blend together into a new *synthesis*. History is driven forward as the synthesis becomes the new reigning thesis and a new antithesis rises to oppose it. Hegel's dialectic demoted the individual—given the highest regard during the Enlightenment. With events driven by the forces of history (i.e., the dialectic), individuals were seen as insignificant as they were swept along by the tides of history. Greatness could be achieved only by those who went with the flow of history as reflected in the belief that great men do not make great history but great history makes great men. Thus, though Hegel shared with Herder an interest in the "individual and unique," such an interest—for Herder as well as Hegel—was not only in the individuality and uniqueness of each person, but also and more so in that of individual nations.

This strong emphasis on collective group identity led to a new emphasis on the state:

> [T]he state became an object of poetry and adoration; they [Romantics] regarded it as something so lofty and wondrous, so full of miracle and mystery, that it could no longer be the work of free men founded for mutual benefit in the way the eighteenth century [Enlightenment] thinkers had imagined. . . . [The state] was, like the human being, a creation of the unfathomable will of God and of the elemental forces of nature, an ethical individual like man himself, only infinitely greater and more powerful. Joseph Freiherr von Eichendorff (1788-1857), a leader of the younger Catholic generation of romanticism, called the state "a spiritual community to make life as perfect as possible by developing the strength of mind and soul in a people, which alone could truly be called life." Zacharias Werner who started as a disciple of the Enlightenment and later joined the Catholic Church and the romantic movement, defined the state as "a union which should make it possible for a group of human beings to fulfill their highest vocation. It isolates this group to give it back to mankind in an ennobled form."
>
> Yet the romanticists were individuals too strongly artistic to allow the state to impose a deadening uniformity. According to their ideal, the individual should serve and love the state with all his soul and mind, yet he should not be a robot but a free man living his own life, united with others without losing his individuality. They praised liberty, but it was a liberty not rooted in reason and equality but in history and peculiarity. In Eichendorff's novel *Ahnung und Gegenwart* Leontin shouted: "Es lebe die Freiheit," but he did not mean universal liberty of 1789, which was the same for everybody and in which everybody felt himself proudly free everywhere.
>
> . . . romantic political philosophy held fast to the thesis that the state was not man's work nor established for the benefit of the individual, who was indissolubly part of the state and inevitably determined by its past. (Kohn 1967b, 187-88)

The glorification of the state came at a time when the solidification of modern state power was reaching a height where it was beginning to pervasively shape human identity. In many ways then, Romanticism was both a reflection of new state power and a legitimizing philosophy for the continued growth and use of state power.

Romantics had a great interest in the past (Craig 1972, 7) but were confronted with a major problem: few had kept a detailed record of the history of European nations and states, especially not in Eastern Europe. Much that had been written was limited to specific times and places, having resulted in a very fragmented historical record. Much known history was that of dynasties and of ancient Greek and Roman scholars. History, therefore, had to be reconstructed, and Herder believed that it could only be done through folk poetry (Wilson 1973, 825). To Herder and his protégés, folk poets were really historians who spoke in a metaphorical language that reflected the very essence of the national soul. Although folklore and folk poetry provided a means for reconstructing history, it was itself very problematic. Often very ambiguous, folklore and folk poetry could be interpreted variously. In an attempt to provide meaning for the past and also fill in the past's numerous gaps, Romantic historicists reconstructed many histories and mythologies that were essentially fabricated. Romantics were not bothered by the lack of hard evidence. Meaningful continuity was more important than unexplained facts. As Anthony D. Smith points out,

> Their aim is to retail the "past," in such a way as to "explain" the lot of their community and prescribe remedies for its ills. To this end, historicists must collate different versions and strands of communal traditions and produce a single, unified "past" which gives a convincing and emotionally satisfying account of the present situation of their ethnic kinsmen. There must be no loose ends, no doubts or conflicting versions, which can blur and erode the "native hue of resolution." (1986b, 191-92)

Smith goes on to outline a series of eight elements that are found in any national mythology or myth of ethnic descent:

1. a myth of origins in time; i.e. when the community was "born";
2. a myth of origins in space; i.e. where the community was "born";
3. a myth of ancestry; i.e. who bore us, and how we descended from him/her;
4. a myth of migration; whither we wandered;
5. a myth of liberation; i.e. how we were freed;
6. a myth of a golden age; i.e. how we became great and heroic;
7. a myth of decline; i.e. how we decayed and were conquered/exiled; and
8. a myth of rebirth; i.e. how we shall be restored to our former glory.
(1986b, 192)

Many of the ideas of Romantics, such as those of natural political boundaries, cultivate deep emotions of national pride that can lead to intolerance of others. Such, however, was not always the case. For example, Herder was a German-speaking Prussian, and his ideas strongly shaped the emergence of the modern German nation, but he can hardly be called a German nationalist. "Each nation was to him a manifestation of the Divine, and, therefore, something sacred which should not be destroyed but cultivated" (Kohn 1955, 31). He despised Prussian militarism and believed that a healthy and prosperous nation could best develop among peaceful peasant peoples such as the Slavs. In fact, Herder greatly admired the folk practices and traditions of the Slavs. He predicted a glorious future for the Slavic peoples and encouraged them and others to collect Slavic folk poetry and information on Slavic traditions and customs. Herder's writings were published in many Slavic languages as well as German, and they were instrumental in stimulating national consciousness among Slavs (Wilson 1973, 830-31).

In summary then, Romanticism stood in sharp contrast to Enlightenment philosophy. Where the Enlightenment stressed universal truths and the rights of the individual, Romanticism emphasized unique truths and the rights of the group. While Enlightenment thinkers valued universal languages of Latin and Greek, Romantics promoted the use of native, vernacular languages. As Enlightenment philosophers insisted on rational, intellectual thought, Romantics cherished the irrational, emotional spirit. While Enlightenment thinkers saw physiographic boundaries as good political boundaries because they helped to provide collective security, Romantics thought of physiographic boundaries as having a more intimate connection to national identity because particular natural environments determined nations' characters/cultures as well as ways of life. While Enlightenment thinkers argued that states existed to provide security for individuals, Romantics believed that states produced individuals and thus deserved human love, adoration, and loyalty. As Enlightenment thinkers preferred urban settings, known for great social interaction and stimulating intellectual environments, Romantics idolized bucolic settings with their close connections with nature; moreover, unlike cities, rural areas were preserves of folk cultures, which in turn provided a means for Romantics to write "histories" for their peoples.

Subsequently, Romantic philosophy has given rise to a number of terms and phrases, which in turn can be employed to identify Romantic thinking. Romantics, for example, speak of "national awakening," as if nations always existed but did not know it. Not surprisingly then, Romantics use the term "historical continuity" to prove that nations have always existed, ignoring that they have to fabricate history to demonstrate its continuity.[16] Historical continuity implies "destiny," and a "glorious" one at that. After all, a linear past, especially a well-constructed one, implies a particular future. Romantics also heavily employ the terms "natural" and "artificial," implying that some historical acts and events, or even current policies and situations, are unnatural.

Romanticism implied a different spatial ordering for nationalism in Central and Eastern Europe than did the Enlightenment in Western Europe. As the idea of the nation evolved, so did the ideas relating to the spatial extent of a nation's territory. The emphasis placed on language, for example, suggests that nationalists might have defined the national territory on the basis of the spatial distribution of language speakers. However, this was not the case. Language was not as simple and as straightforward an issue as it may seem. As already noted, until the rise of Romanticism, language was not thought of as it is today, and certainly not considered to be the basis of identity. Thus, individuals did not feel as strongly attached to certain languages and were more willing to change their language practices. The educated and privileged, for example, routinely learned and spoke many languages and, as noted in chapter 2, saw it as beneath themselves to speak the vernacular languages of their peasants. As a result, some were multilingual, while others, although speaking only one language, did not speak the language of their ancestors and felt no qualms about it. In fact, modern standard languages were not thoroughly in use yet, so language was in constant transition across the landscape.[17] Therefore, language was a very problematic issue for those who wanted to use it as a national determinant.

Romantics were even aware of the fluidity of language and tried to rectify the situation by encouraging individuals to "relearn" their native languages. By doing so, individuals could discover their true national identities. This belief, however, led to other problems: How could individuals identify their proper national languages so that they could learn them, speak them, and thus realize their true national identities? Moreover, if many did not actually speak their true national languages, then how could language be used to map out the spatial distribution of nations? The latter question must be answered before national territories could be mapped out, at least if language was to be used as Romantic philosophy implied. The answer to this question was not easy because it involved an inherent contradiction. Romantics insisted that language was a national determinant, yet many Romantics could not accept that many then must have changed their national identities when they adopted a new language. Instead, Romantics insisted these individuals not speaking their true native languages were oppressed, and could realize their true national identities only when they relearned their native languages.

But again, who were these people—these Russified Poles, Belarussians, Ukrainians, etc.; these Germanized Poles, Czechs, Slovenes, etc.; these Magyarized Slovaks, Romanians, Croats, etc.? How could one distinguish between a Russian-speaking Russian and a Russian-speaking Pole or a German-speaking German and a German-speaking Pole? And where did they live?

Language and shared history were not the concrete issues that they seemed to be and, therefore, were not dependable in delimiting the territories of nations, though Romantic philosophy implied that they should be used for such a purpose. Romantics, nevertheless, were able to identify members of nations and national territories through the existing imperial-territorial order. Indeed, Romantic philosophers were no more able to reject the existing imperial-territorial order than the Enlightenment thinkers who preceded them. In addition, they accepted physiographic boundaries as appropriate political boundaries as Enlightenment thinkers had.[18] Though they emphasized physiographic political boundaries for differing reasons, they nevertheless largely accepted the status quo political-territorial order. Thus, with the rise of Romantic nationalism in Central and Eastern Europe at the beginning of the nineteenth century, the Germans, Austrians, Russians,[19] and even the Hungarians began viewing their imperial states as their new national states. The Germans had more of a problem in this process because they did not have a single imperial state but many small dynastic states. Nevertheless, the modern Romantic conception was not simply a welding together of German peoples based on the notion of a common German language. Such a description would be an oversimplification of the process. Modern national Germany came about from the welding together of numerous German states (Herb 1993, 11; 1997, 8-12), identified to a significant degree by larger territorial configurations.[20]

As dynastic-imperial territories were being redefined into nation-states, a new emphasis was indeed placed on language as a defining national characteristic, thanks to Romantic philosophy. Consequently, many new group identities emerged, and many peoples in Central and Eastern Europe found themselves to be defined as a new class of minorities. In dynastic-imperial times these peoples were simply part of the underclass that labored for the imperial leaders. During the period of growing nationalism, however, some joined the ranks of the ruling group while others were viewed as unwanted minorities who increasingly were seen as outsiders and a threat to the ruling nation.

The minority peoples of Central and Eastern Europe were likewise influenced by the ideas of nationalism. Herder, for example, glorified the Slavs in his writings and encouraged them to cultivate their national identities. However, the newly emerging minorities found that the Germans, the Austrians, the Russians, and the Hungarians increasingly were discriminating against them.[21] In many ways, such discrimination only encouraged these minority peoples to develop their own group identities—national identities. The minority peoples had a problem, however, because most of them did not have an existing state to use as the basis from which a national territory could be defined. However, the emphasis that Romanticism placed on history allowed these peoples to reach back into the past, to the "Golden Age" of their ancestors (see Smith quote, page 162), and choose their ancestors' territories—frequently with boundaries along physiographic features. Because the ancestors of the past were empire builders, not nation builders, the minority nations of Central and Eastern Europe often chose territories that had little relationship to contemporary ethnic distributions. Nevertheless, reaching back into the past gave Eastern Europeans the ability to do what the Western Europeans were doing—redefine an imperial territory as a national territory.[22] Considering that most of Eastern Europe's educated elite received their education in the West, it is no surprise that many Eastern European thinkers would try to emulate Western Europeans. Looking back into the past to a "Golden Age" of a great empire also gave Eastern Europeans parity with Western Europeans by showing that Eastern Europeans had achieved greatness as well.

Romantic ideas first emerged among intellectuals and only spread slowly to more common people. Napoleon was responsible for fanning the spread of nationalism through the general populace, especially in Central and Eastern Europe, and helping the modern state to solidify (Greer and Lewis 1997, 464-65). In France itself, for example, Napoleon ended the attack on Roman Catholicism by the revolutionaries and accepted it as the main religion of France. However, the Roman Catholic Church lost much of its properties, and the French government assumed the right to nominate bishops. These new practices paralleled the similar earlier Protestant practices, both of which contributed to the abolition of the complex medieval structures whereby political power was multilayered and not confined by state boundaries; in this case, whereby the Roman Catholic Church centered in Rome exercised political authority in numerous states. In essence, Napoleon put into practice the modern state idea that the state has total control over affairs—including religious affairs—within its territory. Similarly, Napoleon transferred education from religious authorities, meaning that the state would inculcate patriotism in its citizens rather than the previous church practice of cultivating a broader Christian identity. The Napoleonic Code simplified and standardized laws—a characteristic of modern states—by doing away with centuries-old accumulation of idiosyncratic practices. Correspondingly, regional and local courts were presided over by salaried officials who reported directly to the central government.

Napoleon crowned himself emperor rather than have the pope complete the act. It was a very bold and unorthodox move as it implied that his power originated from himself and his people rather than from God's religious representative on Earth as espoused by the older medieval ideas. Napoleon's act may not have been accepted by commoners, but as his armies swept across Europe, the power of such national ideas was demonstrated every time his national army defeated an imperialist army. Napoleon's victories were swift and decisive, and did more to bring about the questioning of the legitimacy of divine right monarchs in the minds of the masses than the abstract rhetoric of Enlightenment philosophers. At the same time, Napoleon's victories greatly fanned the emerging national sentiments of peoples, especially within the empires of Central and Eastern Europe. In practical terms, Napoleon reorganized the continent's political geography into something more akin to modern statehood as he had done to France itself by reorganizing its internal political geography. For example, he abolished the Holy Roman Empire in 1806 and its complex hierarchy of political-territorial relations. In the process, he consolidated the more than three hundred German states and over one-and-a-half thousand knightly estates (James 1994, 34-35). For the Poles, the Slovenes, and the Croats—those who were particularly receptive and helpful to Napoleon—Napoleon created states. By 1812, Napoleon had completely redrawn the map of Europe (see figure 4.6), and it looked and functioned more like a map of modern nation-states than what had just come before it at the dawn of the French Revolution.

The old dynastic forces obviously were threatened by Napoleon's actions. Though Napoleon had trounced them in battle after battle, he eventually miscalculated with his attack on Russia in 1812. Napoleon was left vulnerable by the loss of most of his army and the dynastic forces regrouped and defeated him. Though he rose again, a coalition of dynastic forces put a final end to his reign at Waterloo in 1815. In what was called the "Concert of Europe," they sought to extinguish national sentiments completely and reestablish the old imperial order at the Congress of Vienna (see figure 4.7). The Poles and Italians lost the states that Napoleon created for them, and the national sentiments of minorities were suppressed throughout the reestablished empires. At first, it seemed that the old dynastic forces would be successful, but the national idea was already born, even among the dominant peoples. The dynastic-imperialist ideas reigned supreme again, but the na-

tionalist idea waited to assert itself while the new ideology of nationalism
began to smolder.

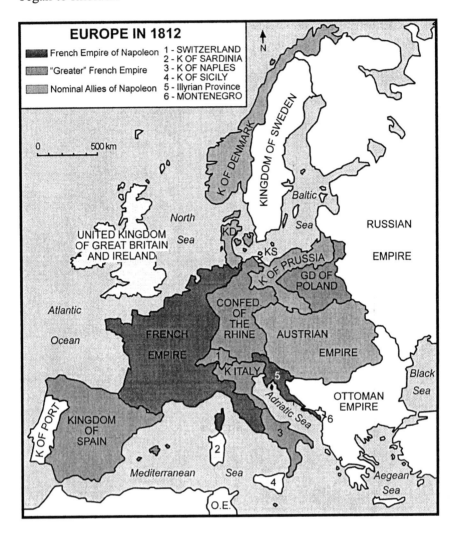

Figure 4.6 Europe in 1812

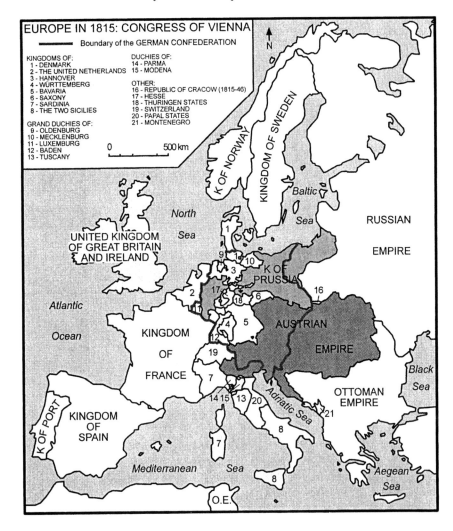

Figure 4.7 Europe in 1815: Congress of Vienna

Notes

1. For more on ethnosymbolism and critiques of it, see Monserrat Guibernau and John Hutchinson's edited volume of *Nations and nationalism* (2004). See also Umut Özkirimli's article "The nation as an artichoke? A critique of ethnosymbolist interpetrations of nationalism" (2003).

2. Perhaps the best example of the complexity of medieval territorial rule is that of Charles V (1519-1556), who in addition to serving as Holy Roman Emperor

also held the following titles: "Emperor of Austria; King of Hungary, of Bohemia, of Dalmatia, Croatia, Slavonia, Galicia, Lodomeria, and Illyria; King of Jerusalem, etc.; Archduke of Austria; Grand Duke of Tuscany and Cracow; Duke of Lorthringia, of Salzburg, Styria, Carinthia, Carniola and Bukovina; Grand Duke of Transylvania, Margrave of Moravia; Duke of Upper and Lower Silesia, of Modena, Parma, Piacenza and Guastella, of Ausschwitz and Sator, of Teschen, Friaul, Ragusa and Zara; Princely Count of Habsburg and Tyrol, of Kyburg, Görz and Gradiska; Duke of Trient and Brixen; Margrave of Upper and Lower Lausitz and in Istria; Count of Hohenembs, Feldkirch, Bregenz, Sonnenberg, etc.; Lord of Trieste, of Cattaro and above the Windisch Mark; Great Voyvod of the Voyvodina, Servia, etc., etc." (Jászi, [1929] 1961, 34; also quoted in Benedict Anderson 1991, 20).

 3. Richard I is one example, as he spent only about ten months of his ten-year reign in the England that we know today. He had so little regard for the island part of his kingdom that he is reputed to have said that he would have sold London had he found a rich enough buyer (Delderfield 1972, 45).

 4. Today, Tyroleans, Styrians, Bohemians, and Moravians seem to be no more than people from places with those names, perhaps leading one to the conclusion that these peoples are not nations or "real" identity categories but just "geographic designations" because no languages by those names exist. However, those identities existed and indicate that place of origin was the basis of identity, perhaps more so than language and culture. Furthermore, the listing of these identities in conjunction with the name Hungarians suggests that Hungarian identity was similarly derived from a place rather than from a language though a Hungarian language existed. Indeed, the latter part of the quote indicates that some Hungarians—not to mention Croats—spoke Slovak. Moreover, Austrians are listed too, and although Austria is a place and not a language, a separate Austrian nation is currently accepted and distinguished from the German nation though Austrians speak German.

 It is interesting that the author points out that historians have overemphasized language and race in identifying groups. Yet just after making the point, the author seems to accept that language and race are the essential basis of identity by first naming such groups, "Germans, Slavs or Magyars," and then stating that they were "much more conscious of being Tyroleans, Austrians, Styrians, Bohemians, Moravians or Hungarians." It is as if the author only superficially accepts that the differing sense of identity resulted in different social groupings by first acknowledging that different social formations existed but then suggesting that they were really organized along our current understandings of nationhood though the people of the seventeenth century were not aware of it.

 5. The Prussian case illustrates this point. At the turn of the eighteenth century, foreigners outnumbered middle-class Prussians in the Prussian army (Benedict Anderson 1991, 22; Vagts 1959, 64 and 85)—hardly a nationalist army as we would conceive of one today.

 6. The idea of equality had linguistic implications as well. In Europe, in particular, Enlightenment philosophy could not recognize the special "sacred" status that Latin, or even Greek and Hebrew, had long enjoyed in the Christian realm up

until that point (Benedict Anderson 1991, 70-71). All languages were equal. However, these languages contained much human knowledge; therefore, Enlightenment thinkers continued to learn and use these languages. Though these languages continued to be used, it is important to recognize that the reasons for their continued use changed as they went from being seen as sacred languages to languages containing much knowledge about the world.

7. The political landscape that Enlightenment thinkers created, still in existence today, demonstrates that Enlightenment thinkers venerated Greek social and political philosophy greatly. Examples are readily seen in the United States, where many federal government buildings and state capitols have a distinct Greco-Roman architectural style.

8. Benedict Anderson makes a very similar argument in the beginning of his book *Imagined communities* (Anderson 1991, 2). Anderson, however, goes on to explore the historical dimensions of this process, while this book explores the geo-graphical dimensions.

9. Benedict Anderson argues that territorial framework created by the great European colonial empires defined the states and nations in Latin America, Africa, and Asia: "In considering the origins of recent 'colonial nationalism,' one central similarity with the colonial nationalisms of an earlier age immediately strikes the eye: the isomorphism between each nationalism's territorial stretch and that of the previous imperial administrative unit" (Anderson 1991, 114). This process occurred first in New Spain. As noted earlier, the Spanish-speaking Roman Catholics did not band together to create a New Spanish state but instead banded together with the indigenous peoples in a number of smaller states. The Spanish administrative-territorial units defined the number and areal extent of the new states (Anderson 1991, 52-53), and with them, the new national identities. In other words, individuals transcended, actually ignored, their linguistic and religious similarities and differences and developed national identities with one another based on the shared experiences of living together in the same places and territories.

10. For more information on Rousseau, see Alfred Cobban's *Rousseau and the state* (1964) and Anne Cohler's *Rousseau and nationalism* (1970).

11. Improvident marriages were those entered into by males under twenty-one years of age (Robinson 1982, 156).

12. For example, he had a great influence on such Romantic poets as Wordsworth, Coleridge, Byron, and Shelley (Sir William Jones, Library of Congress, http://www.loc.gov/law/public/asl/htdoc/asl002.html).

13. Dennis Pringle points out a number of flaws in the natural unit argument and the historical and economic arguments, which are in many ways corollaries to the natural unit argument (1985, 7-10). First, if an island can be a natural political unit, then so can a chain of islands such as Japan and New Zealand. Therefore, it could be argued that Ireland should be together with the other British Isles as one political unit—as it once was under British rule. Furthermore, the argument that the British and Scots-Irish presence in Northern Ireland is unnatural is contradicted by the fact that many parts of Northern Ireland are closer to Scotland than to the rest of

Ireland. Considering also that water transportation and communication was much easier and safer than land routes through most of history, it seems that the British and Scots-Irish presence in Northern Ireland is expected on historical and economic grounds according to natural circumstances rather than somehow a violation of them.

14. The long history of using physiographic features as political boundaries began changing in the nineteenth century. During this time, the decreasing costs of map production made maps more widely available, and the growth of universal education led to a greater demand for maps as the public learned how to read them. Subsequently, reliance on physiographic boundaries seemingly diminished as maps were able to depict boundaries precisely anywhere in earth space. As Guntram H. Herb notes in his research, maps increasingly became the instrument for delineating German territory (1997, 2004). Physiographic boundaries, however, did not completely lose their significance in the human mind. Richard Böckh's use of physiographic boundaries to spatially delineate the German language and the elevation of *Lied der Deutschen* to anthem status in the twentieth century are a few examples. Joseph Stalin's use of the Oder and Neisse Rivers to redraw the eastern boundary of the German Democratic Republic after the Second World War is another example, though Stalin was not concerned about the nuances of German identity and the accurate determination of the German homeland.

15. Modern research has shown that human institutions (e.g., economic and political) and social group formations are human constructs—created in the human mind before made into reality by humans. Therefore, no political boundaries are natural, and no natural political boundaries exist unless one wants to argue that nature and/or God intend for political boundaries to fall in particular locations. Furthermore, when we use terms such as *natural political boundaries* and *artificial political boundaries*, we run the risk of developing the mind-set that nations have existed since the beginning of time and, therefore, any new social group formations are artificial and the members of them are not deserving of the same human rights as the "real," "natural" nations. For those of us who believe that all social group formations and thus political boundaries are artificial because they are all human constructs, we do ourselves and others justice not to speak of natural political boundaries but rather to acknowledge that some political boundaries follow physiographic features without any deeper meaning underlying them.

16. History had to be fabricated because—contrary to Romantic thinking—clear and distinct peoples had not existed through time. The various peoples of the past intermarried, blending both their genes and their cultures. The result has been a diverse human landscape of continual genetic and cultural transition. States homogenize their citizens and leave the impression of distinct human groupings. However, the unified character of modern nations is cultivated by modern state processes and not the result of "historical continuities," as Romantics argue. States cannot unscramble the scrambled eggs of past human cultures. They can only choose surviving elements from various earlier cultures to cook up something new. Modern French nationhood, for example, is a recent blend of Roman, Celtic, and Frankish

(i.e., Germanic) elements, though it is presented as something coherent and eternal. For example, a 130-foot-tall granite cross of Lorraine stands outside the town of Colombey-les-Deux-Eglises in the Champagne region with an inscription that when translated reads "From time immemorial there has been a pact between the greatness of France and the liberty of the world" (Elliot 1995).

17. It was noted in chapter 2, for example (see page 24), that only about 12 to 13 percent of France's population could speak French "correctly" in 1789, and that only 2.5 percent of the population in Italy spoke Italian on a daily basis in 1860 (Hobsbawn 1990, 60-61). These two examples, along with others that Hobsbawn discusses, demonstrate that language was not the primordial essence of nationhood.

18. In many ways, Romanticism conformed to Hegel's dialectic in that Romanticism was a synthesis comprised of the thesis of the old dynastic-imperial order blended together with the new antithesis of the nation based on common cultural characteristics.

19. Benedict Anderson eloquently describes the process for the Russians in the following manner: "stretching the short, tight, skin of the nation over the gigantic body of the empire. 'Russification' of the heterogeneous population of the Czar's subjects thus represented a violent, conscious welding of two opposing political orders, one ancient, one quite new. . . . 'official nationalism' [was a] willed merger of nation and dynastic empire" (1991, 86).

The significance of existing or previously existing territorial configurations is also illustrated in the rise of socialism. Most socialists also conceived of the political-territorial order of the world in terms of the imperialist order (Anderson 1991, 108). In contrast to the Austrian socialists, the Bolsheviks of Russia were more successful in reestablishing the boundaries of the Czarist empire for the new communist state (Schöpflin 1991, 7).

20. The German case excellently illustrates the power that previous territorial configurations hold in people's minds. In the early years of German nationalism, German nationalists defined the German national state in terms of the German Confederation and even spoke of the Holy Roman Empire (Alter 1994, 74-77; Seton-Watson 1977, 94-97). In fact, the very name of the modern German national state—the Second German Empire—demonstrates the power of previous territorial configurations. Although the state came about as a result of the emergence of nationalism, the state was called an empire; indeed, it had many imperial characteristics. The word *empire,* however, not only illustrated the persistence of imperialist thinking, it gave legitimacy to the new state by claiming to be the reincarnation of the Holy Roman Empire, which itself derived legitimacy from an earlier territorial configuration—the Roman Empire. Terms such as Kaiser, which was a reincarnation of the term Caesar, serve as further illustrations. Thus, legitimacy was found in previous territorial configurations, not just the German people, despite the new nationalist idea. The Nazis also legitimized themselves by crafting a name for their state—the Third Reich (meaning the Third German Empire)—based on prior territorial configurations. Such a name was chosen despite all of the nationalist fervor and rhetoric of Nazism.

21. Benedict Anderson argues in the Austrian and Russian cases, however, that nationalism emerged among the minority peoples before it did among the dominant ones (Anderson 1991, 84-88). In these cases then, the minority peoples developed a new sense of alienation from their empires before they were persecuted for not being members of the dominant groups. Nevertheless, even though the Austrians and Russians were late in developing national consciousness, they implemented nationalist policies against their minorities as voraciously as the other dominant groups of Europe.

22. On the surface, the minority peoples of Central and Eastern Europe seemed to be challenging the imperial order by their attempts to carve nation-states out of the existing empires. This challenge was nonexistent from the perspective that they defined their national territories on the basis of previously existing empires.

5

The Maturation of Modern European Nations and States

A nation is a society united by delusions about its ancestry and by common hatred of its neighbors.
—William Ralph Inge

The idea of the *nation* suffered a major setback with the defeat of Napoleon, but modern state mechanisms remained intact. Though they were handed over once again to their dynastic masters, their new mechanisms that touched the daily lives of the masses strengthened and continued to foster the national idea after its birth. The nineteenth century was also a tumultuous time as technological innovations and new scientific discoveries shaped the development of both the national idea and state mechanisms as they matured. Most noteworthy were the Industrial Revolution, the idea of race, and environmental determinism. While these developments unfolded, both new and old paradigms vehemently opposed the new idea of nation. In the meantime, state mechanisms grew more powerful. Of the paradigms, Marxism, established religion, and old imperial forces figured most prominently. Most often independently, sometimes in alliances, but almost always continually, these forces denounced and assailed the concept of nationhood. The early assaults from imperialism and established religion seemed to extinguish the national idea in 1815, but the national idea steadily grew into a pervasive force over the course of the century. As it did so, conflicts with its antagonists intensified and erupted into violence, sometimes across all of Europe, as in the 1848-1849 nationalist revolutions, or in individual cases where German, Italian, and Balkan nationalists sought to create states for their respective nations. By the latter half of the nineteenth century, the tide began to shift for nationalism, but as it battled with old orders and new ideologies for ascendancy, it was likewise influenced and shaped by them. In the end, the idea of nation triumphed, not by defeating and eradicating these other paradigms, but by recasting old systems and integrating new ideas into its own image. Indeed, as the national idea became increasingly dominant, nationalism's adversaries increasingly donned nationalist garb to survive. It was a strategy that succeeded in the short run, but it undermined their resistance to nationalism, assuring nationalism's triumph in the long run.

By the early twentieth century, most old ways and new ideologies were subsumed within the national idea. In the process, many nation-states emerged within old territorial frameworks so that they were in essence rearticulations of older imperial territorialities. However, not all the old paradigms were completely dead. Imperialism and nationalism squared off in a horrific war beginning in 1914, and it took until the end of 1918 for empires to collapse and new nation-states to emerge in their place. The nation-state idea was triumphant, but the geopolitics of favoritism denied many nations the state territories they desired. The fear of Bolshevism also thwarted many nations' claims to territory. In fact, the rise of Bolshevism threatened to extinguish the national idea at the moment that it had reached a new height in sociopolitical-territorial organization. With the First World War failing to satisfy the aspirations of many European nations, nationalism intensified among the defeated and disappointed in the war, even leading to the rise of fascism in some cases. Hitler played on the irredentist feelings of Germans to rise to power and then manipulated the irredentist aspirations of Central and European nations to expand the German Empire, in the process reorganizing the political map of Europe. After Hitler was defeated, the Allies essentially reestablished the old political map of Europe. In the belief that not all nationalists' claims to territory could be satisfied and the fear that attempts to satisfy such claims would only lead to bloodshed, the Allies held firmly to the status quo of boundaries. However, the territorial aspirations denied many nations were not dead, though the Soviet government suppressed nationalist expressions and prevented any nationalist conflicts from emerging. Over the course of the twentieth century, state mechanisms grew stronger and state bureaucracies became increasingly intrusive in individuals' lives. State-centered thinking reached a new height and the national idea grew ever more paramount. Following the end of the Cold War in the last decade of the twentieth century, influential governments continued to hold to the policy of not allowing reterritorialization; national aspirations, nevertheless, led to the dissolution of the Soviet Union, Czechoslovakia, and Yugoslavia, resulting in more nation-states in Europe than ever before.

Though the idea of nation was born at the turn of the nineteenth century and has since captured the imagination of most modern societies, the national idea has certainly evolved and matured over the last two hundred years as it has been shaped by technological innovations and scientific discoveries as well as having had to compete with both old and new paradigms. The state too has developed in tandem with the national idea, experiencing similar pressures, though not assailed directly by formidable opposing forces. This chapter is concerned with the maturation process of nations and states in light of the phenomena they interacted with in the last two hundred years. Thus, we begin at the birth of the modern nation and state, at the turn of the nineteenth century.

The Nineteenth Century

Technological Innovations and Scientific Discoveries

The Industrial Revolution

Capitalism was noted in chapter 4 as having contributed to the emergence of modern nations and states. By the early nineteenth century, capitalism evolved into the Industrial Revolution and became an increasingly pervasive force. In addition to trade and the private accumulation of wealth, the Industrial Revolution added large-scale production of goods using inanimate machinery and fuel sources. Large-scale production led to large-scale migration of people from farms to factories, in turn tremendously transforming the social and political landscape and ending agrarian societies. The remaining vestiges of feudalism, whereby a privileged ruling class of lords oversaw toiling masses, were dismantled as the toiling masses moved to the burgeoning cities. The privileged positions of the upper-echelon lords were safe for a while, but their positions too would eventually be challenged as people came to see their lives differently.

The Industrial Revolution turned agrarian society on its head. Whereas the agrarian world depends on stagnancy, capitalism—especially industrial capitalism—suffocates on stagnancy and seeks to eliminate it. Thriving instead on endless competition, it requires perpetual growth, which is brought about by continual innovation. Unlike in agrarian societies where a son can learn his craft (usually farming) from his father, in industrial societies the father's knowledge is antiquated before he is able to pass it on to his son. In fact, growth and innovation proceed so quickly that the father has to be retrained himself on more than one occasion to remain productive. The speed of change cannot be sustained by knowledge passed down through the generations but by literacy and education. Thus, concomitant with the growth of the Industrial Revolution was the rise of universal education. However, information and knowledge could be disseminated only where language was standardized. The invention of the printing press in the fifteenth century encouraged language standardization, but illiteracy remained high wherever agrarian societies persisted. Thus, the continually changing landscape of language practice persisted. The demand of the Industrial Revolution for more literate societies was more persistent in bringing about total language standardization, especially concerning the masses. By the time of the Industrial Revolution, modern states were more highly developed and pervasive and could ensure language standardization as required by the Industrial Revolution. The general demand of industrialization for standardization increased the powers of states and in turn facilitated more industrialization; both industrialization and the state power were mutually reinforcing. From industrial society's obsession with competition and innovation emerged the broader notion of progress, the idea that life can become better if one learned and applied oneself. The idea of progress, like many other characteristics of the Industrial Revolution, stood in sharp contrast to agrarian understandings. Whereas agrarian society viewed time as cyclical (e.g., birth and death) and linked vertically to God with the notion of simultaneity, industrial society saw time as horizontally connected and contextual; hard work and good investment now mean wealth and prosperity later.

The Industrial Revolution promoted social characteristics that broke down the social hierarchies of the agrarian world. Education was no longer reserved for the privileged and a means for the privileged to separate themselves from the common people. Basic universal education worked to eliminate social differences as it imparted common knowledge to populations defined by states. Universal education also helped states to homogenize their populations as everyone not only learned the same basic material, but also learned to speak and write the same vocabularies and grammars and learned their histories (Rich 1977, 68-69). Education also meant that economic positions were interchangeable through retraining. Gone were the feudal practices of highly guarded "trade secrets" that remained within families and promoted social stratification. Finally, horizontal, progressive time hardly involved God in its construction and operation as agrarian views of cyclical time and simultaneity had by making God the central pivot of time. With God less in the equation, the rigid social hierarchy in which a privileged class ruled in the name of God increasingly lost its legitimacy. Nationhood today is so firmly imprinted with ideas, concepts, and practices of industrial society (e.g., universal education, equality, interchangeability, competition, innovation, and progress) that it is no wonder that some scholars see nationalism as an outgrowth of the Industrial Revolution. For example, Ernest Gellner wrote that

> the age of transition to industrialism was bound . . . to be an age of nationalism, a period of turbulent readjustment, in which political boundaries, or cultural ones, or both, were being modified, so as to satisfy the new nationalist imperative which now, for the first time, was making itself felt. (1983, 40)

Indeed, with many ideas of Romanticism and subsequent philosophies reflecting the social and economic transformations brought about by the Industrial Revolution as it progressed and expanded, it seems more than coincidental that Romanticism, Idealism, and other philosophies existed at the same time as the Industrial Revolution.

The Idea of Race

In the nineteenth century, scientific inquiry led to the idea of *race* and infused it into human identity and the concept of *nation*. As it occurred, attention was refocused in many ways from religion to race as a basis of identity, in turn married to the Romantic emphasis on language. For example, slavery practices of the Europeans in their new world colonies were based on a Christian/non-Christian dichotomy; social class differences too had a religious flavor in that the ruling classes saw their privileges emanating from God. However, the scientific emphasis of the Enlightenment brought attention to human physical and biological differences (Public Broadcasting System, *Race: The power of illusion*). In the British North American colonies, the term *white* appeared in colonial laws in 1680 and began replacing categories of Christian and Englishman. In 1776, Johann Blumenbach coined the term *Caucasian* (Bertoletti 1994, 117; Nott and Gliddon 1854, 88), clearly indicating that the modern concept of race came into practice long after slavery was established. Though Enlightenment thinkers saw whites and Caucasians as superior to blacks and Negroes, they saw the differences as caused by environment rather than something natural or inevitable. However, later in the Romantic period, Romantics saw race as a natural distinction. Through science, figures such as Samuel Morton (1799-1851), Josiah Nott (1804-1873), and Louis Agassiz (1807-1873) developed their belief in white superiority and employed science to defend slavery (Nott and Gliddon 1854). When Charles Darwin (1809-1882) developed his ideas on evolution,[1] he further fueled the concern with race as he focused on physical traits and genetics (1859). More significantly, Darwin's cousin, Francis Galton (1822-1911), coined the term *eugenics*—meaning "the science of good birth" (1883)—and with it a new field of science that emphasized the need for societies, through their governments, to engage in selective breeding by controlling immigration policy while enacting anti-miscegenation laws and forcing its less desirable citizens to be sterilized. The concern with genetics and race equated these concepts with the idea of *nation*, making races, languages, and nations synonymous in the minds of many. Maps too reinforced this interutilization of these terms by depicting the spatial distributions of languages, suggesting they are nations, but labeling them as races.[2] The marriage of race and nation reached its culmination with the Nazis and was discredited at the same time, but a lingering association of nation and race persists to this day.

Environmental Determinism

The interest in race stemmed from the more broadly developing interest in the natural sciences, which coincided with the rise of Romanticism. Still at that point in history, a sharp line did not exist between the natural and social sciences. Many great thinkers pursued work in both these realms, which we consider separate and distinct today. The broad interest meant that scientists usually saw strong connections between natural and social systems. Most studied the natural world and believed that natural laws were the basis of social laws. In many ways, scientists were following the much older path of environmental determinism, which viewed all aspects of the human condition as products of the natural environment. The new science of the late eighteenth century and nineteenth century, however, gave new vigor to environmentally deterministic views and even brought the perspective to the forefront of thinking, not only in scientific research but also in the popular mind.

At the end of the eighteenth and the beginning of the nineteenth centuries, many scientists worked on issues of limited scope, but their research was later pieced together and made the foundation of entirely new and revolutionary theories about the natural and social worlds. In many ways, Darwin's idea of biological evolution as expressed in his work *The Origin of Species* (1859) is the culmination of the new scientific thinking in the nineteenth century. Though Darwin pursued much original research, many of Darwin's ideas came from the research of those before him. Indeed, many of Darwin's ideas on evolution came from works by Jean-Baptiste Lamarck (1744-1829). From a social scientific perspective, before Darwin published his seminal work individuals like Herbert Spencer (1820-1903), Henry Maine (1822-1888), John Lubbock (1834-1914), and Alfred R. Wallace (1823-1913) already had employed evolutionary concepts of natural science to construct ideas and theories concerning the human world (Livingstone 1992, 185). Today, Darwin's ideas are treated as unique when, in reality, Darwin's ideas were firmly built upon the work of his predecessors and contemporaries. Thus, contrary to the depiction of his research, Darwin's ideas were less of a fork in the road of scientific discovery and more of a link in the chain. Perhaps not as original as many may think, Darwin's ideas stimulated the imagination of the scientific community and promoted more research.

The concept of evolutionary biology as expressed by Darwin and many of its associated ideas as articulated by Spencer and others influenced both academic and popular understandings of geographic concepts and processes. One of the most notable geographers to incorporate evolutionary biology into geography was Friedrich Ratzel (1844-1904). Applying the ideas of those already mentioned plus those of Ernst Haeckel (1834-1919) and Moritz Wagner (1813-1887) (Livingstone 1992, 197-98),[3] Ratzel developed Organic State Theory, which posited the idea that states are like biological organisms (Agnew 2002, 56-66; Blouet 2001, 28-30; Glassner and Fahrer 2004, 270-71; Hunter 1983; Martin and James 1993, 170; Pearcy et al. 1948, 14; Ratzel 1882; 1891; 1896a; 1896b; 1897; 1969; Storey 2001, 23-25; Wanklyn 1961). As such, states are born, grow, mature, and die. Fixed to the soil, states derive their sustenance from the natural resources of territory. As the populations of states grow and exhaust their resources, they need to expand like a growing organism, but their expansion is through the consumption of *lebensraum* ("living space"), otherwise known as "geographical area within which living organisms develop" (Dickinson 1969, 71). From this perspective, Ratzel viewed boundaries as the peripheral organs of states, playing a central role in states' growth and consumption. The dynamic of state consumption and growth allows for the health and vitality of states, as well as the nations within them, to be measured according to size. Put simply, the larger the state, the more healthy and vital it is. This view also means that states, just like biological organisms, compete with one another for survival, with larger states devouring smaller ones and also portions of larger ones in the process of decay. This latter idea reflects Darwin's idea of "survival of the fittest."

Organic State Theory not only reflected the ideas of Darwin in geographical ideas, but also fit in well with the world's geopolitical situation of the late nineteenth century (Agnew 2002, 52-56). The Italian and German states had come into being in 1861 and 1871 respectively, and their governments sought colonial possessions. By that time, however, the European colonialist empires had thoroughly divided up the earth's surface among themselves, leaving few unconquered places for the new Italian and German states to colonize. Therefore, if these two new countries were to obtain colonies, they would have to at the expense of the other European empires. In many ways then, Ratzel's Organic State Theory was a reflection of the world's political realities in the late nineteenth century. At the same time, Ratzel's theory legitimized Italy's and Germany's aggressive challenge to the other European powers and also suggested from a scientific perspective that Italy and Germany, as youthful and vigorous states, would inevitably overcome the older and soon-to-be-decaying empires of the United Kingdom, France, and the Netherlands in the same way that these empires overpowered the even older Portuguese and Spanish empires sometime before. In essence, Ratzel made the political and economic competition between the European empires into an inevitable biological struggle.

Whether Ratzel viewed states literally as biological organisms is still a matter of great debate (Agnew 2002, 63-64). He was a prolific writer and not always careful in his writings as his interest in broader processes and universal principles led him to many generalizations, which he himself criticized. At times, he seems to argue that states were literally biological organisms, yet at other times he clearly drew upon the conditions of biological organisms only for analogy while recognizing that states had characteristics not found in biological organisms. For example, Ratzel acknowledged that although states go through a life cycle of youth, maturity, and old age, an old age state can be rejuvenated and begin a life cycle again, perhaps many times, but in any case can experience life beyond the capabilities of real organisms.

What is important about Ratzel's ideas is that they took the conceptions of nations and states a step farther in multiple directions. For example, Fichte and Hegel had seen states as entities of their own but not as biological organisms (Agnew 2002, 58), most likely because they thought about the world before Darwin developed his evolutionary ideas.

Ratzel's use of biological terms, whether applied literally or only as analogies, transformed the idea of states in the minds of many from entities to living organisms. In doing so, Ratzel saw states as organizing units of humanity and thus elevated states to a preeminent position in human affairs (Agnew 2002, 64-65). While states were mere possessions of divine right rulers in medieval times, and Enlightenment and Romantic philosophers turned states over to the "people" (albeit defined differently by each group of philosophers), Ratzel transformed states from possessions to possessors. In many ways, Ratzel merely described the new reality of state power, but his ideas of the Organic State gave philosophical legitimacy to state power as it grew. Indeed, as state power grew, it took possession of knowledge and inquiry, which were then pursued by and on behalf of states. Subsequently, the discipline of geography, as well as all other disciplines, was reorganized to serve the needs of states, both in practical terms of management and in their lines of inquiry. Though geography and other disciplines can trace threads of their intellectual crafts to the beginning of history, their current incarnations trace themselves back only about two hundred years, to the end of the Enlightenment and the beginning of the Romantic period when divine right monarchy came to an end and higher learning was removed from the service of monarchies and the church and became part of the secular state ideally to pursue higher learning in the name of rational and objective thought (Martin and James 1993, 162-63). By the late nineteenth century, states had come to dominate not only general human thinking, but also intellectual thinking and to such a degree that Ratzel saw and described the situation as a biological given. Certainly, the modern era of state-centered thinking described in chapter 3 hit a new zenith.

In describing states as biological organisms fixed to the soil, Ratzel simultaneously fixed the concept of nationhood to the soil:

[The] process of amalgamation of regional districts similarly enjoins the closer relationship of the people to the land. The growth of the state over the surface of the earth can be compared to the downward growth which leads to an attachment to the soil. It is more than a metaphor when one speaks of a people as taking root. The nation is an organic entity which, in the course of history, becomes increasingly attached to the land on which it exists. Just as an individual struggles with virgin land until he has forced it into cultivable fields, so too does a nation struggle with its land making it, through blood and sweat, increasingly its own until it is impossible to think of the two separately. Who can think of the French without France, or the Germans without Germany? (Ratzel quoted in Kasperson and Minghi 1969, 22)

This too went a step further than what the Romantics before him had done. It is true that Romantics were environmentally deterministic in their belief that the cultures and characteristics of nations were derived from specific natural environments that provided particular ways of life. Thus, they argued that state boundaries should follow physiographic features, which they called "natural boundaries." Ratzel took these environmentally deterministic ideas to a higher level with his concept of *lebensraum* and his descriptions of political boundaries as "organs" of states. In essence, Ratzel's ideas—which tied nations to the land—implied that individual nations were better suited to particular natural environments just as individual plant and animal species were better suited to specific natural environments. In some cases, some nations were seen as better adapted to make maximum use of natural environments. These ideas invited further biological research and genetic investigation. These lines of inquiry were readily pursued by the public and academics who were stimulated by Darwin's ideas concerning evolutionary biology and the new and growing interest in race. Thus, Ratzel contributed to the development of the belief that national identity was fundamentally comprised of "blood and soil."

Ratzel had many followers, both across Europe and in the United States. Perhaps the most noteworthy in Europe were Swedish political scientist Rudolf Kjellén (1864-1922) and the German geographer Karl Haushofer (1869-1945), both of whom made their impact through their influence on Adolf Hitler. Such influence, however, occurred primarily after the First World War; so a discussion of how their ideas evolved from Ratzel's will wait to a later section. Suffice it to note at this point that they represented a continued emphasis on the natural environment's role in shaping national identity. For example, Kjellén argued against Norway's independence from Sweden on the grounds that the Scandinavian mountains were not a separate and distinct natural region; seas and rivers were more significant in defining natural boundaries than mountain chains, and thus Norway was naturally a part of Sweden (Agnew 2002, 60). Norway gained its independence from Sweden in 1905, but it should not be forgotten that the ideas of natural boundaries were integral to nationalist debates and arguments.

Ellen Churchill Semple (1863-1932) and Ellsworth Huntington (1876-1947) were two American geographers that Ratzel influenced greatly. As one of Ratzel's most ardent followers, Semple even went to Germany on two occasions to study under him. Her admiration of Ratzel and the most obvious indication of his impact on her are reflected in the title of one of her more significant works, *Influences of Geographic En-*

vironment on the Basis of Ratzel's System of Anthropo-geography (1911). Semple rejected Ratzel's ideas about states being organisms (Martin and James 1993, 329) but along with Huntington was inspired by Ratzel to take an environmentally deterministic perspective on culture—indicated too in her book title. For example, she argued that Tibet's resource-scarce mountains caused the Tibetan Buddhist monks to engage in celibacy and other Tibetans to practice polyandry (1911, 582-86); she likewise argued that celibacy began among Roman Catholic monks and nuns in the resource-scarce mountainous environments of Europe. For other cases, Semple argued that scarce mountainous environments led to the development of cultures noted for lying and stealing. Huntington was more interested in the effects of climate on human society (1907; 1915; 1924) and was known for arguing that civilization could develop only in regions of stimulating climate and that regions of oppressive heat like the tropics could never produce higher civilization (Martin and James 1993, 325-26).

In many ways, these aforementioned scholars are criticized for their environmentally deterministic views. However, their views were by no means unique. As previously noted, though Ratzel's ideas had a tremendous impact on others, he had been influenced by better-known scholars like Charles Darwin and Herbert Spencer. Semple and Huntington too were inspired by others than only Ratzel. Huntington, for example, learned much from the geographer William Morris Davis (1850-1934) (Martin and James 1993, 325), famous for his "geographical cycle" (1899), which described landscapes as going through the evolutionary stages of youth, maturity, and old age;[4] it was a theory clearly inspired by Charles Darwin. Even so, singling out Darwin and Spencer for ideas that are now discredited by what we have since learned from science is in itself unfair. These scholars of the nineteenth century were inheritors of both Enlightenment science and medieval privilege. In many ways, it is not surprising that their ideas and theories were a blend of both traditions, and it would take some time for science to free itself from medieval notions of privilege. Moreover, environmental determinism—the belief that the physical environment shapes culture—underlay human thought since the earliest recorded civilizations. Indeed, when Semple wrote that ancient Alpine tribes were "poor and addicted to robbery," she was quoting the Greek scholar Strabo (ca. 64 B.C.-A.D. 20) (1911, 586). In some ways then, Ratzel, Semple, and their contemporaries only brought the environmentally deterministic viewpoint to the forefront of their research though they likewise certainly took it to new levels.

Interestingly, environmentally deterministic ideas continue to crop up today though they are widely rejected in academic research. For example, it is not uncommon for someone to say that the natives on tropical islands are lazy because the hot weather makes them lazy[5] or to hear about someone's correlating temperatures to crime rates and implying that with increased temperatures people lose their tempers and are more likely to assault or murder their fellow human beings than when the temperatures are cooler. As another example, the Maryland Court of Appeals struck down the governor's legislative redistricting plan in 2002 on the grounds that it violated two constitutional provisions: "that districts be compact and that due regard be given to natural boundaries such as rivers and the boundaries of counties and municipalities" (Stuckey 2002, B2). Such a statement about natural boundaries brings forth questions. For example, do Democrats and Republicans tend to locate on opposite sides of rivers and, therefore, rivers make good voting district boundaries because they encapsulate homogenous political communities within them as desired by districting guidelines? If such is true, then it means that the side of a river that one chooses to live on ultimately determines how one will vote in an election because some sides of rivers make one develop Democratic views while other sides foster a Republican outlook. Obviously environmentally deterministic views still lurk in the popular mind and have yet to be completely expunged from our laws.

As noted, academia eventually rejected environmental determinism, and not much of it is seen in academic research today. Unfortunately, little of its effects on human thinking are taught or remembered outside the field of geography. The consequence of forgetting about environmental determinism is that it is no longer seen as a factor in how the concept of nationhood developed.[6] Today, the ideas of common culture and history (both used here in the broadest sense) receive greater attention as the determinants of nationhood. It is further recognized that these cultural constructs are fluid. However, what is forgotten is that environmentally deterministic views played a major role in framing these fluid concepts of nationhood from the time that the modern national idea emerged at the turn of the nineteenth century through a sizeable period in the early twentieth century—in other words, for most of the existence of the concept of modern nationhood. Though that framework is not there today, it still reveals itself in the numbers, sizes, and characters of nations today.

The Struggle against Old and New Paradigms

From the influence of the technological innovations of the Industrial

Revolution to new scientific discoveries concerning race and environmental determinism, nationhood adopted a form that is recognizable by today's understandings of the concept. Human beings also came to see themselves as fundamentally divided into nations and accepted national identities so thoroughly that it was not only assumed that nationhood effortlessly glided to the forefront of human social organization, but that it was so fundamental to human social organization that human beings were always members of nations and without question could be nothing else. An examination of nineteenth-century and early-twentieth-century history, however, shows that though the rise of nationhood was forceful, it was by no means smooth and effortless. The idea of nation was vigorously denounced by the new ideology of Marxism, assailed by long-established religions like Christianity and assaulted by long-entrenched political systems—namely, the ruling dynastic-imperial monarchies. As nationalism battled against new beliefs and established orders for ascendancy, it was likewise influenced and shaped by them. In the end, the idea of nation triumphed, not by defeating and eradicating these other orders, but by recasting old systems in its own image. From the territorial perspective, nation-states came to be rearticulations of older imperial territorialities.

The Assault from Marxism

"The Concert of Europe," which had been formed by the very conservative dynastic powers of Europe after the defeat of Napoleon in 1815 to suppress emergent nationalist feelings, broke down as nationalist revolutions erupted all over Europe in 1848. The national idea seemed poised for its final triumph. However, in that year of nationalist revolutions, Karl Marx (1818-1883) and Friedrich Engels (1820-1895) published *The Communist Manifesto* ([1848] 1968). In 1867, they published *Das Kapital*. So as the Industrial Revolution was giving the national idea one of its final kiln firings and with it its modern recognizable form, it had also given birth to socialism and communism—philosophies and ideologies that were hostile to the national idea (Greer and Lewis 1997, 510). Marx and those who followed in his footsteps saw the world not as fundamentally divided into nations but into social classes determined by economic processes: "the mode of production in material life determines general character of the social, political and spiritual processes of life" (quoted in Rich 1977, 40). They saw the world as divided into small ruling classes who exploited the working masses, a situation that led to great economic disparities between these two classes and subsequently class struggle.

These ruling classes used state mechanisms to oppress the lower classes, but technological innovations which brought about changing modes of production resulted in social transformations that gave the oppressed classes opportunities to break their chains of bondage and overthrow the ruling classes, themselves become the dominant class and thereby renew the cycle of class struggle. To socialists and communists, history was driven by this cycle of class struggle. The ancient world was comprised of masters and slaves, the feudal age of nobles and serfs, and finally the capitalist age of the bourgeois and proletarians (Greer and Lewis 1997, 511-12).

Viewing the world through the lens of economics, Marx then saw religion as nothing more than an instrument of the ruling classes to suppress the working classes which numerically outnumbered them. Not surprisingly then, Marx and his successors were hostile toward organized religion. The antireligious aspect of socialist and communistic belief garners great attention in the capitalist world though reasons for such views are less frequently recognized. Also noted is the socialist and communist argument that private property should be abolished (Marx and Engels [1848] 1968, 27). What is given considerably less attention is the Marxist desire "to abolish countries and nationalities" (Marx and Engels [1848] 1968, 35). Though the concept of nation is a taken-for-granted concept today, in Marx's time it was more obviously newer and not seen as a given but rather something quite artificial. To Marx, nationalism was the result of the uneven development of capitalism, employed by the ruling classes, just as they had used religion, to oppress the working classes. Considering the social and political circumstances of the nineteenth century, it is not too surprising that Marx and his followers took such a view. On the surface, the ruling classes embraced nationalist ideals, extolling the virtues of their nations and wrapping themselves in their nations' symbols. By doing so, they could turn the attentions of the working peoples away from their oppressed situations and redirect it toward nationalist competition, in turn harnessing the energies of the working classes to expand the empires of the privileged around the world, oppressing more peoples and reinforcing the position of the privileged while doing it all in the name of their "nations." As competition turned to conflict, millions of oppressed took up arms against one another. They could not see that they were of the same social class because their leaders had convinced them that they were fighting other "nations." Marx and his followers knew, however, that while the leaders of countries were calling upon their citizens to make great personal sacrifices to champion their national causes these leaders themselves maintained their familial ties by continuing to intermarry and that they continued to see themselves separate and distinct from the people they ruled. Marx saw these surviving medieval vestiges of sociopolitical rule, but rather than seeing their continued existence as evidence that the idea of nation was a young and uncompleted process, Marx concluded that the ruling classes had fabricated the idea of nation, just as they had religious ideas, to deceive the working classes and perpetuate socioeconomic inequities. Ironically, Marx also could not see that both the dynastic-imperial idea and established religion were hostile to the national idea and that established religion likewise shared the belief that the national idea was a delusion and obscured people's true identity.

Though Marx and the socialists and communists who succeeded him did not believe in the idea of nation, one of their major weaknesses was that they continually framed their thinking and rhetoric in nationalist terms. Most noteworthy, they would continually refer to themselves as "internationalists." In other words, they unceasingly divided themselves into subcategories according to a form of identity that they did not believe in. They might argue that their own persistent use of "national" categories was not their goal but merely the acknowledgment of an existing reality—temporarily brought about by changing modes of production and the manipulations of the ruling classes. However, by using nationalist rhetoric, they ensured that something ephemeral became permanent.

The Battle with Established Religion

The initial reaction of the Roman Catholic Church and the Eastern Orthodox churches to the idea of nation was extremely negative. For example, in 1864, Pope Pius IX launched an attack on new intellectual trends. He considered nationalism to be just as evil as socialism, communism, or the scientific ideas of natural science such as those advocated by Charles Darwin (Rich 1977, 28). Though many nations were in the process of constructing their identities around their religious affiliations, the very idea of nation—even for those nations basing their identities on particular religions—usurped religion's position as the primary locus of group identity. People were beginning to think of themselves as primarily English, French, Dutch, and the like, and then secondarily as Christians rather than as primarily Christians with other forms of identity playing secondary and tertiary roles. Thus, by adopting these national identities, people were turning their main attentions away from God's plan for them and instead becoming distracted by the secular ideas of nationhood tied to states rather than to the church.

As national identities grew, they increasingly led to the rejection of any church's political leadership. Church leaders feared that the national idea would result in situations in which Roman Catholics would turn against and even kill fellow Roman Catholics, as well as Eastern Orthodox Christians and Protestants doing the same. Such a situation arose in the revolutions of 1848, known as the national revolutions. For example, as the wave of Italian nationalism spread across the Italian peninsula, Italian nationalists launched a campaign to drive out the ruling Austrian imperialist forces and found an Italian nation-state. Pope Pius IX was sympathetic to many of the revolutionaries' goals but refused to dispatch papal troops in support of the revolution because it would result in Catholics fighting Catholics, though nationalists viewed such a conflict as Italians against Austrians (Craig 1972, 191; Rich 1977, 27). Italian nationalists did not forget the lack of support from the pope. As their forces were later overwhelmed by the Austrians, they fled into Rome where they had the opportunity to express their anger at the Church. As they took over the city, the pope escaped disguised as a simple priest. The revolution of 1848 failed, but Italian nationhood continued to grow, and it achieved an Italian nation-state in 1861. The pope would use French troops to keep Rome and the papal states out of the Italian nation-state until 1870, when French troops were needed to join in the Franco-Prussian War. After that, the Italian government forcibly incorporated Rome and the papal states into the Italian state against Pope Pius's will; from then until 1929, the popes did not recognize their loss of Rome to the Italian nation-state as they "followed a policy of self imprisonment in the Vatican" (Rich 1977, 28). The Italian nation was Catholic, but even if the pope had supported the Italian nationalist cause, the very nature of nationhood meant that Catholicism would lose its place at the center of the new emerging Italian national identity. Indeed, as the Italian nation-state solidified, the Roman Catholic Church lost its power and authority in directing the lives of individuals.

The demotion of religious identity occurred wherever nationalism arose and nation-states emerged. For example, it was noted in chapter 2 that the American revolutionaries desired to include Quebec in their independence movement. Most of the inhabitants of Quebec, however, did not support the Revolution. Being mostly Roman Catholic, most did not accept the concept of separation of church and state that the revolutionaries advocated. American nationhood tied identity first and foremost to the government of a secular nation-state and would diminish the connections that American Catholics would have with the pope and sharply curtail the pope's influence over Roman Catholics in such a nation-state.

Not surprisingly, Bishop Briand in Quebec threatened excommunication of anyone who aided the revolutionaries (Bercuson et al. 1992, 140). The unwillingness of Quebec's Roman Catholics to join the American Revolution and the general desire for Roman Catholics in the thirteen colonies to maintain their close ties to the pope likely explain why other Americans distrusted Roman Catholics. Indeed, the feelings have been generally described as antipapal as much as they have been described as anti-Catholic, indicating that the distrust centered on the Roman Catholic desire to place their religious loyalties ahead of their national and state loyalties.

The conflict between religious identity and national identity, which would have primacy, also manifested itself in the new German nation-state after it was founded in 1871. Though united around Protestant Prussia, the new German state contained many Roman Catholics. A group of Catholics formed a political party to lobby the German government to support the pope, who had become "the prisoner of the Vatican" following the emergence of the Italian nation-state (Ergang 1954, 195). Bismarck, the chancellor of Germany, saw the Catholic political party as a "mobilization of the church against the state," and began a movement to curb the power of the Catholic Church in Germany in what is known as the *Kulturkampf*. In 1873, the minister of public worship and education created the May Laws, which sought to weaken the power of the Catholic Church by putting education and the appointment of clergy under government control. As a few examples, civil ceremonies became compulsory, candidates for priesthood had to spend three years at a German university—where they learned philosophy, philology, history, and German—and vacant dioceses were to be administered by the German state (Ergang 1954, 195). Resistance to the laws was strong, and the government eventually relinquished its attack, mostly because a new pope in 1878 was more conciliatory to the German government and the German government needed an ally in its struggle against what it perceived to be a greater danger to the German state—socialism (Ergang 1954, 195-96). Though the German state was not entirely successful in its struggle with the Catholic Church, history had essentially run out for a universal Christian identity. Though many Germans remained Catholic, it was not long before they would see themselves as German first and foremost. Though national identity triumphed over religious identity, the fact that the two identities were still struggling in the 1870s illustrates just how young the concept of nation is.

Much as the Roman Catholic Church clung to the long-held idea that religion primarily defined identity, so did the Eastern Orthodox Church.

Eastern Orthodox Christians saw themselves first and foremost as *Pravoslavni* ("true believers") and their Russian, Ukrainian, Bulgarian, Serbian, Romanian, etc., identities serving secondary roles. Though these ethnic terms existed prior to the rise of nationalism, their existence should not lead one to the conclusion that they were as important in defining identity as they are today. One example that illustrates that religious identity superseded these ethnic identities is seen in the proposal of Bishop Jovan Jovanović in 1804 for the creation of a Serbo-Bulgarian state that also would have included Wallachia, Moldavia, and Bosnia (Banac 1984, 82). Obviously, Jovanović's proposal for such a multi-ethnic state would not have conformed to the modern understanding of a nation-state. With most Wallachians and Moldavians speaking non-Slavic languages, the greatest shared cultural characteristic of the people of all these territories was religion, namely, Eastern Orthodox Christianity. Indeed, most of the people within these territories called themselves *Pravoslavni,* and the proposal to unite them in a single state showed that medieval Christian concepts still outweighed modern ideas of nationalism. Only after the rise of Romanticism, with its belief that language could be a shared group characteristic, and political developments that made such a state project based on shared religious identity less and less likely did the idea of a Serbo-Croatian state based on linguistics emerge.

Protestantism was much more compatible with modern nationalism. In fact, Martin Luther's promotion of vernacular languages in worship and his ideas of *summus episcopus* may have helped to foster the ideas of the modern nation and state. Nevertheless, as modern nations and states more fully crystallized in the nineteenth century, Protestant clergy and theologians became just as troubled as their Roman Catholic and Eastern Orthodox colleagues that Christianity was losing its central position in defining identity. Without people seeing themselves as Christians first and foremost, they would subjugate their Christian ethics to less ethical secular ideas of nationalism, in turn leading to un-Christian behavior. William Ralph Inge's definition at the opening of the chapter, which describes national identity as delusionary and leading to hatred, is very indicative of this concern and indicates why many Protestant clergy and theologians opposed the idea of nation.[7]

Obstinate Dynastic Imperialism

Integral to the nation-state ideal is the belief that a nation should rule itself because only the nation knows what is best for itself (Anthony Smith 1994, 3379-80). The ideal implies then that all members of a nation are essentially equal because they all share the same characteristics. Leaders are no exception, though they govern. These nationalist principles are antithetical to the dynastic-imperial paradigm whereby the rulers hold their positions by demonstrating that they are separate and distinct from those they rule, and they are allowed to rule because they have a special relationship with God that their subjects do not. Not surprisingly then, the dynastic-imperialist ruling classes disdained the national idea and fought to preserve their privileged positions by suppressing nationalism wherever it arose. When Napoleon whipped up national sentiments all over Europe, the dynasties of Europe formed an alliance, destroyed Napoleon, and then created the "Holy Alliance" and the "Quadruple Alliance" (of Great Britain, Prussia, Russia, and Austria) in what became known as the "Concert of Europe" to oppress nationalism and secure dynastic-imperialism (Craig 1972, 19-20). The Holy Alliance was particularly reminiscent of medieval times. It was conceived of by Tsar Alexander I of Russia, who used it to assert his belief in divine right rule based on Christianity rather than governance by diplomacy or the nationalist principle (Ergang 1954, 29-30, 38-39). The Quadruple Alliance was the child of Prince Klemens von Metternich, the Austrian foreign minister and president of the Congress of Vienna in 1814-1815. Metternich was a self-proclaimed apostle of conservatism and enemy of nationalist principles. As run by Metternich the Congress was not just about how the victorious powers would deal with defeated France but how the ruling dynasties of Europe would reestablish and then preserve the old status quo of their privileged positions and extinguish their new archenemy nationalism. Indeed, once dynastic rule was reestablished in France, France was allowed into the Alliance—turning it into the Quintuple Alliance—and became part of the effort to suppress nationalism.

Small episodes of nationalist outbursts notwithstanding, nationalism appeared successfully pinned down and seemingly almost completely suffocated until nationalist revolutions erupted all over Europe in 1848-1849. Though the revolutions indicated that nationalism was clearly alive and well and also on the rise, dynastic imperialist thinking still held sway and continued to battle nationalism into the twentieth century. For example, when the Austrian emperor could not contain nationalism within his realm in 1848-1849, he called upon the Russian tsar, who then sent troops to crush the Hungarian nationalists (Craig 1972, 140). Such an act is inconceivable in today's world where the idea of nation is more firmly engrained. Affairs within states are seen as exclusively affairs of the nations that inhabit them. The president of the United States, for example, could not call upon foreign troops to suppress civil unrest within the

United States. Such an act would not even cross his mind. Yet the ruling classes of Europe still saw themselves separate and above the people they ruled. They would still take refuge with one another rather than with the people they ruled, though at other times they fought one another as bitter enemies.

The ruling classes held the upper hand as long as the idea of nation had not taken firm root in the masses. For example, people continued to fight for their rulers though they were often treated poorly in the imperialist armies. More importantly, nationalists themselves were unable to completely break out of the mold of dynastic-imperialist thinking. For example, when the wave of Italian nationalism led to the mustering of Italian popular forces that drove the Austrian armies from the Italian peninsula in 1860, ended centuries of Habsburg rule, and made Italian unification possible, the Italian nationalists crowned a Habsburg—Victor Emmanuel II—the first king of Italy. The victory was a major step forward for Italian nationhood, but certainly dynastic imperialism showed continued life when Italian nationalists chose the cousin of their enemy to be the first Italian king (Hayes 1953, 594).

The Italian case was by no means exceptional. The nineteenth century was noted as a time when many new nation-states were created in Europe, especially in southeastern Europe (see figure 5.1). These newly created nation-states were continually consecrated with the establishment of ruling dynasties and usually with members from outside the nations in question. The Hohenzollerns provided most of the new kings and queens, though other German dynasties provided Albania and Belgium with their first rulers, and it was the Bavarian and then Danish dynasties that provided Greece with its royal lineage. Thus, countries like Romania, Bulgaria, Greece, and Albania had German-speaking rulers (a Danish speaker in the case of Greece after the Danish dynasty began supplying monarchs) who usually never bothered to learn the national language of their people. Because these rulers were Protestant or Roman Catholic and the peoples they ruled usually Eastern Orthodox, these new kings and queens also did not practice the same form of Christianity as their peoples. In the case of Albania, many Albanians were Roman Catholic and some were Orthodox, but the vast majority were Muslim, meaning that their German king was even less like the people he ruled than was the case in the other countries where sharp differences existed between ruler and subjects. Only in Serbia had a native dynasty emerged. Even so, it was antithetical to the nation-state ideal for these nation-states to have dynasties. Many of these new monarchs believed that they ruled by divine right, explaining why they never adopted the cultures of the people

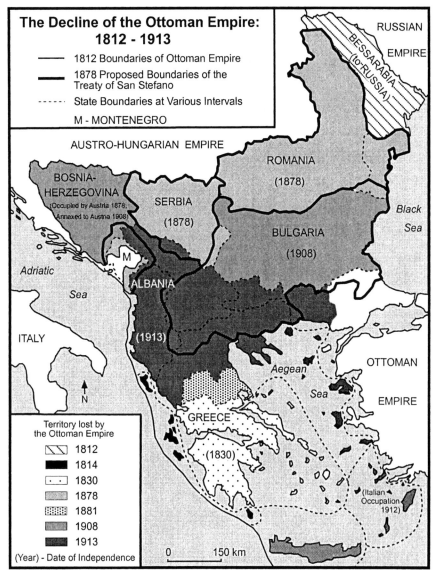

The Decline of the Ottoman Empire: 1812 - 1913

—— 1812 Boundaries of Ottoman Empire

▬▬ 1878 Proposed Boundaries of the
Treaty of San Stefano

----- State Boundaries at Various Intervals

M - MONTENEGRO

AUSTRO-HUNGARIAN EMPIRE

RUSSIAN EMPIRE

BESSARABIA (to RUSSIA)

ROMANIA (1878)

BOSNIA-HERZEGOVINA
(Occupied by Austria 1878;
Annexed to Austria 1908)

SERBIA (1878)

Black Sea

Adriatic Sea

M

BULGARIA (1908)

ALBANIA (1913)

ITALY

N

Aegean Sea

OTTOMAN EMPIRE

GREECE (1830)

Territory lost by
the Ottoman Empire

- 1812
- 1814
- 1830
- 1878
- 1881
- 1908
- 1913

(Year) - Date of Independence

(Italian Occupation 1912)

0   150 km

Figure 5.1 The Decline of the Ottoman Empire: 1812-1913

they ruled. Consequently, most of them never supported political structures that empowered their peoples to participate in their own governance, and instead preferred more medieval forms of governance. It
would seem that the newly created nation-states of Europe in the nine-

teenth and twentieth centuries should have been able to politically constitute themselves as purer forms of the nation-state than many of the older states which were still encumbered with many pre-nation-state vestiges such as dynasties. Yet each one, including Albania—which did not become a country until 1912 and did not receive its first king until 1914—illustrates that dynastic-imperial structures still overpowered national ideas. It took until the mid-twentieth century for most European nation-states to take a more ideal form by casting out their dynasties or reducing them to mere figurehead status.

The creation of dynasties for the new nation-states of Europe shows that dynastic-imperialism was still a potent force, though the national idea was on the rise. Human identity changed tremendously in the time from the French Revolution to the First World War, but in that span of a little over a hundred years, the ruling classes of Europe changed very little. For example, the Russian tsars believed so strongly in their divine right to rule that it took on a mystical quality. They held this belief right up until the demise of the Romanov dynasty in 1917. Also indicative of the lack of change were such figures as Austrian Emperor Francis Joseph and Queen Victoria of England. They completed two of the longest reigns of European monarchs with Francis Joseph ruling from 1848 to 1916 (Rich 1977, 106-10) and Victoria reigning from 1837 to 1901. Though these monarchs reigned into the twentieth century, the span of their reigns coupled with the fact that they were raised and educated by individuals whose ideas were rooted in the seventeenth century illustrates that these individuals were imbued with ideas that predated the national idea. For example, Francis Joseph was a student of Metternich, the man who as a young man lived in Paris and witnessed the French Revolution, disdained its ideas, and subsequently orchestrated the Congress of Vienna in 1814-1815 to extinguish nationalism and reestablish the old dynastic order.

Francis Joseph's antagonism to nationalism came earlier as he rose to power in 1848—the year of nationalist revolutions. Following his suppression of revolutions with the help of the Russian tsar, Francis Joseph implemented or consented to the implementation of policies that sought to eradicate nationalist practices, not to mention remaining feudal vestiges that hampered his rule by divine right. One means was through the use of modern state mechanisms, namely, the bureaucracy, army, police, and a network of spies. The other way was through an alliance with established religion, which too despised the national idea. For example, the Roman Catholic Church was given control over education, Church property was declared sacred, and civil marriage was abolished (Rich 1977,

108). The latter approach illustrates that dynastic-imperialism and established religion allied with each other in their common struggle against
the national idea.

Queen Victoria was perhaps less ideological in her approach, but she
illustrates how some dynastic-imperialist practices not only persisted but
intensified before nationalism and imperialism came to their final blows
in the twentieth century. The dynastic-imperialist practice of intermarriage ran contrary to nationalist principles because it diluted and confused national identities and loyalties. Yet despite the rise of nationalism,
it continued and turned most of the European dynasties into one big family, reaching across national lines. Victoria was one of the figures most
responsible for not only perpetuating the practice but for perfecting it as
she became known as the grandmother of Europe. Most of her thirty-six
grandchildren married into or took over many of the royal houses of
Europe (Dorothy Thompson 1990, xiv). For example, Sophie married
Greece's king, Marie became the queen of Romania, Maude the queen of
Norway, Margaret the crown princess of Sweden, and Victoria the queen
of Spain (Van der Kiste 1986, 166-68; 1993, xi, 116). Numerous others
went to such German states as Prussia, Hesse and the Rhine, Schleswig-
Holstein, Saxe-Meiningen, Saxe-Coburg, Anhalt, Schaumburg-Lippe,
and Battenberg. In addition, Victoria's son Edward, who succeeded her
on the English throne as King Edward VII, married Princess Alexandra
of Denmark. Victoria's uncle became Belgium's first king, Leopold I.
This intertwining of family trees meant that many of the monarchs of
Europe were related, not just distantly but closely enough to be uncles,
aunts, and first cousins to one another. Perhaps the most noteworthy of
Victoria's relations were George V (successor to her own English throne
via her son Edward VII), William II (kaiser of Germany), and Alexandra
(tsarina of Russia, married to Tsar Nicholas II). Thus, the English king,
the German kaiser, and the Russian tsar were all in effect first cousins
and knew one another so well they called one another by such names as
"Georgie" and "Nicky" (Van der Kiste 1993, 105). So close were their
ties that Kaiser Wilhelm of Germany was also a field marshal in the British army and King George V of Great Britain was a field marshal in the
German army (Van der Kiste 1993, 105). It was an interesting situation
considering that Russia and Great Britain went to war against Germany
in World War I, forcing their cousins reigning in other countries to
choose sides.

With nationalism near its ascendancy in World War I, the monarchs
of Europe had to quietly disguise their close relations, take down from
their mantels the crests of their cousins who chose the other side in the

war, and champion their nations' war efforts. In 1914, Tsar Nicholas II of Russia changed the name of Russia's capital from the German sounding St. Petersburg to the Russian derived Petrograd. In 1917, King George V of Great Britain changed the name of the British royal house from the German name Saxe-Coburg-Gotha to the more English sounding Windsor. In many ways, these acts showed that the remaining horizontal structures of medieval states were realigning themselves to the vertical structures of modern nation-states (see figure 4.1). However, such behavior appeared very chameleon-like, and perhaps explains why socialists and communists believed that the national idea was fabricated by these ruling classes who stayed in comfort far from the battlefronts and many of whom profited from war, both financially and by turning the attention of the masses from their luxurious lives. The close alliance of dynastic-imperialism with established religion led socialists and communists to believe that religion too was nothing more than a tool of the ruling classes to preserve their privileged ways. However, perhaps socialists and communists had overstated the situation. Both the ruling classes and established religion had contempt for the national idea and suppressed it whenever they could but increasingly embraced it when it was their only means of survival. It was a strategy that socialists and communists eventually took as well, though they have yet to admit it. Such short-term strategies, however, were counterproductive over the long run and forced the ruling classes to contribute to their own demise.

The Twentieth Century

The growing tendency for Marxism, established religion, and dynastic-imperialism to articulate their positions and goals within nationalist rhetoric and the national framework only hastened their own demise and ensured the eventual victory of the national idea as the nineteenth century wore on. On the other hand, because these paradigms came to embrace the national idea—though simultaneously opposing it—the national idea did not eschew these other paradigms but incorporated them within itself. Thus, for example, the ideas of social class and religious identity are still relevant and vital. However, it is important to note that they primarily exist within national containers. More poignant, the national idea took for itself imperialism's political-territorial framework. Dynasties persisted into the twentieth century, but by the late nineteenth century dynastic empires increasingly became national empires with imperial competition likewise increasingly becoming national competition.

Dynastic imperialism also fanned the national idea by recruiting it in its own imperial causes. Nowhere was this tendency more persistently employed than in the Balkans. Since the demise of Napoleon, the political-territorial landscape of the Balkans was directly controlled by three dynastic states: the Austro-Hungarian (Habsburg prior to 1867), Russian, and Ottoman Empires (see figure 1.1). In addition, Great Britain, France, and Germany (the Kingdom of Prussia before 1871) exerted their imperial influence as well. The Ottoman Empire stood out in that it was Islamic while the others were Christian. Long a threat to the Europeans as the Ottomans had steadily advanced deeper and deeper into Europe for centuries, the Islamic presence helped the Europeans to transcend their differences and resist the Ottomans in a common Christian cause. After the Ottoman Empire reached its territorial maximum in Europe in 1683, it began a slow decline. By the late nineteenth century, it was known as the "Sick Man of Europe" (Ergang 1954, 316-23).

The European dynasties worked individually and in tandem to roll back the Ottoman Empire. After the ideas of Romanticism spread into the Balkans in the nineteenth century, the subject peoples of the empire began to develop national identities and subsequently began to rebel in nationalist movements and insurrections. The situation only hastened the decline of the empire and provided a strong tool for the other empires to leverage against the Ottomans. The Russians long had a religious connection with their fellow *Pravoslavni* ("true believers," used by Eastern Orthodox Christians to identify themselves), but with the rise of Romantic beliefs the Russians also were able to build on their Slavic connections, namely, with such peoples as the Serbs and Bulgarians. Being Roman Catholic and Germanic, the Austrians had fewer cultural connections to the peoples of the Balkans; they, nevertheless, found ways to build relations. Along their borders where their ethnic minorities spread into the territories of the Ottoman Empire, the Austrians promoted the culture of their minorities in an attempt not only to garner the support of their own minorities, but also to cultivate among their brethren across the border the desire to be incorporated into the Austrian Empire. Thus the Austrians built schools, theaters, and other cultural amenities in the hopes of promoting pro-Austrian feelings. To bridge the gap between their own Roman Catholic beliefs and the Eastern Orthodox beliefs of most Balkan peoples, the Austrians promoted the Uniate Church—a blend of Roman Catholicism and Eastern Orthodoxy. It was particularly attractive to the Austrians because the church was easily recognizable to Eastern Orthodox Christians as it contained mostly Eastern Orthodox beliefs and practices yet recognized the Roman Catholic pope as the church's true spiritual leader. Thus, unlike Eastern Orthodox Christians, who tended to look to the Russian tsar as the protector of their faith, Uniate Christians tended to look to the Austrian emperor—a Roman Catholic—as their protector. Perhaps the most poignant example was the Austrian promotion of the Transylvania school, rooted in the Uniate Church, which promoted a Romanian national identity, one that saw its connections with Rome. The effects of this effort are still seen today in that the Romanian language is written in the Latin alphabet rather than the Cyrillic alphabet as customarily used by Eastern Orthodox Christians like the Romanians. Perhaps the Transylvania school was most effective, but the Austrians also promoted the Uniate Church among the Eastern Orthodox Southern Slavs in their realm in the hopes of making a Serbian identity that was anti-Ottoman and pro-Austrian.[8] The Austrians succeeded in cultivating an anti-Ottoman Serbian identity, but it eventually became anti-Austrian too.

Russian and Austrian inroads alarmed the other empires of Europe, most notably Great Britain and France, all of whom feared that if either Russia or Austria were to gain control of Ottoman territory and resources, then that empire could become the dominant European power. Thus, whenever an empire began to seriously exploit the weakness of the Ottomans, the other empires rushed in to prop up the "Sick Man" in hopes that it would last until an opportunity arose for one of them to move in. The Austrians and Russians too joined in on the strategy if the other had the upper hand. For example, after the decisive Russian victory against the Ottomans in the Russo-Turkish War of 1877-1878, the Russians proposed a rather large Bulgarian state, obviously to be its client state in the Balkans. The move would have given Russia control of the Balkans and access to Constantinople and the Middle East. Great Britain almost declared war on Russia, but with added pressure from the other empires, the Russians agreed to a congress in Berlin (Ergang 1954, 321). Contrary to Russian desires, a smaller Bulgaria was created and left as an autonomous province within the Ottoman Empire. Great Britain was granted the right to occupy Cyprus and Austria-Hungary the permission to administer Bosnia-Herzegovina (see figure 5.1). Such action meant that the Ottoman Empire lasted longer in the Balkans than it would have without such support, though dubious support. More importantly, Romania and Serbia achieved independence with Serbia enlarging its territory at the same time. Montenegro's independence was affirmed and its territory almost doubled in size.

The imperial strategy in the Balkans, though perhaps necessary in the short run, was shortsighted, a double-edged sword that was ultimately self-defeating and eventually led to the destruction of most of Europe's great empires. While the empires kept each other out of the Balkans, fanning nationalism to weaken the Ottomans without annexing territories meant that the national idea grew among peoples until they no longer desired to join the empires to which they were religiously akin (an integral idea of the old imperial paradigm). Instead, the peoples of the Balkans clamored for their own nation-states. In fact, the strategy of keeping opposing empires out of the Balkans soon included the acceptance of nation-states—as already noted with the Congress of Berlin and its recognition of Romania's, Serbia's, and Montenegro's independence. So as the Russians pursued their imperial project, they did so by fanning Serbian nationalism to block the Austrian imperial project (Craig 1972, 443, 447). In retrospect, the strategy is mystifying, but it illustrates how entrenched ideas were among Europe's imperial leaders and how young the national idea was. Though despising the national idea, imperial leaders saw nationalism as an effective weapon without realizing that it eventually would lead to the permanent creation of nation-states; indeed, as will be seen, nation-states also were not what Woodrow Wilson foresaw when he spoke of self-determination. Even after nation-states emerged, imperial leaders were opposed to the national idea. They continued to use nation-states as instruments of foreign policy with plans to forcibly annex and destroy them when the opportunities presented themselves. Nation-states, however, became a force unto their own. In the Balkans, they waged their own wars against the Ottoman Empire in 1912 and 1913, with concern from Europe's imperial powers. Thus, after the Ottoman Empire was essentially pushed out of Europe by 1913 (barring a small toehold across the Dardanelles and Bosporus), imperial designs turned to the new nation-states of the Balkans and ignited a world war.

The First World War

In one way, the First World War can be described as a war that ensued from a complex web of alliances. Additionally, it can be depicted as the outcome of increasing global competition that became hostile after the land available for colonization precipitously diminished, leading to the drive for autarky and the reliance on protectionism. While these views are valid, it is also worth considering that the First World War was the culminating struggle between dynastic imperialism and the national idea. Dynastic imperialism had long tried to suppress the national idea, but it took a new turn at the beginning of the twentieth century when imperial and national projects ran directly into each other, most notably over reterritorialization. Interestingly, the conflagration ignited between an empire and a nation-state, namely, Austria-Hungary and Serbia. As previously noted, Francis Joseph was the emperor of the Austro-Hungarian Empire. As one of Europe's longest-reigning monarchs, he came to power during the national revolutions in 1848 and set out to crush the national idea as one of his first acts as a new monarch. The Serbian nation-state came into being only in 1878 but was, nevertheless, one of the older nation-states of the Balkans and arguably the center of fervent nationalism imbued with Romantic ideals. As the Ottomans lost their grip on their Balkan territories, Bosnia-Herzegovina figured prominently in both the Austro-Hungarian Empire's and the Serbian nation-state's projects. The Austro-Hungarian Empire moved first as it was able to formally occupy the territory in 1878 as recognized at the Berlin Congress following the Ottoman defeat at the hands of the Russian imperial army. Despite losing Bosnia-Herzegovina, the interest of Serbian nationalists in the territory only grew. Thus, Serbian nationalists were outraged when the Austro-Hungarian Empire annexed the territory in 1908. Following successful wars to its southeast in 1912 and 1913, the Serbian nation-state increased in size, became a more formidable force, and more of an obstacle to further Austrian imperialist expansion in the Balkans. With a larger Serbian state, Serbian nationalists waited for an opportunity to oust the Austrians from Bosnia-Herzegovina. They exploited one on June 28, 1914, by assassinating Archduke Francis Ferdinand and his wife while they were on a visit to Sarajevo. Blaming the Serbian government for its role in facilitating the assassination, the Austrian-Hungarian government delivered an ultimatum, which if fully met would have deprived Serbia of its independence (Craig 1972, 445). Outmatched in direct military conflict, the Serbian government agreed to most of the ultimatum's demands and offered to negotiate the remaining points. Not satisfied, the Austro-Hungarian government declared war on Serbia on July 28.

Though the empire (i.e., Austria-Hungary) was much larger than the nation-state (i.e., Serbia), the behavior of imperial leaders (as it had been for some time) only ensured the victory of the national idea by the end of the war. As noted, the dynastic-imperialist disdain for the national idea resulted in a disregard for the potency of the national idea and a blindness to the dangers of fanning nationalism, though it was an effective imperial tool. Thus, the Russian Empire came to the aid of the Serbian nation-state rather than allow itself to be outmaneuvered by a competing empire. It did so to protect its own imperial drive toward Constantinople by blocking Austro-Hungarian expansion into the Balkans. This act, however, triggered the intricate system of imperial alliances that quickly dragged Europe's other empires into a massive war, disproving the belief at the time that the impending war could be localized. In the beginning, leaders also thought that the war would be short, but they had underestimated the new technological advances, particularly in weaponry. As new technologies resulted in massive carnage and even stalemate conditions—to the further demise of the imperialist paradigm—imperial leaders turned ever more to the national idea in the search to bring about victory. Namely, imperial leaders increasingly supported national projects (Sharp 1991, 10-11, 130-31). The most notable example was the Treaty of London in 1915 (Temperely [1921] 1969, 4: 278-347), in which the Entente powers lured Italy to their side by promising it the right to annex Austrian territories, many of which it saw as rightfully Italian. A similar treaty was granted to Romania in 1916 (Temperely [1921] 1969, 4: 216-17), granting Romania the right to annex from Hungary territories that the Romanians saw rightfully as theirs. Offers were made to Bulgaria, but Bulgarian leaders were more attracted to the offers of the Central Powers; most of the territories that Bulgarians desired were held by the Allied and Associated Powers and thus could only be obtained by an alliance with the Central Powers. Great Britain and France also solicited help from the Czechs and then the Poles after Russia withdrew from the war. The Central Powers also promised lands desired by nationalist projects. Offers were made to Italy and Romania, but as noted these countries were more attracted to the offers of the opposing side. However, Bulgaria was attracted by the offers. As the stresses of the war increased, so did the offers. Because many of the territories desired by nationalist projects were desired by minorities of the Austro-Hungarian Empire, the Austro-Hungarian government was forced into the position of conceding greater and greater autonomy to its minorities to counter the offers made by its enemies. Though many deals were made, negotiations continued, and newer deals were being hammered out when the Central Powers collapsed and the war finally ended. What was left ranged from formal agreements like the Treaty of London to partially worked out deals and promises, many of which were not agreed upon by all parties and sometimes made by individuals who did not have the full consent of those they represented. The situation was complicated by the fact that some of the agreements contradicted one another. The victorious powers intended to compensate those who supported them though they had not necessarily foreseen that their promises implied the creation of nation-states. The arrival of Woodrow Wilson, however, firmly pushed Europe down that pathway.

The Paris Peace Conference

A look at the map of Europe's political geography before the war and
another after the war highlights that three empires collapsed (Russia,
Austria-Hungary, and Germany) and nation-states arose in their place
(see figures 1.1, 5.2, and 5.3). In Southwest Asia, the same occurred with
the Ottoman Empire. Moreover, France and Great Britain, though victorious, were seriously weakened with the British Empire fighting a defen-

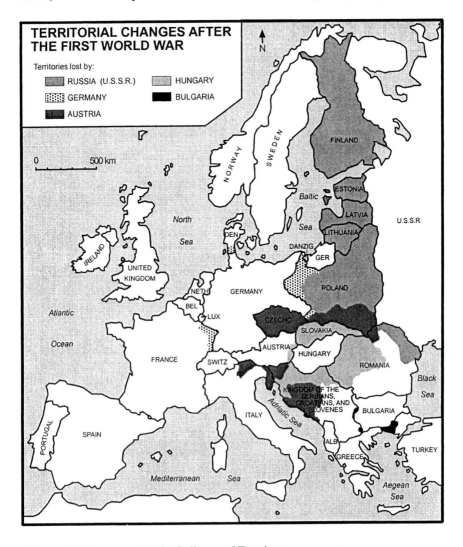

Figure 5.2 Europe in 1919: Collapse of Empires

sive battle to keep Irish nationalists from creating an independent Irish nation-state. In retrospect, it seems obvious that the national idea won out over the imperialist paradigm. However, a closer examination of the postwar years, especially the Paris Peace Conference in 1919, illustrates that the national idea was perhaps victorious but that the application of the national idea in creating nation-states was very problematic. Imperialist and state-centered thinking and the fear of Bolshevism played significant roles in creating a new Europe of nation-states. Even when the nationalist principle was applied, national identity proved to be subjec-

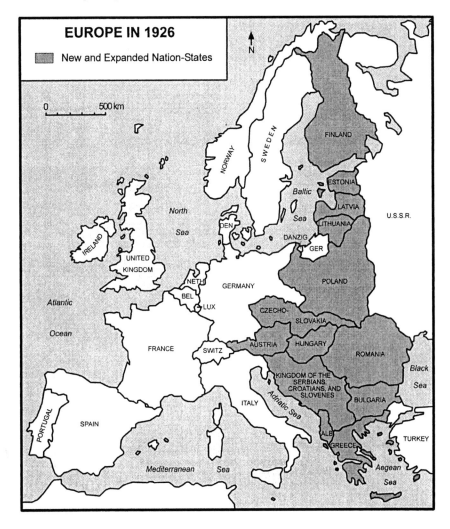

Figure 5.3 Europe's New Nation-States

tive and difficult to define rather than clearly understood and concrete as often treated.

In the aftermath of the war, national groups within the crumbling empires were mobilizing, setting up provisional governments, and attempting to stake out their territories. Unable to stop or fully control these actions, France, Great Britain, the United States, and Italy, nevertheless, were the presiding powers at the Paris Peace Conference. The leaders of the aspiring nation-states, though frequently able to act in a de facto manner, generally continued to seek the support and approval of the established states. Of the ideologies represented on the decision-making councils at Paris, the French leader, Georges Clemenceau, and the British prime minister, Lloyd George, both represented the imperialist mind-set. Not only did they blame Germany for the war, but they also sought to fulfill the war goals of their respective empires. The French, for example, sought Alsace-Lorraine, and the British desired Germany's colonies. Despite their common mind-set, the two leaders were not united in their approach, and their goals were not always complementary. For example, Clemenceau wanted to weaken Germany as much as possible, but Lloyd George was concerned with a balance of power in Europe, seeing the rise of French power to be as threatening as German power had been (Ergang 1954, 401-2). Thus, Lloyd George was not always supportive of Clemenceau's plans for Germany. Although not opposed to the creation of nation-states, both leaders tended to think of nation-states as tools of imperialist projects.

One of the more interesting examples of the imperialist mind-set was Sir Halford J. MacKinder (Martin and James 1993, 205-8). He was Britain's top geographer and as a member of Parliament had influence beyond the academic realm. In 1904, he published his paper "The geographical pivot in history," in which he espoused his Heartland Theory. MacKinder pointed out that a significant amount of the world's resources was contained in the interior of the Eurasian landmass, mostly within Russia. The remote interior of this part of the world left many of the heartland's resources untapped because they were out of the reach of maritime shipping, but the advent of new technologies like the railroad could quickly make them easily accessible and change geopolitical relations. MacKinder continued to develop these ideas, most notably in his book *Democratic Ideals and Reality* (1919). He noted, for example, that the Himalayas and other physiographic barriers made it difficult to access the Heartland. The exception was the easy route across the North European Plain in Eastern Europe. By 1919, MacKinder developed the following dictum:

Who rules East Europe commands the Heartland
Who rules the Heartland commands the World Island [Eurasia/Africa]
Who rules the World Island commands the World.

MacKinder worried less about the Russians exploiting the Heartland's resources and threatening the British Empire, though he became concerned about the rise of Bolshevism, than he worried about the German Empire. With the German Empire bordering the Russian Empire, Germans could easily gain access to the Heartland, apply their superior technology, and seriously threaten Great Britain. To protect British imperial supremacy, MacKinder argued that the Germans had to be prevented from gaining access to the Heartland. To do so, MacKinder proposed the creation of a "Middle Tier" of states from Finland to Greece (Blouet 2001, 51). After the rise of Bolshevism in Russia, the middle tier of states likewise served to buffer Western Europe from Bolshevist aggression. The map of nation-states that were actually created at the Paris Peace Conference in 1919 so closely resembles MacKinder's proposal that the differences are hardly worth mentioning (see figure 5.3). It would be an overstatement to say that MacKinder's proposal was so influential that it was adopted by the peacemakers. To avoid such an overstatement, it is worth noting that MacKinder's proposal reflected national aspirations; therefore, it could be stated that MacKinder simply proposed what many desired. However, MacKinder's proposal is noteworthy for other reasons; it illustrates that those set in imperialist thinking supported the creation of nation-states not because they believed in self-determination but because nation-states could be employed as tools to implement imperial policy. In this case, with the collapse of the Russian Empire and the rise of Bolshevism, France and Great Britain could use the newly created nation-states to contain both Germany and Russia. French leaders in particular supported the creation of these new nation-states because these states could serve as replacements of their former ally Russia on Germany's eastern flank to contain Germany (Blouet 2001, 48). Clemenceau himself articulated this belief frequently:

> [U]ninterested as he was in geographic detail, there was no one who perceived more clearly the relations of geography and political power in their larger strategic aspects. The essence of his policy concerned the defense of France. For her protection from the assault of a revivified Germany he recognized two key positions: first, a demilitarized Rhineland on the German western frontier; second, a fortified bastion in Bohemia under Czechoslovakia as an ally of France. "He who holds Bohemia controls Central Europe."

He had pulled out a map of Central Europe and put his forefinger on
Bohemia and his thumb on the Rhineland. "Look," he said, "so long as
Germany is contained on the Rhine she cannot expose her western front
by a move against the stronghold of the Czechs. These are the critical
points, the Rhineland and Bohemia. This is security. But if Germany is
allowed to fortify the Rhineland, then she will move against Bohemia,
will be free to raise the issue of the Sudetenland, settle the question of
Anschluss, and take off in any direction she may decide. For the moment," he added, "we are secure, but I fear that weaker men are going
to follow me." He put the safety of France on a geographic foundation.
(Seymour 1951, 10-11)

On the other end of the spectrum was Woodrow Wilson, president of
the United States. Known for his catchword "self-determination," Wilson
seemed to dream of the creation of nation-states at the Peace Conference.
However, a closer examination of Wilson's beliefs and his knowledge of
European peoples illustrates that the political map of Europe as it
emerged from the conference by no means resembled Wilson's initial
conceptions. Contrary to what many histories have reduced Wilson's
ideas to, Wilson's own understanding of self-determination of peoples
did not mandate or initially include the creation of nation-states. As an
American, his ideas of political liberties were rooted in Enlightenment
thinking, meaning that he believed that people should have a voice in
their own governance. As Robert Lansing, the secretary of state under
Wilson, noted in his narrative on the conference, Wilson's term "self-
determination" was merely his own expression of the much older
Enlightenment phrase "the consent of the governed":

> The two phrases mean substantially the same thing and have to an ex-
> tent been used interchangeably by those who advocate the principle as a
> standard right. "Self-determination" was not a new thought. It was a re-
> statement of the old one. (Lansing 1921, 96)

As a person with ideas rooted in the Enlightenment, Wilson did not see a
people (e.g., "we the people") as defined by common language and culture but rather by a common political culture, ideally rooted in democracy. Self-determination to Wilson was the empowerment of individuals
to vote for their leaders and express their political opinions, which he
saw as having been sorely lacking in Europe, and the root of conflict.
Typical of an Enlightenment thinker, Wilson tended to accept current
state boundaries while promoting democratic ideals. Indeed, Lansing
further made the point that Wilson no more advocated independence and

the creation of nation-states in Europe with his talk of self-determination than he would have argued for the South's secession from the United States during the American Civil War as the desirable means for resolving that conflict (Lansing 1921, 100-101).

Austria-Hungary serves as an illustration of Wilson's conception of "self-determination." While frequently applying the term, Wilson also stated in his annual message on the State of the Union on December 4, 1917, that,

> We owe it, however, to ourselves to say that we do not wish in any way to impair or to rearrange the Austro-Hungarian Empire. It is no affair of ours what they do with their own life, either industrially or politically. We do not purpose or desire to dictate to them in any way. (Link 1984, 45: 197)

Clearly Wilson did not see national independence or the creation of nation-states as a solution to the problems of this very multiethnic country fraught with internal tensions and disputes. A month later, on January 8, 1918, the same year that the war ended, Wilson delivered his now-famous Fourteen Points speech. Again, while highlighting his concept of self-determination, Wilson did not speak of national independence or the creation of new nation-states to replace Austria-Hungary as his Point X stated that "The peoples of Austria-Hungary, whose place among the nations we wish to see safeguarded and assured, should be accorded the freest opportunity of autonomous development" (Walworth 1977, 280-81).[9] Indeed, Wilson's plan for Austria-Hungary, which was later drawn up in the spring of 1918, called for Austria-Hungary to be federalized, not broken up into nation-states (Ádám 1995). Interestingly, the plan delineated the federal units along historic boundaries, many of which lay along physiographic features.

The leaders of the U.S. allies, namely, of Great Britain and France, were leery of Wilson's talk of self-determination because applying the term as universally as he did suggested that the peoples within the British and French empires deserved self-determination as well. Self-determination may not have meant independence, but it certainly implied that subjects should have more voice in their governance than the British or French were willing to grant. Robert Lansing noted British concerns and objections to Wilson's proposals for formal declarations that ensured or expressed ideas of self-determination (1921, 93-95) and likewise articulated similar concerns himself, as indicated by his notes from the very beginning of the conference in 1919:

What effect will it [self-determination] have on the Irish, the Indians, the Egyptians, and the nationalists among the Boers? Will it not breed discontent, disorder, and rebellion? Will not the Mohammedans of Syria and Palestine and possibly Morocco and Tripoli rely on it? How can it be harmonized with Zionism, to which the President is practically committed? (Lansing 1921, 97)

Ironically, British and French war obligations and imperial strategy promoted the idea that Wilson's term *self-determination* meant national independence and the creation of nation-states. As noted previously, British and French wartime solicitations of help from the Italians, the Romanians, and the minorities of the German and Austro-Hungarian Empires left them in debt to these peoples' desires, which were to create or expand their nation-states. The granting of these desires was not ideal imperialist strategy, but because these nation-states could serve British and especially French imperial strategy, as they could in this case to pin Germany, then the British and French felt obligated to support the creation and expansion of these nation-states. The British and French saw little contradiction in supporting the independence movements of peoples in opposing empires while denying similar movements within their own empires. Such was the double-standard nature of imperialism. Wilson, however, complicated British and French imperial strategy because his talk of self-determination broadened the practice of creating nation-states beyond an imperial strategy employed in specific and limited circumstances to a universal operating principle. As a double irony, though Wilson himself did not equate his own term *self-determination* with national independence, the combination of British and French support for the creation of nation-states in East Central Europe and the subsequent interpretation of Wilson's catchword by the minority peoples themselves turned Wilson's concept of self-determination into the idea of national independence and the necessary creation of nation-states. Thus, Wilson's rhetoric coupled with British and French obligations and actions, despite their own intentions and desires, promoted the national idea and became catalysts for the creation of nation-states. These actions would come to haunt the British and French Empires in the coming decades.

Woodrow Wilson slowly and awkwardly came to the realization that his term *self-determination* meant national independence and the necessary creation of nation-states. This change is seen in Wilson's handling of the Austro-Hungarian Empire. For example, the emperor of Austria-Hungary tried to conform to Point X of Wilson's Fourteen Points (see above) by producing a plan—called the Manifesto—that would federalize the Austro-Hungarian Empire. The Manifesto appeared on October

16, 1918, only weeks before the end of the war (Temperley [1921] 1969, 4: 101).[10] Within a matter of days, Wilson responded by stating that the demand of Point X had become out of date as the United States had subsequently allied itself with the Czechoslovaks and the South Slavs, and it would be they who would determine what was required from the Austro-Hungarian government (Nowak [1924] 1970, 304). With the Czechs desiring independence and including the Slovaks in their plans and the South Slavs likewise seeking to create their own state(s), Wilson's demand for self-determination moved from a vision of turning empires into federalized states to the practice of dismantling empires and erecting nation-states in their place. The Austrian emperor failed to conform to Wilson's idea of self-determination because he waited until Wilson changed the meaning of his own concept.

In accepting the desire of Central Europeans to create nation-states, Wilson approached boundary delineation for new states with the typical Enlightenment concern for economic viability and defense rather than with the Romantic emphasis on ethnicity defined by language and other cultural criteria. To Wilson, every new national state had to have unfettered access to the "great highways of sea" so that it could engage in global trade (Baker and Dodd 1926, 2: 412). For those states that could not reasonably possess coastlines with good harbors, access could be gained via major rivers. Thus, Wilson fought for the internationalization of major rivers like the Rhine and Danube. Though it may seem contradictory to some, Wilson's concept of self-determination—which was rooted in the concern of economic viability and defense as much as ethnicity—led him to advocate or accept boundary proposals that violated the ethnic principle.

By the time Woodrow Wilson arrived at the Paris Peace Conference in 1919, it became clear that one of the major tasks of the conference was to delineate the boundaries for the new nation-states. Until then, Wilson acted on principle but had long known that he lacked the detailed knowledge to make the right decisions at an ensuing peace conference. To remedy his own weakness, Wilson assembled a group of specialists, mostly academics, to collect information that would be crucial to making postwar decisions that would ensure a lasting peace. The group was assembled in early September 1917, shortly after U.S. entry into the war (Gelfand 1963, x-xi, 44). The group became known as the Inquiry and was headed by a close confidant of Wilson, Edward Mandell House, more commonly known as "Colonel" House. Geographers played an important role in the Inquiry with Isaiah Bowman, president of the American Geographical Society, topping the list and holding a crucial position

(Heffernan 1998, 88). The Inquiry was soon housed in the offices of the American Geographical Society, where the society's cartographers produced over 1,200 maps as well as numerous documents and reports. When the war was over, Bowman and many other members of the Inquiry boarded the *George Washington* for the sea voyage over to the Paris Peace Conference. While on board, Wilson told his panel of experts, "Tell me what is right and I'll fight for it. Give me a guaranteed position" (Seymour 1951, 17; Miller 1924, 1: 373). It became clear that Wilson did not know much about the peoples and places of Europe. Thanks to the efforts of Bowman and the other geographers, Wilson learned a great deal. For example, he found out that a large number of Germans lived in northern Bohemia and was surprised that the Czech leader Masaryk had never told him that fact when he laid claim to the territory for the Czechs (Seymour 1951, 17). He also learned the locations and details of places such as Silesia and Teschen (Czech: Těšín/ Polish: Czieszyn). The contribution of the Inquiry did not end with the sea voyage either. Members of the Inquiry were present at the negotiations. They listened to the highest level discussions with Wilson, Lloyd George, and Clemenceau, injected their wisdom when solicited, and brought forth their maps from back rooms and spread them before these world leaders. These experts of Wilson became so invaluable to the peace process that Lloyd George and Clemenceau summoned and consulted with these experts on their own.

The idea of self-determination immediately opened the question of national identity itself. The existence, number, spatial distribution, and character of national groups were not clear. Consider, for example, the Duchy of Teschen (see figure 3.6). The people of the duchy considered themselves to be their own people: *Slazacy* (Slonzaks) (Temperley [1921] 1969, 4: 351-52). Ninety percent of them preferred to remain independent of both Czechoslovakia and Poland though both countries claimed the duchy on historic and ethnic grounds (Mamatey and Luža 1973, 33; Perman 1962, 230-31). An Inter-Allied Commission was sent to the duchy to investigate the matter and subsequently recommended that an independent state be created for these people because the duchy had "for ethnographic and geographic reasons a special physiognomy" (quoted in Perman 1962, 231). The French representative, however, disagreed on the grounds that the independence of such a small territory was not practical because German capitalists would essentially take control over the duchy in time. Thus, the duchy should be divided between Czechoslovakia and Poland, the two states that laid claim to the territory. With the *Slazacy* having no political institutions at their disposal, the duchy was eventually divided between Czechoslovakia and Poland following a long political dispute between the Czech and Polish governments coupled with internal disagreements between the Allied representatives, each of whom had their own geopolitical visions that were in part entangled with Czech and Polish national projects.

The Teschen case illustrates that though the leaders of the Allied Powers came to support national independence for the peoples of Central Europe—primarily prompted by ethno-nationalists in Central Europe—they viewed national identity through the lenses of economics and politics, both rooted in long-held ideas of natural territories bounded by physiographic features such as rivers and mountain ranges and reaffirmed in historic boundaries and state-centered thinking. Enlightenment thinking certainly asserted itself as nations were thus seen as groups of people bound together for security, in turn giving weight to the economic viability of any state (old or newly created) and the reliance on physiographic boundaries for defense. The preference for historic boundaries was thought to be tied to issues of economic viability and defense because many of them followed physiographic boundaries; however, historic boundaries had more profoundly contributed to state-centered thinking and the assumption that the functional economic regions they had created were somehow givens, thus natural, and had to be preserved. Romanticism, too, certainly had its effects on thinking as seen in the emphasis placed on language. A deeper analysis, however, shows that language, though spoken of as a national identifier, was circumscribed within these aforementioned ideas of identity and territory, flavored with environmental determinism. Leon Dominian, one of the geographers of the Inquiry, perhaps best typifies the ideas concerning language and its significance in his book *The Frontiers of Language and Nationality in Europe* (1917):

We therefore turn to the land for intimate acquaintance with man and his culture. His very character is shaped in the mold of his habitual haunt. (2)

Language areas, in common with many other facts of geography, have been largely determined by the character of the surface or climate. (2)

Considered as political boundaries, linguistic lines of cleavage have twofold importance. They are sanctioned by national aspirations and they conform to a notable degree with physical features. Every linguistic area considered in these pages bears evidence of relation between language and its natural environment. (3)

The beauty of modern French, as well as the attraction it exerts on cultivated minds, is due to its well-balanced blend of northern and southern elements. . . . In it the sunshine of the south pierces with its warm rays the severity of northern earnestness. No other European language can boast of an equally happy composition. (11)

The picture of linguistic evolution can be painted only with the colors of geography. (17)

Nationality cannot depend on language alone, for it is founded on geographical unity. The past thousand years of European history contain sufficient proof of the fact. The three southern peninsulas Spain, Italy and Greece are homelands of an equal number of nations. A single language is current in each. To the north a similar differentiation of nations adapts itself to regional divisions. Plains, mountains and seas have limited European nationalities to definite number and extension. (315)

A literary history of a country is, in great measure, the mirror of its political growth. The development of social aptitudes, of intellectual faculties or of material wants within a given area is, in the last resort, an expansion of the living forces which make for nationality and which, ultimately, find their way into literary records. Nationality and literature are thus bound together by geography and history. (317)

So because it is part of life and a living influence, literature has always consolidated the nation-forming power of language. Poetry, especially, is often an intensified reflection of national thought and life. In the words of Irving, "Poets always breathe the feeling of a nation." The cultivation of literature serves national ends.
    Belgium is fathomed in their [Belgian] hearts. Their eyes lingered lovingly on the scenery in the midst of which they lived. Flat roads winding interminably over flat lands, chimes whose tones mellow with age ring from the crumbling tops of old towers, rustic feasts enlivened by the roaring mirth and joviality celebrated by Flemish painters, these are the visions which are evoked by the French works assembled by Belgian writers in their compositions. One would seek in vain, however, for these Belgian scenes in French literature. . . . The same subtle sensation of the living earth has been felt on the troubled surface of mountainous Switzerland. For of Swiss lands and life few descriptions will ever combine the charm and faithfulness which characterize the works of Gottfried Keller, foremost among the country's writers who drew on the joint inspiration of flaming patriotism and the incomparable beauty of Swiss landscape. (318-19)

One of the most remarkable instances of the influence of poetry on national destiny is found in Serbian nationality, which has been cast altogether in the mold of the country's epic ballads or "pjesmes." Although primarily inspired by the valorous deeds of legendary heroes, these indigenous compositions describe Serbian life and nature with extraordinary verisimilitude and beauty. (321)

Replete with the glow and color of Serbian lands, the pjesme voices Serbia's national aspirations once more in the storm and stress of new afflictions. Its accents ring so true that the geographer, in search of Serbian boundaries, tries in vain to discover a surer guide to delimitation. For Serbia extends as far as her folk-songs are heard. From the Adriatic to the western walls of Balkan ranges, from Croatia to Macedonia, the guzlar's ballad is the symbol of national solidarity. His tunes live within the heart and upon the lips of every Serbian. The pjesme may therefore be fittingly considered the measure and index of nationality whose fiber it has stirred. To make Serbian territory coincide with the regional extension of the pjesme implies defining of the Serbian national area. And Serbia is only one among many countries to which this method of delimitation is applicable. (322)

In dealing with the varied influences which engage attention in a study of linguistic areas the student is frequently compelled to pause before the importance of economic relations. (325)

A national frontier in the strictest sense of the term cannot, therefore, be limited by the surface feature which has shaped its development. It has generally outgrown this phase of its extension together with the constantly increasing range of activity of the peoples it once inclosed [*sic*]. Factors of an ethnological, economic or linguistic nature must, therefore, be considered. Then only will the new delimitation be entitled to be qualified as natural. (328)

Germany's expansion is a natural phenomenon. The country is overpopulated. It must expand. The sea is a barrier to its westerly expansion. The north is uninviting. The south is being drained of its resources by active and intelligent inhabitants. The "Drang nach Osten" of German Imperialism is therefore inevitable. The line of least resistance points to the east, where fertile territory awaits development. (331)[11]

The practical value of linguistic frontiers as national boundaries is due to their geographical growth. They are natural because they are the result of human intercourse based largely on economic needs. Having developed naturally, they correspond to national aspirations. Such being the case, the task of frontier delimitation can be made to assume a scientific form. . . . The clear duty of statesmen engaged in a revision of boundaries is to put the varied interests at state into harmony with the facts of nature as they are revealed by geography. . . .

The preceding remarks should not be considered as implying that a mountain, or a river, or even the sea are [*sic*] to be arbitrarily regarded as frontiers. Lines of water-parting deserve particular mention as having provided satisfactory national borders in history. But in boundaries each case should be treated upon its own merits. (332-33)

These views are seen in the newly constructed political map of Europe (see figure 5.4). France, for example, regained Alsace-Lorraine and extended its boundaries east to the Rhine River though much of Alsace-Lorraine predominantly spoke German.[12] Italy received South Tyrol from Austria and extended its boundaries north to the higher peaks of the Alps to fulfill the Italian nationalist program of *Italia Irredenta* though South Tyrol was inhabited by many German speakers.[13] For the Czech portion of the new Czechoslovak state,[14] the boundaries for the new state were primarily those that separated Germany from Austria-Hungary, themselves very historic boundaries following the ridges of the Bohemian, Ore, and Sudeten Mountains, though many Germans were left within the new Czechoslovak state. In the south, the boundary for the Czech part of the state was drawn along the internal boundary between the provinces of Austria and Bohemia, also the historic boundaries of the Grand Duchy of Austria and the Kingdom of Bohemia; these boundaries likewise left many Austrian Germans within the new Czechoslovak state (Bowman 1928, 329). Leon Dominian, the great advocate for drawing political boundaries along historic boundaries, exemplified much of the underlying thought for such action when he stated, "Bohemia, which has been shown to be splendidly laid off on a physical map, deserves political independence because it is endowed with geographic individuality" (1917a, 341). In addition to the concern with economic viability framed within state-centered thinking of historic boundaries and seen through the lenses of environmental determinism, boundary delineation concerning Germany was also influenced by the perceived need to punish the Germans and ensure that the German Empire would not be a threat in the future, particularly to France.

The ideas of natural boundaries underlay the view of Hungarians and political boundaries perceived to be appropriate for the new Hungarian state:

Agreement between the land and its inhabitants appears to exist here, for the Magyar is, in the first place, a lowlander accustomed to live within the precincts of a fertile plain. He has always shunned the moun-

Figure 5.4 Spatial Disjunctions of the New Nation-States

tain and is rarely to be met above the 600-foot contour. . . . On the western side, west of the Raab, the heights drained by the river are peopled by Germans and, in spite of a complex boundary zone, a convenient line of demarcation can be drawn upon the basis of elevation. Southward the old-time utility of the Drave [Drava] as the dividing line between Croat and Hungarian remains unimpaired to this day. (Dominian 1917a, 338-39)

Interestingly, no historic boundaries were used in conjunction with these perceptions to delineate the political boundaries of the new Hungarian state as had been the case with other countries. The fringes of the Hungarian kingdom had until that point been occupied by non-Hungarians, most of whom desired independence. The Slovaks, for example, opted for a union with the Czechs. The northern boundary of the kingdom, with minor exception, was used for the northern boundary of the Slovak part of the new Czechoslovak state. In the south, however, no historic or internal boundaries existed that could lend themselves to a boundary between the new Czechoslovak and Hungarian states. It is noteworthy to point out that one of the Czech leaders, Eduard Beneš, argued that the Slovaks should be united with the Czechs in a common state not only because they were similar ethnically, but also because they together formed part of a "Czecho-Slovak" in the tenth century before it had been destroyed by the Hungarians (Deák [1942] 1972, 35). Beneš, however, did not point to any historic boundary between this supposed medieval Czecho-Slovak state and the Hungarian one. Beneš's claim was questionable, amorphous at best, and it may seem odd that he would try to make such a questionable claim when the ethnic argument for united Czechs and Slovaks was so strong. His claim, however, underscores how powerful historic boundaries were in framing thinking and legitimizing territorial claims though they were ultimately not used for the new Hungarian state.

Though historic boundaries were not used for the boundaries of the new Hungarian state, neither were ethnographic boundaries beyond a general notion. On the one hand, the large exclave of Hungarians in eastern Transylvania separated by Romanians and others from the main group of Hungarians made it nearly impossible to draw a practical boundary line to bring all Hungarians together in one state. Ethnically complex southern Hungary (which became the Vojovodina of Yugoslavia and the Banat of Romania) presented similar difficulties. On the other hand, despite these difficult situations, the newly drawn boundaries of Hungary also clearly left outside of the new Hungarian state Hungarians whose distributions were compact and whose location was adjacent to the new state's boundaries. On ethnographic grounds, these Hungarians easily could have been included within the new Hungarian state. However, the concern of economic viability and defense coupled with a negative view of Hungarians because they had been the enemy in the war[15] and the additional negative attitude, which emerged after a Bolshevist regime came to power in 1919—which coincided with the peace negotiations—colored the views of the decision makers at the peace conference. Thus, the boundaries of the Slovak portion of Czechoslovakia were moved south to the Danube, well into territory clearly inhabited by Hungarians, to give the Czechoslovak state access to this international waterway to engage in trade. This Hungarian-inhabited territory also gave the state a major east-west rail connection, seen as an economic necessity (Macartney and Palmer 1962, 123). The decision to draw the Hungarian-Romanian boundary so that Hungarians fell within the Romanian state was made for the same reason, to give the Romanians an important rail link to ensure the viability of the Romanian state (Deák 1942, 28, 49-50, 67, 69).

Romania also received the whole of Bessarabia though it was occupied by other national groups, because the territory, bounded by the Prut and Nistru (Dniester) Rivers, was seen as a natural territory historically belonging to Romania (Temperely [1921] 1969, 4: 228). With Bolshevism governing in Russia, no attempts were made to discuss with Russian officials the issue of detaching this territory from the Russian Empire. Indeed, with Bessarabia incorporated into Romania, Romania could then be linked with Czechoslovakia and Poland, allowing the three states to serve as a buffer against the spread of Bolshevism into the rest of Europe as well as to block German advance into Eastern Europe. For a time, the French even used Romania as a staging ground to fight the Russian Bolsheviks with the hope of restoring the Tsarist Russia, partly in hopes of protecting France from Germany by restoring its old alliance with a country that could threaten Germany's eastern flank (Macartney and Palmer 1962, 100). After it became clear that Bolshevism was in firm control of Russia, French leaders leaned more heavily on Romania, Czechoslovakia, and Poland as allies to encircle Germany. To make such an alliance effective, French leaders saw the need to make these new states large enough to be as effective as the Russian Empire formerly had been. Thus, for example, the French representatives at the peace conference supported the proposal to include Ruthenia within Czechoslovakia. Ruthenia was seen as too small to be viable. It was also a crucial geostrategic link between Romania, Czechoslovakia, and Poland. The decision clearly violated the ethnic principle as the Ruthenians were most ethnically akin to the Ukrainians. However, Entente leaders believed that the allotment of Ruthenia to Ukraine could have provided the Bolsheviks with a major passageway into the rest of Europe. The decision may have also violated the principle of self-determination because, given a choice, the Ruthenians may have opted to stay within Hungary (Macartney and Palmer 1962, 124). Entente representatives saw that possibility as equally unpalatable because the Hungarians had recently had a Bolshevist government of their own, and that government attempted to send its armies into Ruthenia to link up with the Russian Bolsheviks to ensure its long-term survival. Some of the Entente representatives expressed reservations about awarding Ruthenia to Czechoslovakia. However, they shared many of the French concerns about Bolshevism in Russia and Hungary. In addition, the Czech representatives launched a very effective lobbying effort to include Ruthenia within their new state.

Geopolitics also played a role in the demarcation of the Polish state's boundaries. As noted, Poland fit well into French plans to contain Germany and then later to serve as a buffer to Soviet Russia (Ergang 1954, 495). Initially, however, Entente diplomats focused on physiographic boundaries, economic viability, and ethnic distributions when considering Polish state boundaries. All three of these concerns, as already noted more generally, were intertwined concepts. The Poles were seen as the "people of the field" as *pole* translates as "field." Following from this, their rightful home was seen as the fields, so to speak, of the Vistula River basin of the North European Plain (see figure 5.5). Once again, Leon Dominian expresses these blended concepts most succinctly:

> In sum, the valley of the Vistula, from the Carpathians to the Baltic, constitutes the field of Polish humanity and institutions. In spite of the remoteness of the period when they first occupied the land, these children of the plains never attempted to scale the mountainous slopes. The solid wall of the Carpathians, . . . with its abrupt slopes facing the north, forms the southern boundary of the country. (113)

> Within this marshy country, a Polish folk has maintained its own institutions ever since the consolidation of the Poles into a distinct people within the drainage area of the Vistula. (133)

> The western linguistic boundary of Poland extends through the German provinces of Silesia and Posen. Here replacement of the language by German since the sixteenth century is noticeable. At that time the Oder constituted the dividing line. (116)

> The advance of the area of Polish speech, in the form of a tongue of land, to the Baltic coast, is proof of intimate dependence between Polish nationality and the basin of the Vistula. This northernmost section of the territory in which Polish is spoken, lies entirely within Prussian territory. Centuries of Teutonic influence failed, however, to eradicate completely Slavic language or customs in the valley of the great river. (117)

> In the eastern field the basin of the Dnieper merged without abrupt transition into that of the Vistula, just as the basin of the Oder[16] on the west formed the western continuation of the Baltic plain. Four centuries

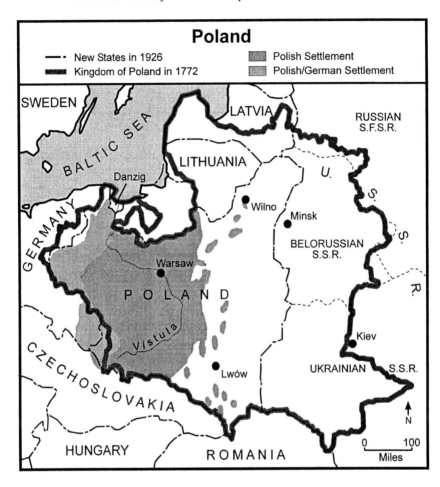

Poland

— · New States in 1926 ▨ Polish Settlement
▬ Kingdom of Poland in 1772 ▨ Polish/German Settlement

Figure 5.5 The Polish Nation and State

of struggle with Russia ensued until the Mucovite Empire absorbed the greater portion of Poland. (121)

The problem of delimiting Polish national boundaries is complicated on the east and west, as has been stated, by the absence of prominent surface features. On both sides the lines of linguistic parting provide the only practicable demarcation. On the north and south, however, the Baltic and the Carpathians may be utilized advantageously as natural frontiers. But the fate of the Polish region is strongly outlined by nature, for the entire basin of the Vistula is a regional unit. Any partitioning of this basin would probably be followed by political conflicts. (136)

These ideas are seen in the Allied decisions when they decided to demarcate the new Polish state's boundaries. The Carpathians were used for the
southern boundary. Much of the boundary likewise followed the historic
boundary of the Kingdom of Hungary. The concern for access to the Baltic Sea was addressed by the award of the lower Vistula to the new Polish state. In addition, Danzig (now Gdańsk) was internationalized in the
spirit of free international trade (Bowman 1928, 418-19). Where physiographic boundaries were no longer reliable (thanks to the alleged unnatural easterly thrust of Teutonic aggression), the Entente leaders tended
to award the mixed German-Polish speaking areas to the Poles because
the Poles had joined the Entente during the war while the Germans had
been the enemy. In some cases, especially those in which the Germans
protested impending decisions, plebiscites were employed. In the eastern
regions, Entente specialists delineated on the map the eastern boundary
of continuous Polish speech. The line later became known as the Curzon
line (Macartney and Palmer 1962, 112). Entente leaders considered how
much farther they would extend the line to form the Polish state's eastern
boundary, either to include Polish exclaves and/or to adjust the line to
conform to physiography and/or to ensure economic viability. The discussions were rendered moot as Polish and Russian Bolshevist armies
clashed in a series of wars. While not disputing the aforementioned conceptions of Polish territory, Polish leaders believed that historic boundaries were paramount in defining the Polish state's boundaries. Thus, they
saw the rightful boundaries of their state as those of the Kingdom of Poland before it was first partitioned in 1772 by Prussia, Russia, and the
Habsburgs (see figure 5.5). Thus, Polish armies drove east, deep into
lands inhabited by Belarussians, Russians, Ukrainians, and Lithuanians
and incorporated Vilnius (Wilno in Polish) and Lvov (Lwów in Polish)
(Macartney and Palmer 1962, 109).[17] Entente leaders did not approve of
the military campaigns but had no troops in the region to prevent the
moves and likewise were not going to aid the Russian Bolsheviks in
resisting. Thus, Entente leaders waited for the Russo-Polish wars to burn
themselves out, following which they accepted the boundary negotiated
by Russian and Polish leaders as the boundary decided upon at the Paris
Peace Conference. Polish leaders had failed to set the new Polish state's
boundaries along the old kingdom's boundaries in the east, but these
boundaries were clearly much farther east than Polish settlement (Macartney and Palmer 1962, 114-15).

The case of the South Slavs also illustrates the prevailing aforementioned conceptions of nationhood but in particular most poignantly underscores the role that state-centered thinking played in shaping national

identity and the creation of nation-states. South Slavic intellectuals were stimulated by Romanticism after it emerged in the early nineteenth century. Various nationalist movements subsequently arose, each inspired by the existence of shared cultural characteristics and each attempting to build differing sets of these shared cultural characteristics in order to define and construct distinct national identities. Many of these conceptions of nationhood and their subsequent nation-building projects were overlapping. The term *Yugoslav,* which means *South Slav* in the Slavic languages, most clearly illustrates the overlapping character of these identities because it does not refer to a single coherent group. Instead, it refers generally to all those movements that attempted to build national identities from the same bank of cultural characteristics and likewise to each of those specific movements striving for the same. *Illyrian* is a similar such term and movement.[18] Such terms as *Serb* and *Croat* also included conceptions that were broad and overlapping. Today, *Serb* refers to a South Slavic speaker who is an Eastern Orthodox Christian, and *Croat* identifies a South Slavic speaker who is a Roman Catholic. Though they are separate and distinct identities today, their distinctiveness is the result of nearly two centuries of nation-building—a process that itself testifies to the fluidity of identity. In the early twentieth century, and still partially true today, Serb and Croat national identities overlapped much more than they do today. For example, many Serb nationalists saw Croats and South Slavic Muslims as nothing more than Catholic Serbs and Muslim Serbs respectively. Similarly, many Croat nationalists saw Serbs and South Slavic Muslims as Orthodox Croats and Muslim Croats respectively. Leon Dominian expresses the Serbian nationalist perspective and the one that in one way or another was accepted by Entente diplomats:

We are in the presence of Serbians, disguised under various appellations, among which the most familiar are Croatians, Slavonians, Bosnians, Herzegovinians, Montenegrins, Dalmatians and Illyrians. . . .[19]

Schemes for the formation of an independent Jugoslavia were naturally thrown into sharper relief through the medium of linguistic unity.

Such a south Slavic political entity must necessarily be identified with Serbia. Its extent is admirably defined by geographical, ethnographical and linguistic lines all of which coincide, thereby pointing irrefutably to national unity. The Drave, Morava, Drina and Lim rivers, with the Adriatic Sea, encircle this genuine Serbian area. It comprises the entire system of parallel ranges which form the mountainous rearland of the Adriatic. (1917a, 338)

Dominian and other Entente diplomats most likely adopted the Serbian conception of identity because Serbia manifested itself as a state while the others had not.[20] Since the Treaty of Westphalia in 1648, international relations were tied to states, not peoples, though many states came to represent specific peoples.[21] Thus, individuals in one country, especially governmental representatives, were overwhelmingly inclined to think of other peoples in terms of their states, whether they were the dominant group or minorities within those states. Thus, the coupling of the Romantic emphasis on language as the basis of national identity with the Serbs' possessing a state led Allied diplomats to equate most South Slavic peoples with Serbian identity. This belief was reinforced by parallels drawn between the Italian peninsula and the Dinaric Ranges. Just as the Piedmont had forged the states of the Italian peninsula (e.g., Lombardy, Tuscany, Naples, Sicily, etc.) into a single, naturally defined Italian state with a new Italian identity, Serbia was dubbed the "Piedmont of the Balkans" and seen as the inevitable unifier of the South Slavs (Petrovich 1976, 1: 231-32). Under Serbian tutelage, it was believed that the other South Slavs would assimilate into a single nation called the *Yugoslavs* (or perhaps simply continue with the name *Serb*) as Lombards, Tuscans, Neapolitans, Sicilians, etc., were developing a common Italian identity under the tutelage of the Piedmont.

The state-centered thinking of Allied diplomats was reinforced by the practical aspects of the war. The Serbian state had been an ally and the country belligerently attacked by Austria-Hungary. Thus, the Entente community had sympathy for the Serbs and subsequently for their views and actions. Interestingly, people within the Entente were sympathetic to the Slovenes, Croats, and other South Slavic peoples within Austria-Hungary. However, state-centered thinking and state mechanisms worked against these peoples' desires as well. As noted, France, Great Britain, and the United States accepted Austria-Hungary as a given. As such, they sought to democratize the country rather than dismantle it. Therefore, despite the sympathies for the South Slavs within Austria-Hungary, the Entente powers directed the South Slavs to work out their differences with the other peoples of Austria-Hungary. Indeed, Harold Temperley noted that,

> The governing classes in both countries [Great Britain and France] were inclined to be favourable to Austria-Hungary, which was widely regarded as a European necessity in her character as a reconciler of many races, as conservative and normally peaceful by reason of her internal difficulties. ([1921] 1969, 4: 176)

After the collapse of Austria-Hungary and the end of the war, the Serbs continued to benefit by having a state, and the South Slavs of the former Austria-Hungary continued to be disadvantaged by state-centered thinking and state mechanisms, both on the military front and the diplomatic front. The Serbian army rushed in and secured the South Slavic lands of Austria-Hungary (Temperely [1921] 1969, 4: 194-96) while the empire's South Slavs were hampered by the double standard of state mechanisms. Though an oppressed minority with international sympathy, the South Slavs of Austria-Hungary were citizens of an enemy state and, therefore, were directed to disarm, though they were willing to take up the Entente cause. The Italians, who laid claim to much of the South Slavic lands of the Dalmatian coast, used their state's mechanisms in the international arena to ensure that the South Slavic units of Austria-Hungary disarmed. The Italian action only aided the Serbian army in securing the lands that the Serbian government desired. On the diplomatic front, the South Slavs of Austria-Hungary had formed the Yugoslav Committee, composed not of individuals with primarily Serbian views but with Croat and more broadly defined and inclusive Yugoslav views. However, because it represented the views of minorities within a state and did not officially represent a state itself, the Yugoslav Committee made few inroads in promoting its views as diplomatic doors were continually shut in its face. Even after the Yugoslav Committee worked more closely with the Serbian government and received the sanctioning of that government, Entente representatives refused to give the Yugoslav Committee official recognition at the Paris Peace Conference[22] (Temperley [1921] 1969, 4: 131, 200), instead allowing the officials of the Serbian government to represent South Slavic views and aspirations.[23] Thus, thanks to state-centered thinking and the operation of state mechanisms in the international arena, the new Yugoslav state (initially named the Kingdom of the Serbs, Croats, and Slovenes) was defined in terms of Serbian views. It was a process that later came back to haunt the Yugoslav state.

It may be tempting to point to the cases of the Czechs and the Poles to refute the aforementioned argument that state-centered thinking and state mechanisms played such a large role in defining nations and nation-states. However, if the Czechs and the Poles are the exception because they did not possess states prior to the end of the war, then they are the exception that proves the rule. As already noted, the Entente powers initially directed the Poles and Czechs to work out their problems with the governments of the states in which they resided. It was only after the collapse of Tsarist Russia and the disintegration of Austria-Hungary, both of

which occurred toward the end of the war, that Entente leaders enter-
tained the idea of creating nation-states for the Czechs and Poles. Even
then, Entente support for Czech and Polish aspirations was supplemented
by the fact that Czech and Polish military units had joined the Entente
cause, many of which had gone to France to fight alongside Entente
forces in the trenches. The South Slavs of Austria-Hungary were in a
much more complicated situation. Because many were suspicious of the
Greater Serbian idea and its claim to their lands and also the Italian
claims to their land, many preferred to stay within Austria-Hungary and
thus fought for it. Moreover, as noted, the Italian intention to annex their
lands led the Italian government to use its state mechanisms to push for
the disarmament of these Slavs. Thus, in contrast to the Czechs and
Poles, many of whom more squarely fought on the side of the Entente,
and were thus allowed by the Entente to return to their homelands to secure them, the South Slavs of Austria-Hungary were disarmed. In addition, with a nonexistent Austro-Hungarian Empire and a weak Russia—
as it was embroiled in revolution and then civil war—the Czechs and
Poles were not threatened by the encroachment of an Entente country. If
the Russian state had been stronger, its leaders could have claimed Czech
lands and even more Polish lands than it possessed at the beginning of
the war on the grounds of cultural affinity. Certainly, the Russian army
had moved into Austrian Galicia, inhabited by Poles, early in the war and
again toward the middle of the war. At the end of war, however, the Russian army was barely able to control Russia itself and thus no longer was
in position to claim Czech or Polish lands. In contrast, the South Slavs of
Austria-Hungary were confronted on the one hand by Italy, an Entente
member, and on the other by Serbia, also an Entente state, in this case
claiming their land by virtue of common ethnicity. Further indication of
the power and role that state mechanisms played in the territorial settlement is also seen in the Czechs and Poles. Both were more politically
organized and more quickly and effectively took control of governing
structures within their lands to establish statehood, which in turn was
employed to further their national projects. The Czechs quickly forged a
dominant partnership with the Slovaks and Ruthenians, and the Poles
swiftly dominated the Karzuby (Kashubians) and other similar peoples,
though these peoples had not necessarily and unconditionally adopted
Polish national identity. As also noted previously, the overwhelming
force of the Czech and Polish institutional mechanisms tore the much
smaller Duchy of Teschen, rendered its institutions ineffective, and began assimilating the duchy's people, though the people of the duchy saw
themselves as separate and distinct. Moreover, their unique identity was

acknowledged by most Entente diplomats.

Diplomats at the Paris Peace Conference delineated additional nation-states and other politically organized territories for the peoples they acknowledged. Though the discussion on this subject has been extensive so far, the point here has not been to give a detailed description of the emergence of every nation-state in Central and Eastern Europe. The first point of discussion was to emphasize that the national idea emerged victorious from the First World War and the ensuing subsequent Paris Peace Conference while one of the national idea's opponents, dynastic imperialism, suffered a major setback. On a general level, it may have been sufficient to point to a map of Europe before the war and another after the war to show the destruction of empires and the emergence of nation-states (see figures 1.1 and 5.3). However, the triumph of the national idea was much more complicated than that. First, the conceptions of nationhood were not simple, as often viewed in hindsight. Second, many of the decisions at the Paris Peace Conference demonstrate that the triumph of the national idea was not yet complete. It would take at least another world war.

The views of nationhood at the Paris Peace Conference reflected a blend of ideas from both the Enlightenment and the Romantic periods. From the Enlightenment came the notion that nations were groups of people bound together for security, in turn creating a concern for the economic viability of any state (old or newly created) and a reliance on physiographic boundaries for defense. Thus, Wilson, for example, did not initially equate his concept of self-determination with national independence. Only with the agitation of Central and Eastern Europe nationalists imbued with Romantic ideas did these two concepts merge into one, and only at the end of the war and during the ensuing peace conference. The Romantic view of nationhood also was not a simple one, based only on what can be described as a neo-Romantic reductionist view that defines nationhood primarily by common language tempered by religion and some collection of lesser important cultural characteristics. Language was seen as important, but, as noted before, it was ensconced in economics and politics, both rooted in long-held environmentally deterministic ideas that bound people to places and advocated the concept of natural territories. These Romantic views coupled with Enlightenment ones gave further credence to historic boundaries as well as perpetuating and deepening state-centered thinking.

Interestingly, the Paris Peace Conference was both a success and a disappointment for the national idea. It was a success in that nation-states emerged out of the ashes of empires. However, the aforementioned discussion concerning boundary delineation highlights the fact that nations' claims to territory were undermined by both the fear of the spread of Bolshevism and by geopolitics, both of which led to the preferential treatment of friends versus foes in territorial settlements, especially in disputed areas. Consequently, the foes, though imbued with the same views of nationhood and having similar kinds of national aspirations as the friends, had their desires dashed with the harsh punishment meted out to them. For example, the German state was not only stripped of lands not inhabited by Germans, but many lands with Germans also were taken away. The new Austrian state of German speakers was likewise denied many territories of the Austro-Hungarian Empire inhabited by German speakers. Furthermore, the self-coined term *German-Austria* was denied the representative government of that new state and so was the desire to unite with Germany (Lansing 1921, 99; Temperley [1921] 1969, 4: 479). Similarly, the new Hungarian state was denied many lands of the Austro-Hungarian Empire inhabited by Hungarians. In contrast, many of the friendly states like Poland, Romania, and the Kingdom of the Serbs, Croats, and Slovenes gained many territories not inhabited by the nations they represented. The preferential treatment is clearly seen in the spatial disjunctions that appeared on Europe's new political-national map (see figure 5.4). Thus, the war and the peace conference had not brought for them the fulfillment of the national principle, especially not in terms of territory. As Woodrow Wilson feared, resentment brewed in their hearts until Europe erupted in war again. The war was not simply revenge, but also an attempt by the losers in the First World War to fulfill their national aspirations denied them, again especially in terms of territory.

The Continuing Struggle with Established Religion and Marxism

Before moving on to the territorial aspirations of the defeated, it is worth mentioning the situation of the other opponents of the national idea. The First World War had been the manifestation of the culminating struggle with dynastic imperialism. Certainly dynastic imperialism had suffered a major defeat with the war, though a few empires persisted. However, the conflagration that ignited from the conflict between the national idea and imperialism tends to overshadow the conflict with established religion and Marxism—including the descendants of Marxism, such as Marxist-Leninism. In many ways, established religion lost the struggle against the national idea with a whimper rather than with a bang. People continued to be religious, but nationhood crept to the position of primacy in the hierarchy of identity, leaving religious identity circumscribed within national identity containers. The First World War had accelerated the last stages of this process. As the intensity of fervent nationalism increasingly focused attention on the struggle between national identities (e.g., French against German, and Austrians against Serbs), little concern was expressed for the consequences of Christians taking up arms against Christians, whether it was Protestants against Protestants, Roman Catholics against Roman Catholics, or Eastern Orthodox against Eastern Orthodox, as such concerns had been expressed only a few decades earlier. Established religion's acquiescence to the national idea and modern statehood is seen in 1929 when the Vatican finally recognized the Italian state in the Lateran Treaty and Concordat and resigned itself to the enclave of Vatican City (Greer and Lewis 1997, 565), one of the smallest states in the world.

The conflict between the national idea and Marxism was much more complicated. Marxism, as rearticulated through the ideas of Lenin and the other Russian Bolsheviks, seemed to have achieved its own victory as the first socialist/communist state emerged out of the ruins of Tsarist Russia. In 1923, the Russian Socialist Federated Republic (R.S.F.R.) merged with the Ukrainian, Belorussian, and Azerbaijani Soviet republics to form the Union of Soviet Socialist Republics (U.S.S.R.) (Ergang, 1954, 448). This state, founded on Marxist-Leninist ideas, preached world revolution and steadily expanded over subsequent years, growing to eleven republics by 1936. Occupying as much if not more of the earth's surface as the new nation-states of Europe and expanding, communism seemed to be a wave overtaking the surging tide of nationalism.

Despite the explosive emergence of the Marxist ideal, Marxist-Leninism and its successor Stalinism failed to appreciate how much the national idea had permeated thinking, including their own. Thus, despite believing that nationhood was a fabrication of the uneven development of capitalism that would fade away when socialism created an equitable reality, the Russian Bolsheviks came to accept the idea of nation. Lenin, for example, believed that the Soviet state should be "national in form and socialist in content" (Schöpflin 1991, 7). Stalin went on to compose a definition of nation similar to those constructed by nationalists themselves:

A nation is an historically evolved, stable community of people arising on the basis of a community of language, territory, economic life, and psychological makeup as manifested in a community of culture. (quoted in Wixman 1980, 22)

Furthermore, as Ronald Wixman notes, Soviet scholars went on to develop the general idea of the *socialist nation*, and specifically the concept
of the *Soviet people*, "said to be the basis for the future monolingual,
mono-cultural, new Soviet society" (1980, 26). The language and culture
for the new Soviet nation were never defined, but the governmental policies indicated that the new Soviet nation had the same characteristics as
the Russian nation. The old national policies of *Russification* had not
died but simply found new expression (Wixman 1980, 26-43). Thus, despite the rise of socialist states, socialist governments continued to promote the national idea. In time, failed economic policies eventually
would contribute greatly to the demise of socialist states in Europe at the
end of the twentieth century, but the continued promotion of the national
principle meant that these socialist states would unravel along nationalist
lines.

Unfulfilled and Fervent Nationalism

As established religions resigned themselves to the national paradigm
and socialists and communists continued to rail against it while persisting
in framing their rhetoric and actions according to nationalist conceptions
despite the gloss of their new terminology, the losing nations of the First
World War were dissatisfied because their nationalist aspirations were
not fulfilled at the Paris Peace Conference. Embitterment soon followed,
and from it nationalism intensified ·and new extreme forms such as fascism developed.[24] Fascist movements were a curious blend of nationalism and socialism (e.g., National Socialism [or Nazism]), otherwise opposing ideologies, but, as noted, socialists frequently framed their
thinking and rhetoric along nationalist lines. Until the end of the First
World War, the national idea existed side by side with dynastic imperialism and established religion. However, with many monarchies destroyed,
others highly ineffective, and established religion no longer in charge of
the social institutions that it once operated, few entities—especially democracy, which develops slowly—could solve the economic problems
caused by the war. With disastrous economies undermining governmental effectiveness, in turn promoting political chaos, a blending of ideologies occurred in response to both the economic and political troubles.
Socialism focused heavily on economics. Anticapitalist in its origins,
socialism argued that the means of economic production should be taken
out of the hands of individual capitalists, who were exploiting the
masses, and placed under the collective ownership of the people. Nation-

alism had been more politically oriented in that it believed that a people should govern itself rather than be ruled by a privileged few or by foreign rulers. Though socialism and nationalism were contradictory in many ways, the socialist belief that a people should own the means of economic production fit well with the nationalist belief that a people should govern itself. Nationalism, however, was not necessarily anti-capitalist as it had developed in tandem with capitalism, perhaps even as an outgrowth of capitalism, as suggested in chapter 4. Thus when nationalism merged with socialism, capitalism was accepted though capitalists within society had to pursue their trades in the interests of their nations, at least nominally if not literally. This expected alignment of national and capitalist interests was a negligible restriction to many capitalists who feared pure socialism, which advocated public ownership of all businesses and thus would have stripped capitalists of their wealth. Finding fascism preferable to socialism and also to democracy, which was feeble at the time and struggling to protect the free marketplace, many industrial capitalists bankrolled aspiring fascist leaders, in turn helping them to seize political power.

Fascism also came along at a time when the development of new technologies and the growth of bureaucracies reached a level that allowed modern state mechanisms to involve themselves in the daily lives of individuals to a greater degree than ever before. With their new ideology, fascist leaders were able to take full control of the economic and political lives of their nations from the broad societal level down to the individual. It ushered in the era of totalitarianism, and was adopted not only by fascist regimes but by the new socialist government in the Soviet Union, especially under Joseph Stalin. Though very intrusive in people's lives, fascism was welcomed by many who saw it as a preferable alternative to the economic and political chaos of the postwar years. Fascism further ingratiated itself with people by glorifying and extolling national virtues while blaming foreigners for national problems. It built on Romanticism, for example, with its heavy emphasis on such phrases as "national awakening." The Nazis especially were fond of the phrase "*Deutschland erwacht*" ("Germany awakens"). Frequently, however, fascism pushed Romantic ideas to their extreme. The state was gloried and treated as the embodiment of the nation to a degree not seen before. Nazism in particular went yet a step further than some of the other fascist movements by also rooting itself in scientific ideas concerning race, most notably eugenics, itself a nineteenth-century pursuit like Romanticism but having many of its originators and strong proponents in the United States (Kühl 2002). Fascism's exhibition of excessive nationalist pride played especially well among the humiliated nations of the war, but it was also popular in some of the victorious countries like Italy where the stresses of the war caused much hardship and the people were dissatisfied with many of the outcomes of the war, such as the limited territorial gains, despite victory.

Adolf Hitler, of course the preeminent fascist leader in Germany, catapulted to power by railing against the injustices of the war guilt and war reparations. Just as importantly, he rose to power by fanning irredentism, inciting outrage among many Germans at the loss of German territories. Reincorporating lost German territories, adding other German-settled lands, and settling lands with Germans seen rightfully to become German lands became the centerpiece of Hitler's regime and the cause of another world war.

A frequently overlooked figure connected to Hitler was the geographer Karl Haushofer (1869-1946). Haushofer played a role in turning geographical concepts and theories into governmental practice. He had read Friedrich Ratzel's Organic State Theory, and particularly noted the idea of *lebensraum*. He was well aware of Halford J. MacKinder's Heartland Theory. Furthermore, he had read the works of the Swedish political scientist Rudolf Kjellén (1864-1922), who also had read Ratzel's Organic State Theory but unlike Ratzel saw the state as literally a biological organism. Rudolf Kjellén also coined such terms as *geopolitics* and *autarky*. Haushofer folded many of the ideas of these men into his own in what became known as the school of *Geopolitik*. He was bitter about Germany's loss in the war (Haushofer and Trampler 1931) and began lecturing on the principles of geography at the University of Munich beginning in 1919 in the hopes of helping Germans understand their place in the world. In 1924, Haushofer founded the academic journal *Zeitschrift für Geopolitik*, published by a National Socialist (i.e., Kurt Vorwinckel) (Herb 1997, 89), also publisher of many of Haushofer's other written works (1927, 1937, 1939).

One of Haushofer's students, Rudolf Hess, introduced him to Adolf Hitler (David Murphy 1997, 107). He visited Hitler several times while Hitler was incarcerated in the Landsberg fortress following the famous Beer Hall Putsch in 1923. Hitler was writing *Mein Kampf* at the time, and many ideas similar to Haushofer's are seen in the work. For example, Hitler's use of Ratzel's term *lebensraum* probably came to Hitler via Haushofer. Following Hitler's rise to power in the 1930s, Haushofer's position was elevated and his school of geopolitics received great support from the Nazis. Haushofer's influence on Nazi thinking is highly debatable, but it is clear that Haushofer and his followers helped the Nazi war effort. At the same time, it is possible that Haushofer's influence on the Nazis is exaggerated. Certainly Haushofer had many disagreements with the Nazis. Inspired by MacKinder's Heartland Theory, Haushofer saw a close relationship with Russia as crucial for Germany and became extremely troubled after Hitler ordered the invasion of the Soviet Union in 1941. Similarly, Haushofer likely placed more emphasis on environmental determinism than race and thus saw the concept of *lebensraum* somewhat differently, namely, that Germans were only destined to settle certain lands rather than any lands they could conquer, as advocated by the more racially obsessed Nazis. In fact, Haushofer held the Japanese in high regard and thought they were destined by *lebensraum* to settle certain lands that the Germans were not (1931). He may have been instrumental in forging the German-Japanese alliance, but the Nazis pursued the alliance as strategy rather than out of admiration. The argument that Karl Haushofer had limited influence on the Nazis gathers more strength over the course of the Nazi era. A turning point, as suggested, was Hitler's decision to invade the Soviet Union in 1941. Until about then, Haushofer praised Nazi expansionist policies as in line with his geographic theories. Afterwards, however, Haushofer began to rapidly fade from the public scene—where he had a high profile—especially after Rudolf Hess, Hitler's deputy führer but also Haushofer's former student, made his mysterious trip to Great Britain to supposedly negotiate an armistice or ceasefire of some sort (David Murphy 1997, 244-45). Furthermore, after Karl Haushofer's son, Albrecht—also a geographer—was linked to the assassination attempt on Hitler's life in July 1944, Albrecht was sent to prison and Karl was sent to Dachau concentration camp. Albrecht did not survive his experience, but Karl did. Following acquittal at the Nuremberg War Crimes Tribunal, Karl Haushofer and his wife committed suicide.

Though Karl Haushofer and many other German geographers had their differences with the Nazis, their shared ideas illustrate that Nazi ideas, though extreme, were outgrowths of broader environmentally deterministic views of nations and territories and the connections linking the two. Nazi views on race too were not unique but a product of the more general concept of race as it emerged in the late eighteenth century and grew in the nineteenth century with the eventual development of such sciences as eugenics. Most significantly, these ideas were elements of the broader and more mainstream concept of *nation* as it manifested itself in the early twentieth century. Thus, though the Nazis were extreme in their beliefs, their ideas were founded in familiar concepts that resonated with people, not only with Germans, but with other peoples as well. The "N" in Nazi represented "national," and the Nazis appealed to national sentiments to rise to power and then fuel their conquest.

Outside of Germany, Hitler's nationalistic rhetoric, which included talk of self-determination, played well in Central and Eastern Europe with both the defeated nations of the First World War and those who were disappointed with their experience of victory. After annexing Austria in the name of self-determination, Hitler then advanced his plan to incorporate additional German lands by soliciting help from the defeated and disappointed with opportunities to annex their lost national lands. Focusing first on Czechoslovakia, Hitler easily persuaded the Poles and Hungarians to advance claims against Polish- and Hungarian-occupied lands of Czechoslovakia in tandem with his claims to the German-inhabited Sudetenland (Macartney and Palmer 1962, 386-91). Hitler probably could have gained the Sudetenland on his own, but his luring the Poles and Hungarians into alliance meant that the collective claims pressed by all three would have likely forced the collapse of Czechoslovakia, in turn allowing Hitler the opportunity to annex all of Bohemia and Moravia—crownlands of the former Austrian Habsburgs. Moreover, Poland and Hungary would have been brought into Hitler's political alliances if the plan worked. The plan failed as initially conceived, but with the help of Mussolini, the Munich Conference (September 29, 1938) was held and Germany gained the Sudetenland. A few days later, Polish troops occupied the lands they claimed, the portion of the duchy of Teschen which they claimed at the Paris Peace Conference in 1919 but were not awarded. The Hungarian claims took longer to obtain because Czech representatives felt that they could resist as their army was stronger than Hungary's. With continued support from Hitler, Mussolini, and Polish leaders, the Czechs acquiesced to Hungarian demands for southern Slovakia. With continued pressure from Hitler on the Czechs, Slovakia and Ruthenia achieved autonomy and moved toward independence. Hitler's efforts garnered lands that German, Polish, and Hungarian nationalists all deemed to be theirs, and the Slovaks, disappointed by their relationship with the Czechs within Czechoslovakia, gained more control over their lands.

The Second World War

Hitler then used the tactic to gain what he saw as the rightfully German lands of Poland by negotiating a deal with the Soviets—laid out in the Molotov-Ribbentrop Non-Aggression Pact—which gave the Russians the opportunity to attain the lands they thought rightfully theirs. These lands included eastern Poland, Finland, the Baltic states, and Bessarabia (Macartney and Palmer 1962, 409). Though Czechoslovakia had been dismantled solely by diplomatic negotiation, the negotiated plans to divide Poland were put into effect by military invasion on September 1, 1939. The joint Nazi-Soviet attack on Poland ignited the Second World War as the British and French governments declared war on Germany a couple of days later. The British and French, however, only launched a blockade instead of an attack. It was a course of action that allowed Hitler to contemplate his response to the threat from the west while continuing to pursue his strategy in the east. In the spring, Hitler's armies conquered Denmark and Norway, followed by the Netherlands, Belgium, Luxembourg, and then France in June. With the threat from the west neutralized, Hitler could turn his attentions back to the east and continue with his strategy of claiming German *lebensraum* and using territories desired by nations of Central and East Europeans as incentives to achieve this goal.

In the meantime, Stalin decided to finally take Bessarabia from Romania and also Bukovina, the historic crownland of the Austrians. At the same time, the Bulgarians took the opportunity to claim the southern Dobrudja, and the Hungarians received northern Transylvania (Macartney and Palmer 1962, 425-27). With the Russians apparently reinvigorating their century-old drive toward the Holy Land via the Balkans and having occupied a former Austrian crownland, Hitler felt that German *lebensraum* was being transgressed. In a speech in early 1940, Hitler stated that "We Germans lay no claim to world domination. We only ask to be left alone in our own living space. But, as far as this living space is concerned, we permit no interference" (quoted in Fifield and Pearcy 1944, 63). Generally distrustful of the Russian Bolsheviks, who were now within German *lebensraum* as the Nazis saw it, Hitler began making plans to invade the Soviet Union (Macartney and Palmer 1962, 427-28).

Hitler's ally Mussolini, however, hampered Hitler's plans as he was obsessed with gaining lands Italian nationalists thought rightfully theirs in Greece and Yugoslavia. Without Hitler's consent, eliciting help from the Bulgarians by offering them the opportunity to advance their irredentist claims against Greece, the Italian military attacked Greece. However, Mussolini's army was unable to fully subdue Greece, and help from the Germans seemed necessary. Concerned that Mussolini would launch a military campaign against Yugoslavia and that the Hungarians, Romanians, and Bulgarians would join because they were looking to claim lands from Yugoslavia they saw as rightfully theirs, Hitler went to great pains to counter the possibility by forging a series of agreements—mostly non-aggression pacts—in order to maintain peace in the Balkans (Macartney and Palmer 1962, 434-47). He even went so far as to suggest to the Yugoslavs that they could extend their boundaries down to Salonica (Thessaloníki), appeasing the irredentist claims of Serb nationalists. Hitler seemed successful, and his timetable for the invasion of the Soviet Union remained intact. Then Yugoslav public dissatisfaction with the compromises led to the overthrow of the king in Yugoslavia. The new regime, though more oriented to the West, did not abrogate the agreements Hitler arranged. However, loud street demonstrations in favor of Great Britain and the United States, coupled with rumors that the Russians had helped to engineer the coup, incensed Hitler. No longer holding the Italians, Hungarians, Romanians, and Bulgarians back from asserting their territorial claims against the Yugoslavs, Hitler reversed direction and essentially demanded that they invade with an invitation for them to "satisfy [their] territorial ambitions" (Macartney and Palmer 1962, 442). This strategy of playing to territorial claims of nationalist aspirations, however, was somewhat of a two-edged sword. Though it could be used to provoke an attack, the directions of attack on such grounds were limited to specific territories defined by irredentist claims. Thus, the Italians took the coastal areas and allowed their Albanian provinces—annexed before the war—to move into Kosovo. The Bulgarians occupied Macedonia, and the Hungarians claimed only small territories along the fringes of their state's boundaries, which had previously been within their former kingdom. These claims included the Banat, which was the only territory the Romanians desired. Hitler himself only desired for Germany the Slovene lands, former crownlands of the Austrian Habsburgs. Having been dissatisfied with their relationship with the Serbs in the Yugoslav state, the Croats were allowed to declare an independent, fascist state under the tutelage of Italy. However, no nation desired the Serbian heartland (other than the Serbs, of course) or Montenegro, and it seemed absurd to Hitler, who saw the Hungarians and Romanians preparing to fight over the Banat when the neighboring Serbian heartland was much larger and offered much more. Outraged, Hitler was forced to send additional German troops to take the Serbian heartland, Montenegro, and likewise the Banat. At the same time, German troops were dispatched to Greece, to finish what the Italian military could not do. Hitler then awarded to the Bulgarians the lands they claimed in eastern Macedonia and western Thrace and allowed Italy to annex the Ionian Islands. In the end, these military campaigns in the Balkans delayed Hitler's invasion plans for the Soviet Union.

By the end of April 1941, the political map of Europe was turned inside out as it now reflected the territorial aspirations of the defeated and disappointed at the end of the First World War rather than a map of the victorious (see figure 5.6). The Poles, Czechs, Estonians, Latvians, and Lithuanians had lost their states completely while the Serbs and Greeks found their states occupied by foreign nations. The Romanians had fared better, having lost mostly what they had gained at the Paris Peace Conference in 1919 but keeping some of the awards of the time such as the southern part of Transylvania. The Slovaks and Croats, disappointed by their experience with being placed in states with the Czechs and Serbs respectively, achieved their independence. The Germans, Hungarians, and Bulgarians profited the most by having regained most of their former lands. The Russians too reclaimed much of their former empire though now doing so as Soviets, nominally antinationalist in perspective. The role of the great powers was also reversed. Germany and the Soviet Union were now dominant, 'and the United Kingdom and France were in the prone positions.

It is important to note that Hitler's success until this point was not just the matter of German military technological superiority, the willingness of Hitler to abrogate any agreement as if it were just a piece of paper, or the political blunders of British and French leaders. Certainly these factors were important, but it is also necessary to recognize that Hitler played to the national aspirations, specifically territorial claims, of other European peoples. One look at the political map of Hitler's Europe illustrates this point (see figure 5.6). Interestingly, Hitler abandoned this strategy after he ordered the invasion of the Soviet Union with Operation Barbarossa in June 1941 (Clark [1965] 1985). He only invited the Finns and the Romanians to advance their territorial claims against the Soviet Union as he had solicited other nations against an intended target. But even in these cases, their claims were highly limited to negligible percentages of the Soviet Union's territory. Hitler had the opportunity to employ his strategy by offering the Baltic peoples, the Belarussians, and the Ukrainians their own independent states. Indeed, the Ukrainians suffered greatly under Stalin's rule, most notably under an engineered famine in the early 1930s that starved one to three million Ukrainians to death. With Hitler having satisfied nationalist aspirations in East Central Europe, most notably having given autonomy to the Ruthenians—the close ethnic kin of the Ukrainians—many Ukrainians welcomed German troops into their lands (Milner-Gulland and Dejevsky 1991, 173-75); many even threw roses at the feet of German soldiers. Very dissatisfied with Russian rule, many certainly expected that they would receive their

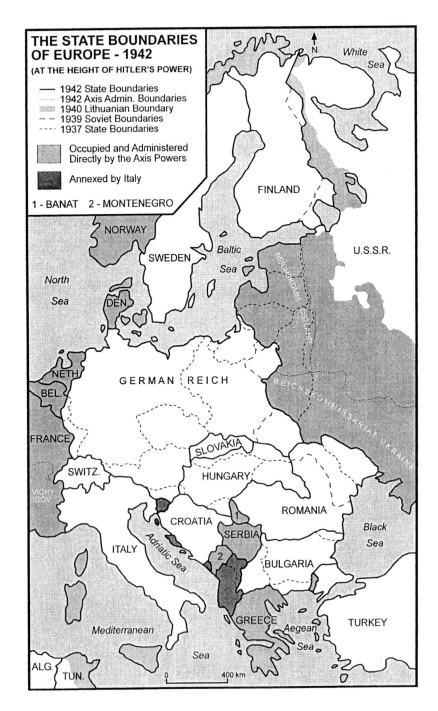

THE STATE BOUNDARIES OF EUROPE - 1942
(AT THE HEIGHT OF HITLER'S POWER)

— 1942 State Boundaries
····· 1942 Axis Admin. Boundaries
▓▓▓ 1940 Lithuanian Boundary
– – 1939 Soviet Boundaries
- - - 1937 State Boundaries

▒ Occupied and Administered
Directly by the Axis Powers

■ Annexed by Italy

1 - BANAT   2 - MONTENEGRO

White Sea

FINLAND

NORWAY

SWEDEN

Baltic Sea

U.S.S.R.

North Sea

DEN.

NETH.

BEL.

GERMAN REICH

REICHSKOMMISSARIAT OSTLAND

REICHSKOMMISSARIAT UKRAINE

FRANCE

SLOVAKIA

SWITZ.

HUNGARY

VICHY GOV

ITALY

Adriatic Sea

CROATIA

SERBIA

1

2

ROMANIA

Black Sea

BULGARIA

GREECE

Aegean Sea

TURKEY

Mediterranean Sea

ALG.

TUN.

0   400 km

Figure 5.6 Hitler's Europe

own nation-states, or quasi nation-states, as did the Slovaks and Croats following their disappointment with Czech and Serbian rule respectively. Curiously, Hitler did not pursue this course. Instead, beyond eastern Karelia, which the Finns claimed, and Bessarabia, northern Bukovina, and Transnistria, which the Romanians claimed, Hitler organized the bulk of conquered Soviet territory into two administrative districts: Reichskommissariat Ostland and Reichskommissariat Ukraine (see figure 5.6). He then persecuted, condemned, and even began exterminating the inhabitants. Certainly, his actions conformed to his racial ideology, but his racial beliefs existed when he fulfilled the nationalist territorial aspirations in the Balkans. Many of these people were Slavs like the Belarussians and Ukrainians whom he now treated so harshly. Perhaps Hitler had a particular hatred for the Russians, whom he saw as a real menace; and typically racist, he saw little difference between the Belarussians and Ukrainians who lived in the same state as the Russians. Perhaps Hitler had been so successful in conquering countries until that point that he no longer saw it necessary to implement every detail of his previous strategy, in this case granting national independence to a minority to overcome an enemy. Conceivably, Hitler was just becoming more and more irrational as time went on. These possibilities are left to the speculations of history. What is clear, however, is that by abandoning the practice of granting minorities greater control over their territory, Hitler's war effort suffered several consequences. First by denying nationalist aspirations and persecuting, Hitler turned these sympathetic and hopeful people into an enemy whom he then had to fight as organized guerilla bands behind his lines. Second, as the front moved farther and farther east, he had not cultivated new allies to secure the newly conquered territories or to help protect German troops spearheading onwards. Moreover, minorities across the lines, learning of Nazi persecution, had no incentive to welcome the German advance into their lands as Ukrainians and others initially had. It meant that Hitler had to rely on old allies such as the Italians, Hungarians, and Romanians, who became less and less willing to support German troops the farther they ventured from their own homelands (Palmer 1970, 259-62). Indeed, as the front pushed farther east, the promise of territorial rewards in the Steppe became meaningless to these peoples. Thus, Hitler had to coerce support by threatening to take away lands previously awarded. On the other hand, the Ukrainians most likely would have been willing to protect the lines which lay near their boundaries if they had been given independence and treated better. The Italians, Hungarians, and Romanians, being so far from home, were unenthusiastic and provided unreliable support to German troops, especially to the

German flank at Stalingrad (Beevor 1998, 81-83, 181-84, 322, 355, 365; Clark [1965] 1985, 269). Indeed, Stalingrad was the high water mark of Nazi expansionism. Following the German defeat in the city in January 1943, German forces were rolled back over the next two years, and a new territorial order emerged in Europe.

The New Peace after the Second World War

Though Hitler was defeated, the national idea only reinforced its grip on human thinking and bound itself more tightly to the modern state and its mechanisms. Great Britain, France, and the Netherlands were victorious in the war, but war effort had seriously damaged their economies and hence their ability to maintain their rule over their colonial possessions abroad. With the national idea having spread to their subject peoples, the British, French, and Dutch were in no position to suppress rising national aspirations for independent nation-states. Beginning in the late 1940s and proceeding through the 1950s and 1960s, the British and French governments voluntarily gave up most of their colonial possessions. Having remained neutral during the war, Portugal was not devastated like the others, but it too could not hold back the rising tide of nationalism within its colonies and likewise began relinquishing its control over them. Thus, the remaining European empires crumbled before another surge of nationalism with little resistance to offer. Dynastic imperialism was barely a residue with its last vestiges existing as little more than anachronistic relics performing ceremonial and symbolic roles for the modern nation-state.

Noteworthy, the new nation-states were the colonial territories that the British and French had created. They were drawn during European imperial competition with the intent of extracting natural resources and with little regard to the peoples who lived within them. Indeed, most contained highly multiethnic/multitribal populations, many of whom were divided among differing colonial possessions. Yet, the colonial possession functioned as quasi states, meaning that they were functional regions comprised of pathways of spatial interaction that brought these heterogeneous peoples together in common political, economic, and educational systems. In time, the peoples of each of these spatial units developed a layer of identity tied to and circumscribed within these geographic units. Thus, when the national idea was encountered and accepted, the general nationalist aspiration was to free these units rather than to delineate a territory from scratch. As a result, few calls have been advanced to change the colonial boundaries, though they bear little to no resemblance to the political geographies that existed prior to the arrival of Europeans. The European practice of marrying the national idea to state territories spread rapidly.

Hitler's defeat also did little to mitigate the competing nationalists' claims to territory within Europe. Obviously, it was not possible to draw boundary lines that would satisfy all nationalists' aspirations. That had been the strategy of the Paris Peace Conference in 1919, and clearly it failed. Rather than reopen the boundary issue, it was decided by the Western Allies that the boundaries before the war would be reconstructed and no further revisions would be accepted. Furthermore, if ethnic exclaves were used as excuses to extend boundaries, as Hitler had done, then attainment of peace following the Second World War would be to move ethnic groups to their titular states. Thus, over thirteen million Germans, one-and-a-half to two million Poles, several hundred thousand Hungarians, and tens of thousands of other groups were forcibly moved (De Zayas 1988; Kosiński 1969; Mellor 1975, 120-23; Reardon 1998; Rugg 1985, 258; Schechtmann 1963). By 1960, the collective number of minorities in Eastern European countries had decreased from thirty-four million to seven million, from 36 percent of the aggregate population to 7 percent. The idea was to remove, or at least minimize, the argument for extending boundaries in the name of self-determination. Alexander Murphy points out that after the Second World War, the only legitimate justification for territorial claims rested in the argument that a "territory itself had been wrongfully seized" (1990, 532). Long gone were the days that a state leader or government could claim a territory on economic or strategic grounds, though these reasons may underlie a historical claim; even so, such a claim would have to be couched within and limited to a historical claim. The ethnic/national argument, though recent in human history and state relations, also was not acceptable outside the parameters of a historical argument. The historic argument created an interesting duality. First, it reinforced centuries-long ideas concerning the nature of territories where boundaries still lay along physiographic features. Second, it brought state-centered thinking to a new height as it treated the postwar political map as a given, placing it outside the bounds of consideration as a contributor to state and/or national conflicts and likewise removing its alteration as a solution to those conflicts.

The idea to reconstruct the boundaries as they were before the Second World War and then not revise them again witnessed one major exception. Stalin altered the boundaries of the Soviet Union, which likewise changed the boundaries of Finland, the Baltic states, Poland,

Czechoslovakia, and Romania (see figure 5.7). Stalin was a communist, supposedly not believing in the national idea and instead believing that humanity was fundamentally divided into social classes. Interestingly, despite these communist ideals, Stalin redrew the Soviet Union's boundaries not according to how they were after the rise of Bolshevism in Russia, but how they were for the Russian Empire prior to the rise of Bolshevism.[25] Only after doing so did he accept the principle that boundaries should not be redrawn.

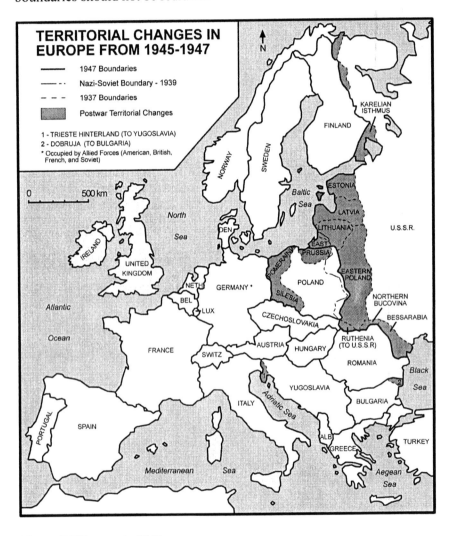

Figure 5.7 Europe in 1947

The claim can be made that the Soviet Union's governments did not allow expressions of nationalism. In many ways, such was the case. Certainly, the government in Moscow was unsympathetic to nationalist claims and did not allow nationalist conflicts to emerge. However, putting a lid on nationalism did not preclude the Soviet government from fanning the flames of nationalism at the same time, if inadvertently. The Soviet government was dominated by Russians who continually pursued Russification policies, both within the Soviet state (Wixman 1981 and 1984) and within satellite states within Eastern Europe. The policies were aimed at creating a Soviet society composed of Soviet men and women, but, lacking obvious details of such a society, officials—who were mostly Russian—fell back on Russian norms and national characteristics to construct their ideal Soviet society. Though the non-Russian peoples were not allowed to express their own nationalisms openly, Russification policies agitated the nationalisms of these peoples, though the intent of communist practice was to dilute and completely dissolve any sense of national identity. So while the Soviet authorities kept one foot firmly on the brakes of nationalism, their other foot pushed the accelerator of nationalism to the floor. Much like a race car in the same situation, it appeared to be motionless until the one foot came off the brake. Indeed, when the Soviet government showed obvious signs of weakening with the opening of the Berlin Wall in 1989, the foot on the brake fell way, allowing the race car of nationalism to surge ahead once again. The satellite nation-states asserted their independence, and before long the Soviet Union itself disintegrated.

Significantly, though the U.S. government had not accepted the forceful incorporation of the Baltic states after the Second World War, it did not support the attempts of Lithuanian leaders to gain independence for their republic through 1990 and most of 1991 on the grounds that Lithuanian independence was a decision for the Soviet people to make.[26] The U.S. government extended its recognition to Lithuania only after the Soviet Union was clearly disintegrating in the fall of 1991, after other states had extended their recognition and other Soviet republics began treating Lithuania as an independent state. Ironically, state-centered thinking had done as much to construct the idea of a Soviet people within the minds of people outside the Soviet Union as Soviet authorities had been able to do within the minds of its own citizens. Despite the lack of support from the outside world, the Lithuanians and other peoples pushed for and achieved national independence.

It is noteworthy that despite there being more than one hundred differing peoples within the Soviet Union, the Soviet state broke apart along its republics' boundaries. State-centered thinking certainly was not dead as the Soviet state's provincial boundaries were used for the boundaries of the new states that emerged in its place. Such was also true with further conflict in East Central Europe. Czechoslovakia broke along its two main constituent parts, leaving separate and independent Czech and Slovak republics. When conflict arose in Yugoslavia, the initial response of the U.S. government and many other Western governments was to express their support for the territorial integrity of Yugoslavia while arguing for the need for demographic reforms to bring about peace. Again, the U.S. and other Western governments recognized the seceding republics only after the republics had essentially gained independence on their own. When recognition was given, the U.S. and Western governments insisted that Yugoslavia disintegrate along the lines of its republics.[27] Even in Bosnia-Herzegovina, where conflict brought about the greatest bloodshed since the Second World War, the United States and other governments worked to preserve the territorial integrity of Bosnia-Herzegovina, finally doing so with the Dayton Peace Accord.

As we move into the twenty-first century, much attention is given to globalization and the European Union, both of which transcend and challenge the national idea. Yet while these two forces erode the national idea, they likewise agitate it. Indeed, the national idea threatens the success of the European Union. More importantly, despite the rise of new forces that undermine nationalism, Europe has more nation-states than ever with a dozen created or re-created in Eastern Europe in the last fifteen years and fervent nationalist-separatist movements showing increased intensity in Western Europe. Clearly, the national idea is not dead. However, the relationship between nations and their territories is still underappreciated.

Notes

1. Though Charles Darwin is generally thought of as a biologist, it is interesting to note that he was elected to the Fellowship of the Royal Geographical Society, publishing some of his works in that society's journal (Livingstone 1992, 180).

2. This practice continued to gain momentum in the early twentieth century. One of the more notable examples comes from *National Geographic* magazine. The December 1918 issue is titled "The Races of Europe." The entire issue is devoted to the subject, and a special map supplement is included. The map, also titled "The Races of Europe," seems to depict languages.

3. Haeckel's statement that "politics is applied biology" indicates the close connection of natural and social scientific thinking. Wagner was impressed by Darwin's theory of evolutionary biology but believed that Darwin underappreciated the role of geographic isolation, migration, and the general principles of diffusion and space.

4 Interestingly, both Davis and Ratzel adapted their theories of the "geographical cycle" and Organic State Theory to Darwin's ideas of evolutionary biology by adding the possibility of "rejuvenation."

5. This reasoning follows the argument that if necessity is the mother of invention then abundance is the mother of laziness—that is, the abundance of a tropical paradise.

6. This statement applies whether one is a modernist, a primordialist, or anywhere between because—as already noted—environmental determinism has been a pervasive way of thinking since the beginning of recorded history.

7. The Romantic nationalist belief that the past is all important to identity was also seen as un-Christian because Christians should focus on obtaining salvation. Such a view is also illustrated by Inge as he said that "Events in the past may be roughly divided into those which probably never happened and those which do not matter" (http://www.quotationspage.com/quotes/William_Ralph_Inge/).

8. The Austrians also promoted the Uniate Church in Galicia, but that effort was against the Russian Empire rather than the Ottoman Empire in that it promoted a Ukrainian identity separate from the Russian one.

9. Only a few days before, the British leader echoed the same view: "The break-up of Austria-Hungary is no part of our war-aims, [and that, if genuine self-government on democratic principles were given to nationalities,] Austria-Hungary would become a Power whose strength would conduce to the permanent peace and freedom of Europe" (Tempereley [1921] 1969, 4: 176).

10. The attempt of the Austrian emperor to propose a federal plan to save the empire so late in the war seems pathetically futile. Yet it was not the first attempt of the Habsburgs to negotiate a reconstruction of the empire. Indeed, the Habsburgs attempted to broker agreements throughout almost the entire war. However, as imperial leaders, they could not break free of imperialist thinking in their attempt to satisfy the growing nationalist aspirations within their realm, though they were willing to fan nationalism to further their own imperialist goals when it suited them. More poignantly, though ethnically German, the Habsburgs could not even reconcile themselves with the German nationalists within their realm. For example, when the details of secret negotiations that had taken place between the French and the emperor in 1917 were revealed, the German nationalists turned their backs on the emperor because, "They [the Habsburgs] had gone far to renounce their own distinct German nationalism and had forgone German national re-union in favour of the autonomous Austrian State, trusting that in reality they remained in exclusive control of the State. Here in the middle of a war which was to have led to a consolidation of the German *Mittel-Europa*, they found the Habsburgs, who had often done lip-

service to the German idea and the German Alliance, conducting a purely dynastic policy of their own. . . . It was with the cold eyes of estrangement that the German Nationalists watched henceforth the fate of the Habsburg dynasty" (Temperley [1921] 1969, 4: 84).

Temperley previously explained the character of the "Austrian State" as conceived by the Habsburgs themselves:

"The idea of the Austrian State" (*die österreichische Staatsidee*) was in recent years habitually in the mouth of those who defended Austria-Hungary's existence. The concrete meaning of the term was never explained; in fact, it had none which its votaries would have cared to explain, and the Austrian State, to which it primarily referred as being conterminous with the Habsburg dominions, did not exist except in reminiscences of the past and pious wishes for the future. The Habsburg Monarchy consisted of two separate, sovereign States, Austria and Hungary, with Bosnia-Herzegovina held by them in common. Since 1867, Austria was that which remained of the amorphous mass of the Habsburg possessions, the "home-farm" of the dynasty, after national States had arisen in Germany, Italy and, in certain aspects, also in Hungary; for nearly fifty years (until 1916) this residuum, which in proportion to its size displayed more frontier and less coherence than any other State in Europe, went officially by the colourless designation of "the Kingdoms and Provinces represented in the Reichsrat". The name of Austria, currently given to them, was kept in reserve in the hope that some day it might once more cover all the dominions of the Habsburgs, *des Hauses Oesterreich.* The Austria of 1867 was regarded by the Habsburgs as but a phase in the history of their dynastic power, their *Hausmacht*; for them there was nothing final about it, indeed they shunned finality—principles when arranged suggest or imply limitation. Every piece of driftwood carried to their shore was to them a promising sprig which might yet grow into a crown. Their outlying western possessions were gone, their age-long dreams of dominion over Germany and Italy were dead; their face was now to the east. Through Galicia and Dalmatia, Austria's fantastically shaped body, enveloping the massive block of Hungary, stretched out its arms towards Poland, the Ukraine, Rumania, and Serbia, which all found their place in the war-dreams and schemings of the Habsburg dynasty. The Habsburgs were the one dynasty which had never linked up its fate with that of any single nation; they had a capital and a territorial base, but no nationality; they had developed schemes territorially coherent, though devoid of all national idea. Their instincts were purely proprietary, the one meaning of an Austrian State to them was that they possessed it; to the outside world, that it existed. For the few, and mostly interested, exponents of an Austrian State, its existence was an aim in itself; and this was the pivot of all that there was in the alleged Austrian *Staatsidee.* But it was by no means this exceedingly frail basis which sustained Austria-Hungary's continued existence. (Temperley [1921] 1969, 4: 58-59)

Temperley's description is not only apt for Austria-Hungary, but also illustrates just how young the national idea was as the leaders of the other dynasties in Europe were able to reinvent themselves and their states in the national framework and even claim a long history of national existence.

11. This paragraph and the previous one echo Ratzel's ideas of *lebensraum*. Interestingly, despite Dominian's support of "German imperialism," he generally considered French culture as superior (as noted in a previous paragraph and again in the subsequent endnote) and supported French claims to territory (e.g., Alsace-Lorraine) over German claims.

12. Leon Dominian, a great advocate of delineating political boundaries along linguistic boundaries, also argued that Alsace-Lorraine rightfully belonged to France though the people spoke German: "To this day the [Rhine] valley province owes more to France in thought and ideals than to any other country. The Alsatian temperament has much of that mental sunshine which Mirabeau calls the 'fond gaillard.' This is assuredly not derived from Germany. His wit is of the true Gallic type—mocking, and tending to the Rabelaisian; its geniality is reserved for France and French institutions, its caustic side for Germany and Germans. It could never have proceeded from the ponderous Teutonic mentality. Alsatians are French in spirit because they know how to laugh well, to laugh as civilized men with the cheer that brightens the good and the irony that draws out in full relief the ugliness of evil" (1917a, 47).

Furthermore, while acknowledging that German was spoken much longer in these territories and that the French language established a strong foothold only after the French Revolution, Dominian takes a Ratzelian perspective: "In Lorraine, the steady expansion of French over German territory reveals the assimilative capacity of French civilization. France, unable to send forth colonists because of her lack of numbers, nevertheless contains within herself by virtue of superior civilization the ability to absorb the foreigner. Of this, evidence is to be found in the Alsatian's sympathy for France no less than in the unanimous verdict of impartial foreigners" (1917a, 334-35).

13. Both Leon Dominian and Isaiah Bowman noted that the Austrians offered to cede the Italian-speaking areas of South Tyrol to Italy in the early days of the war in an attempt to prevent Italy from abandoning the camp of the Central Powers and joining that of the Entente (Bowman 1928, 238-39; Dominian 1917a, 335-36). The decision of the Italian government to switch sides in the war indicates that the Italian government was not satisfied with the Austrian offer. Indeed, the Italian government claimed much more territory, much of which included many German speakers: "Italian demands presented then were based, however, upon strategic necessities as well as linguistic considerations. Italy therefore outlined a frontier much nearer to the Adriatic watershed. . . . The boundary revision will give political validity to the Italian Alps, a region which is geographically Italian" (Dominian 1917a, 335-36).

It is interesting that Dominian, again a great advocate of drawing political boundaries along linguistic boundaries, supported the Italian claim because the Italian proposal created more linguistic minorities: 88,229 versus 32,755 in the Austrian proposal. The Italian proposal left 14,229 Italian speakers in Austria and 74,000 German speakers in Italy while the Austrian proposal would have left 18,863 Italian speakers in Austria but only 13,892 German speakers in Italy (1917a, 337). At the peace conference, the Italian government extended its territorial claim to include more land not inhabited by Italian speakers (Temperely [1921] 1969, 4: 280-87). Clearly, notions of language were embedded in other overriding conceptions.

14. Originally the name of the new state was written *Czecho-Slovakia*, reflecting the equal status of Czechs and Slovaks within this new state.

15. Lloyd George notes this attitude in his memoirs, as noted in a comment by a French representative: "Having a choice to make between an Allied and an enemy country, the Commission must not hesitate, however strong its desire of legitimate impartiality may be, to favour the Allied side" (Lloyd George 1939, 1: 597; also quoted in Deák 1942, 53).

16. Interestingly, Stalin chose the Oder River for the eastern boundary of Germany after the Second World War.

17. These two cities, which Lithuanians and Ukrainians respectively considered rightfully theirs, were incorporated into the Lithuanian and Ukrainian Soviet Socialist Republics after the Second World War and renamed to the Russian Vil'no and Lvov respectively. Both republics retained these cities following independence from the Soviet Union in 1991, but the Lithuanians renamed their city Vilnius and the Ukrainians renamed their city L'viv.

18. For more information on these movements, see the "National Ideologies" section of Ivo Banac's *The national question in Yugoslavia: Origins, history, and politics* (1984, 70-115).

19. Notice again that the common denominator for most identities was territory rather than language and culture.

20. Interestingly, most of the other identities that Dominian notes in his statement are tied to provinces, illustrating that states' spatial subsets played a role in defining identity. Unfortunately, the simplistic view that national identity is defined overwhelmingly by language, religion, and other cultural characteristics leads those imbued with such thinking to conclude that these identities are not real identities, just geographic regions, though the people in these regions defined themselves according to those regions.

21. As noted in chapter 2, this is still seen today in such institutions as the United Nations. Though the name of the organization implies that membership is comprised of nations, members are in fact states. Nations without states have very little voice.

22. Serbs advocating the Greater Serbian view have been accused of undermining the efforts of the Yugoslav Committee. If such is true, such intrigues were certainly helped by state-centered thinking and state mechanisms.

23. Here, too, professional geographers played a major role in defining nationhood and territory. The memorandum containing the territorial claims of the

new Yugoslav state "bore obvious traces of the hand of M. Cvijić, the most learned and enlightened not only of Serbian, but of all the Balkan geographic experts" (Temperely [1921] 1969, 4: 207).

24. For more on fascism, see the following: F. L. Carsten's *The rise of fascism* ([1967] 1980), Aristotle Kallis's *Fascist ideology: Territory and expansionism in Italy and German, 1922-1945* (2000), and Detlef Mülhberger's *The social basis of European fascist movements* (1987).

25. The line deviated in that it included Ruthenia, a territory not previously part of the Soviet Union or the Russian Empire. The territory was valuable because it gave the Soviet Union a common border with Hungary. However, it could also be pointed out that although Ruthenia was not previously part of the Russian Empire, the tsar's armies had occupied the territory on more than one occasion during the First World War, suggesting that the tsar would have incorporated the territory into his empire if the war had gone differently. So it could be stated that Stalin was fulfilling the tsar's goals.

26. The following statements made by officials of the U.S. government illustrate the contradictory nature of U.S. policy toward the Baltic states:

On January 28, 1991, by James Baker, secretary of state, reflecting the belief that the Baltic peoples needed the consent of their fellow Soviet citizens to declare independence though the United States never recognized the forceful annexation of the Baltic states by the Soviet Union: "So, we'll continue to make our views known to the Soviet Union in the hopes that there can be a peaceful resolution to this situation and that the hopes and aspirations of the Baltic peoples to determine their own future can be given effect. . . . We are supporting the efforts of a variety of international organizations to drive home the point to the Soviets that the legitimate aspirations of the citizens of Latvia, Lithuania, and Estonia must not be denied" (Situation in the Baltics 1991, 58).

On February 14, 1991, in [U.S.] Presidential Proclamation 6520: "The United States has never recognized the forcible incorporation of Lithuania and the other Baltic States into the USSR, and we have consistently supported the Baltic people's right to determine and control their own future. . . . The Lithuanian people have used the democratic process in what they hoped would be a peaceful, disciplined effort to gain recognition of their right to independence. Soviet authorities responded in January with the use of force, killing at least 20 people and injuring hundreds of others. The United States has condemned as inexcusable that action against a peaceful and democratically elected government, and we have called on the Soviets to eschew further use of intimidation and violence in the Baltic States. We urge the Soviets to pursue constructive negotiations with the elected representatives of the Lithuanian people" (Lithuanian Independence Day 1991, 134).

On March 4, 1991, by Robert B. Zoellick, counselor of the state department: "It is clear, however, that the Soviet Union has not progressed far in defining appropriate concepts of power-sharing, federalism, or individual rights" (Zoellick 1991, 146).

27. As in the previous case of the Soviet Union, the knowledge that Yugoslavia was inhabited by a multiethnic/multinational population where dominant groups violated the basic human rights of minorities, state-centered thinking and behavior overrode this knowledge and led the U.S. government to treat all the peoples of the Yugoslav state as a single Yugoslav people and to work to maintain the territorial integrity of the Yugoslav state. The following statements made by officials of the U.S. government illustrate this point:

On February 21, 1991, by Richard Schifter, assistant secretary for human rights and humanitarian affairs: "Our response to the problems which I have here described [humans rights violation committed by Serbs against Albanians in Kosovo and violence between Serbs and Croats in Croatia] has been to call attention to them, express our concern to the Yugoslav authorities, and, as my testimony shows, to offer support to those who are trying so hard to steer Yugoslavia toward democracy, the free market, and respect for the dignity of every single individual. Whether these leaders will succeed will depend on the support that they receive from the people of Yugoslavia. The Yugoslavs themselves will have to set their house in order" (153).

On June 3, 1991, by Margaret Tutweiler, state department spokeswomen, in light of Slovenia's and Croatia's intention to declare independence at the end of the month: "By unity, we mean the territorial integrity of Yugoslavia within its present borders. . . . The United States will not encourage or reward secession; it will respect any framework, federal, confederal, or other, on which the people of Yugoslavia peacefully and democratically decide. We firmly believe that Yugoslavia's external or internal borders should not be changed unless by peaceful consensual means" (Tutweiler 1991, 395).

On April 3, 1992, by the White House Office of the Press secretary, several months after Slovenia and Croatia had effectively seceded from Yugoslavia and violence erupted in Bosnia-Herzegovina: "The United States recognizes Bosnia-Hercegovina, Croatia, and Slovenia as sovereign and independent states and will begin immediately consultations to establish full diplomatic relations. The United States accepts the pre-crisis republic borders as the legitimate international borders of Bosnia-Hercegovina, Croatia, and Slovenia" (US Recognition of former Yugoslav Republics 1992, 287).

On June 8, 1992, by U.S. ambassador Edward J. Perkins after months of bloodshed in Bosnia-Herzegovina with the Yugoslav government in Belgrade lending its support to Serb nationalists in the seceding Yugoslav republics who demonstrated their desire to secede from those republics: "Belgrade must clearly and unequivocally demonstrate respect for the independence, borders, territorial integrity, and legitimate sovereign Governments of Bosnia and Hercegovina, Croatia, and other former Yugoslav republics" (Perkins 1992, 448).

6

Interlogue

Men love their country, not because it is great, but because it is their own.

                                                                                    —*Seneca*

The major purpose of this book has been to illustrate that sense of territory and emotional attachment to place are integral components of national identity, that place and territory are as much a part of national identity as language, religion, and shared history. In exploring the place and territorial components of national identity, it becomes clear that it is a fluid and evolving concept that overlaps other forms and layers of human identity. Chapter 2 explored the dynamic character of national identity and how it evolves and intersects with other forms of human social identities. However, the fluidity of national identity means that it is susceptible to the influencing forces of states and history. Chapter 3 examined the role of states in shaping national identity. In addition to illustrating how states help to determine the character of national identity, it showed how the functional regions of states encourage and limit the directions of people's movement, in turn helping to determine which places and territories individuals and then peoples will bond to. Thus, they have acted as broad spatial frameworks for the development of senses of territory and emotional attachments to place. Chapters 4 and 5 illuminated the fact that national identity is a historically contingent phenomenon, not existing in pure ideological form but carrying with it characteristics that pre-dated the national idea. The chapters also pointed out that the state is an evolving concept and entity. Moreover, states' boundaries have not been static; thus, their influences on people have been highly variegated geographically, having led to complicated senses of territory and emotional attachments to place.

Clearly, many factors determine any given nation's sense of territory and emotional attachment to place. More significantly, the timing and degree to which each of these factors shapes any given nation's sense of territory and emotional attachment to place vary considerably from nation to nation. Many unique synergies emerge from the interaction of nation, state, and territory. Thus, the place and territorial components of nationhood are very contextual. To fully understand and appreciate the place and territorial components of nationhood, it is necessary to move beyond an examination of the factors that shape their development and their synergies and consider individual nations. The next volume takes up this task by applying the concepts explored in this volume to nations in Southeastern Europe.

Selected Bibliography

Ádám, Magda. 1995. Plan for the rearrangement of Central Europe, 1918. In *Hungarians and their neighbors in modern times, 1867-1950.* Ed. Ference Glatz. Boulder, Colo.: Social Science Monographs.

Adams, Paul C., Steven Hoelscher, and Karen E. Till, eds. 2001. *Textures of place: Exploring humanist geographies.* Minneapolis: University of Minnesota Press.

Agnew, John A. 1987. *Place and politics: The geographical mediation of state and society.* Boston: Allen and Unwin.

———. 1994. The territorial trap: The geographical assumptions of international relations theory. *Review of International Political Economy* 1:53-80.

———. 2002. *Place and politics in modern Italy.* University of Chicago Geography Research Paper no. 243. Chicago: University of Chicago Press.

Agnew, John A., and James S. Duncan, eds. 1989. *The power of place: Bringing together geographical and sociological imaginations.* Boston: Unwin Hyman.

Agnew, John, Katharyne Mitchell, and Gerard Toal, eds. 2003. *A companion to political geography.* Malden, Mass.: Blackwell Publishers.

Alexander, Oliver. 1999-2002. *"Deutschland über alles": The Song of the Germans—A short history of the national anthems of Germany.* http://alexander.nu/deutschlandlied/index.html (11 November 2003).

Alland, Alexander, Jr. 1972. *The human imperative.* New York: Columbia University Press.

Alter, Peter. 1994. *Nationalism.* 2d ed. London: Edward Arnold.

Anchor, Robert. 1967. *The Enlightenment tradition.* New York: Harper and Row.

Anderson, Benedict. 1991. *Imagined communities: Reflections on the origin and spread of nationalism.* Rev. ed. London: Verso Edition and New Left Books.

Anderson, James, ed. 1986a. *The rise of the modern state.* Brighton, G.B.: Harvester Press.

——. 1986b. Nationalism and geography. Chap. 6 in *The rise of the modern state.* Ed. James Anderson. Brighton, G.B.: Harvester Press.

——. 1988. Nationalist ideology and territory. Chap. 2 in *Nationalism, self-determination and political geography.* Ed. R. J. Johnston, David B. Knight, and Eleonore Kofman. New York: Croom Helm.

——. 1996. The shifting stage of politics: New medieval and postmodern territorialities. *Environment and Planning D: Society and Space* 14 (2): 133-53.

Anderson, Malcolm. 1996. *Frontiers: Territory and state formation in the modern world.* London: Polity Press.

Andrews, Howard F. 1986. The early life of Paul Vidal de la Blache and the makings of modern geography. *Transactions, Institute of British Geographers* 11 (2): 174-82.

Ardrey, Robert. 1966. *The territorial imperative.* New York: Atheneum.

Armstrong, John A. 1982. *Nations before nationalism.* Chapel Hill: University of North Carolina Press.

Asher, R. E. 1995. The rise and fall of language. *The Geographical Magazine* (August): 18-21.

Associated Press. 2002. More citizens simply "American": Census shows fewer remembering old country ancestors. *Cumberland Times,* 8 June, 3A.

Ayto, John. 1990. *Dictionary of word origins.* New York: Arcade Publishing.

Bachelard, Gaston. 1964. *The poetics of space.* Trans. Maria Jolas. New York: Orion Press.

Baer, John. 1992a. *The Pledge of Allegiance: A short history.* http://history.vineyard.net//pledge.htm (3 July 2002).

——. 1992b. *The Pledge of Allegiance: A centennial history, 1892-1992.* Annapolis, Md.: Md. Free State Press, Inc.

Bailey, Thomas A. 1963a. *Woodrow Wilson and the lost peace.* Chicago: Quadrangle Books.

——. 1963b. *Woodrow Wilson and the great betrayal.* Chicago: Quadrangle Books.

Baker, Ray Stannard. 1923. *Woodrow Wilson and world settlement.* 3 vols. New York: Doubleday, Page and Company.

Baker, Ray Stannard, and William E. Dodd. 1926. *The public papers of Woodrow Wilson.* 6 vols. New York: Harper and Brothers Publishers.

Balakrishnan, Gopal, ed. 1996. *Mapping the nation.* London: Verso Press.

Banac, Ivo. 1984. *The national question in Yugoslavia: Origins, history, politics.* Ithaca, N.Y.: Cornell University Press.

Barber, Richard. 1964. *Henry Plantagenet: A biography.* London: Barrie and Rockliff with Pall Mall Press.

Barnard, F. M. 1965. *Herder's social and political thought.* Oxford: Clarendon Press.

Barnes, Trevor, and Derek Gregory, eds. 1997. *Readings in human geography: The poetics and politics of inquiry.* New York: Arnold.

Bartelson, Jens. 1995. *A genealogy of sovereignty.* Cambridge: Cambridge University Press.

Barth, Fredrik, ed. 1969. *Ethnic groups and boundaries.* Boston: Little, Brown, and Company.

Bassin, Mark. 1987. Imperialism and the nation state in Friedrich Ratzel's political geography. *Progress in Human Geography* 2:473-95.

Beevor, Anthony. 1998. *Stalingrad.* New York: Penguin.

Beiner, Ronald, ed. 1999. *Theorizing nationalism.* Albany: State University of New York Press.

Beiser, Frederick C. 1992. *Enlightenment, revolution, and romanticism: The genesis of modern German political thought, 1790-1800.* Cambridge, Mass.: Harvard University Press.

———, ed. 1993. *The Cambridge companion to Hegel.* New York: Cambridge University Press.

———, ed. 1996. *The early political writings of the German Romantics.* New York: Cambridge University Press.

Bell-Fialkoff, Andrew. 1996. *Ethnic cleansing.* New York: St. Martin's Press.

Beloff, Max. 1954. *The age of absolutism, 1660-1815.* New York: Harper and Row Publishers.

Bercuson, David J., et al. 1992. *Colonies: Canada to 1867.* New York: McGraw-Hill Ryerson Limited.

Bertoletti, Stefano Fabbri. 1994. The anthropological theory of Johann Friedrich Blumenbach. In *Romanticism in science, science in Europe, 1790-1840.* Ed. Stefano Poggi and Maurizio Bossi. Boston: Kluwer Academic Publishers.

Biersteker, Thomas J., and Cynthia Weber. 1996. *State sovereignty as social construct.* Cambridge: Cambridge University Press.

Billig, Michael. 1995. *Banal nationalism.* London: Sage.

Binkley, Robert C. [1935] 1963. *Realism and nationalism, 1852-1871.* New York: Harper and Row Publishers.

Biography of the Millennium: 100 people—100 years. 1999. Produced by Working Dog Productions and History Television Productions. 4 vols. 200 min. A&E Network. Videocassettes.

Blouet, Brian W. 2001. *Geopolitics and globalization in the twentieth century.* London: Reaktion.

Böckh, Richard. 1869. *Der Deutschen Volkszahl und Sprachgebiet in den europäischen Staaten Eine statistische Untersuchung.* Berlin: Verlag von J. Guttentag.

Bonsal, Stephen. 1946. *Suitors and Suppliants: The Little Nations at Versailles.* New York: Prentice Hall.

Botsford, Florence Hudson, ed. 1931. *Northern Europe.* Vol. 2 of *Botsford collection of folk songs.* New York: G. Schirmer.

———, ed. 1933. *Southern Europe.* Vol. 3 of *Botsford collection of folk songs.* New York: G. Schirmer.

Bowman, Isaiah. 1922. *The new world: Problems in political geography.* New York: World Book Company.

———. 1928. *The new world: Problems in political geography.* 4th ed. New York: World Book Company.

Bradley, John. 1989. *War and pace since 1945.* New York: Columbia University Press, East European Monographs.

Breuilly, John. 1994. *Nationalism and the state.* 2d ed. Chicago: University of Chicago Press.

Brigham, Albert Perry. 1919. Principles in the determination of boundaries. *Geographical Review* 8 (April): 201-19.

Brown, Peter G., 1981. Introduction to *Boundaries, national autonomy and its limits.* Edited by Peter G. Brown and Henry Shue. Totowa, N.J.: Rowman & Littlefield.

Brubaker, Rogers. 1992. *Citizenship and nationhood.* Cambridge, Mass.: Harvard University Press.

———. 1996. *Nationalism reframed, nationhood and the national question in the new Europe.* Cambridge: Cambridge University Press.

Brunn, Stanley D., and Ernie Yanarella. 1987. Towards a humanistic political geography. *Studies in Comparative International Development* 22 (Summer): 3-49.

Burg, Steven L., and Michael L. Berbaum. 1989. Community integration, and stability in multinational Yugoslavia. *American Political Science Review* 83 (June): 535-54.

Burghardt, Andrew F. 1973. The bases of territorial claims. *Geographical Review* 63 (April): 225-45.

Cahman, Werner. 1949. Frontiers between East and West in Europe. *Geographical Review* 39 (October): 605-24.

Cannon, Garland, and Kevin R. Brine, eds. 1995. *Objects of enquiry: The life, contributions, and influences of Sir William Jones (1746-1794).* New York: New York University Press.

Canovan, Margaret. 1996. *Nationhood and political theory.* Cheltenham, UK: Edward Elgar.

Carmichael, Cathie. 2002. *Ethnic cleansing in the Balkans: Nationalism and the destruction of tradition.* New York: Routledge.

Carr, William. 1969. *A History of Germany, 1815-1945.* New York: St. Martin's Press.

Carsten, F. L. [1967] 1980. *The rise of fascism.* 2d ed. Berkeley: University of California Press.

Cartledge, T. M., W. L. Reed, Martin Shaw, and Henry Coleman. 1978. *National anthems of the world.* New York: Arco.

Cassirer, Ernst. 1967. *The myth of the state.* New Haven, Conn.: Yale University Press.

Chamberlin, E. R. 1979. *Preserving the past.* London: J.M. Dent and Sons.

Chirot, Daniel. 1996. Herder's multicultural theory of nationalism and its consequences. *East European Politics and Societies* 10 (1): 1-15.

Christopher, A. J. 1999. New states in a new millennium. *Area* 31: 327-34.

Clark, Alan. [1965] 1985. *Barbarossa: The Russian-German conflict, 1941-1945*. New York: Quill.

Clark, Robert T., Jr. 1955. *Herder: His life and thought*. Berkeley: University of California Press.

Coakley, John, ed. 1993. *The territorial management of ethnic conflict*. London: Frank Cass.

Cobban, Alfred. 1964. *Rousseau and the modern state*. London: George Allen and Unwin.

Cohen, Anthony. 1985. *The symbolic construction of community*. New York: Tavistock.

Cohler, Anne. 1970. *Rousseau and nationalism*. New York: Basic Books.

Commager, Henry Steele. 1978. *The empire of reason: How Europe imagined and America realized the Enlightenment*. Garden City, N.Y.: Anchor Books.

Comrie, Bernard, ed. 1987. *The world's major languages*. New York: Oxford University Press.

Connor, Walker. 1978. A nation is a nation, is a state, is an ethnic group is a . . . *Ethnic and Racial Studies* 1 (January): 377-400.

———. 1990. When is a nation? *Ethnic and Racial Studies* 13 (January): 92-103.

———. 1994a. *Ethnonationalism: The quest for understanding*. Princeton, N.J.: Princeton University Press.

———. 1994b. When is a nation? Chap. 9 in *Ethnonationalism: The quest for understanding*. Princeton, N.J.: Princeton University Press.

Conversi, Daniele, ed. 2002. *Ethnonationalism in the contemporary world: Walker Connor and the study of nationalism*. London: Routledge.

Conzen, Michael P. 1993. Culture regions, homelands, and ethnic archipelagos in the United States: Methodological considerations. *Journal of Cultural Geography* 13 (Spring/Summer): 13-29.

Cooper, J. P., ed. 1970. *The new Cambridge modern history*. 14 vols. Cambridge: Cambridge University Press.

Cox, Kevin R. 2002. *Political geography: Territory, state, and society*. Oxford: Blackwell.

Craig, Gordon A. 1972. *Europe, 1815-1914*. 3d ed. Hinsdale, Ill.: The Dryden Press.

Crampton, Jeremy. 2003. Cartographic rationality and the politics of geosurveillance and security. *Cartography and Geographic Information Science* 30 (2): 135-48.

Crampton, R. J. 1994. *Eastern Europe in the twentieth century*. London: Routledge.

Cunsolo, Ronald. 1990. *Italian nationalism: From its origins to World War II*. Armonk, N.Y.: M.E. Sharpe.

Czepeli, György, and Antal Örkény. 1997. The imagery of national anthems in Europe. *Canadian Review of Studies in Nationalism* 24 (1-2): 33-42.

Dahbour, Omar, and Micheline R. Ishay, eds. 1995. *The nationalism reader.* Atlantic Highlands, N.J.: Humanities Press.

Darwin, Charles. 1859. *On the origin of species by means of natural selection, or the preservation of favoured races in the struggle for life* microform. London: J. Murray.

Davies, Norman. 1972. *White eagle, red star: The Polish-Soviet War, 1919-1920.* Foreword by A. J. P. Taylor. New York: St. Martin's Press.

————. 1982. *God's playground: A history of Poland.* 2 vols. New York: Columbia University Press.

Davis, William Morris. 1899. The geographical cycle. *Geographical Journal* 14: 481-504.

Dawkins, Richard. 1976. *The selfish gene.* Oxford: Oxford University Press.

Dawson, Christopher. 1994. *The making of Europe: An introduction to the history of European unity.* New York: Barnes and Noble.

Deák, Francis. [1942] 1972. *Hungary at the Paris peace conference: The diplomatic history of the treaty of Trianon.* New York: Morningside Heights, Columbia University Press.

Delderfield, Eric R., ed. 1972. *Kings and queens of England.* New York: Stein and Day.

Desmond, Cosmas. 1971. *The discarded people: An account of resettlement in South Africa.* Baltimore: Penguin.

Deutsch, Karl. 1966. *Nationalism and social communication.* Cambridge, Mass.: MIT Press.

————. 1969. The growth of nations: Some recurrent patterns of political and social integration. Chap. 17 in *The Structure of Political Geography.* Ed. Roger E. Kasperson and Julian V. Minghi. Chicago: Aldine.

Deutsch, Leonhard. 1967. *A treasury of the world's finest folk songs.* New York: Crown.

De Zayas, Alfred M. 1988. *Nemesis at Potsdam: The expulsion of the Germans from the east.* 3d ed. Lincoln: University of Nebraska Press.

Dickinson, Robert E. 1969. *The makers of modern geography.* New York: Frederick A. Praeger.

Dijkink, Gertjan. 1996. *National identity and geopolitical visions: Maps of pride and pain.* New York: Routledge.

Dijkink, Gertjan, and Hans Knippenberg, eds. 2001. *The territorial factor: Political geography in a globalising world.* Amsterdam: Vossiuspers UvA.

Doob, Leonard W. 1964. *Patriotism and nationalism: Their psychological foundations.* New Haven, Conn.: Yale University Press.

Dominian, Leon. 1917a. *Frontiers of language and nationality in Europe.* New York: Henry Holt.

————. 1917b. *The nationality map of Europe.* Vol. 1 of *A League of Nations.* Boston: World Peace Foundation.

Dorpalen, Andreas. 1966. *The world of General Haushofer: Geopolitics in action.* Port Washington, N.Y.: Kennikat Press.

DuBois, W. E. Burghardt. 1970. The Pan-African movement. Chap. 15 in *Nationalism in Asia and Africa*. Ed. Elie Kedourie. New York: Meridian Books.

Duncan, David Ewing. 1998. *Calendar: Humanity's epic struggle to determine a true and accurate year*. New York: Avon.

East, William Gordon. 1961. The concept of political status of the shatter zone. In *Geographical essays on Eastern Europe*. Ed. N. J. Pounds. Bloomington: Indiana University Press.

————. 1966. *An historical geography of Europe*. 5th ed. New York: E.P. Dutton.

Eberhardt, Piotr. 2002. *Ethnic groups and population changes in twentieth-century Eastern Europe: History, data, and analysis*. New York: M.E. Sharpe.

Edwards, John, ed. 1984. *Linguistic minorities, policies and pluralism*. New York: Academic Press.

Egri, Peter. 1988. *Literature, painting and music: An interdisciplinary approach to comparative literature*. Budapest: Akadémiai Kiadó.

Einstein, Alfred. 1947. *Music in the Romantic era*. London: J.M. Dent and Sons.

Eley, Geoff, and Ronald Grigor Suny, eds. 1996. *Becoming national: A reader*. New York: Oxford University Press.

Elliot, Michael. 1995. Gallic pride is (surprise!) a good thing. *Newsweek,* 22 May, 32.

Emerson, Ralph Waldo. 1838. *War*. Boston, Mass.: Lecture. *See* http://www.rwe .org/works/other_works/war_delivered_in_march.htm (17 December 2003).

Emerson, Rupert. 1960. *From empire to nation: The rise to self-assertion of Asian and African peoples*. Cambridge, Mass.: Harvard University Press.

Ergang, Robert Reinhold. 1954. *Europe since Waterloo*. Boston: D.C. Heath.

————. 1966. *Herder and the foundations of German nationalism*. New York: Columbia University Press.

————. 1971. *Emergence of the national state*. New York: Van Nostrand Rheinhold.

Eriksen, Thomas Hylland. 2002. *Ethnicity and nationalism.* 2d ed. London: Pluto Press.

Esman, M., ed. 1977. *Ethnic conflict in the Western world*. Ithaca, N.Y.: Cornell University Press.

Evans, R. J. W., and T. V. Thomas Crown, eds. 1991. Church and estates: Central European politics in the sixteenth and seventeenth centuries. New York: St. Martin's Press.

Febvre, Lucien. [1925] 1974. *A geographical introduction to history*. Westport, Conn.: Greenwood.

————. 1929. *Martin Luther: A destiny*. New York: E.P. Dutton.

Febvre, Lucien, and Henri-Jean Martin. [1958] 1997. *The coming of the book: The impact of printing 1450-1800*. Trans. David Gerard. New York: Verso.

Fehér, Ferenc. 1989. On making Central Europe. *East European Politics and Societies* 3 (Fall): 412-47.

Feiler, Bruce. 2001a. The Bible: Myth or truth? *USA Weekend,* March 9-11, 6-8.

————. 2001b. *Walking the Bible: A journey by land through the five books of Moses.* New York: HarperCollins.

Fellman, Jerome D., Arthur Getis, and Judith Getis. 2003. *Human geography: Landscapes of human activities.* New York: McGraw-Hill.

Fenton, Steve. 2003. *Ethnicity.* Malden, Mass.: Blackwell.

Fifield, Russel H., and G. Etzel Pearcy. 1944. *Geopolitics in principle and practice.* New York: Ginn and Company.

Fishman, Joshua A. 1972. *Language and nationalism: Two integrative essays.* Rowley, Mass.: Newbury House.

————. 1974. The sociology of language: An interdisciplinary social science approach to language in society. *Current Trends in Linguistics* 12: 1629-1784.

————, ed. 1999. *Handbook of language and ethnic identity.* New York: Oxford University Press.

Floto, Inga. 1973. *Colonel House in Paris: A study of American policy at the Paris Peace Conference 1919.* Princeton, N.J.: Princeton University Press.

————. 1982. *Woodrow Wilson and a revolutionary world, 1913-1921.* Ed. Arthur S. Link. Chapel Hill: University of North Carolina Press.

Ford, Franklin L. 1970. *Europe 1780-1830.* London: Longmans, Green, and Company.

Forsberg, Tuomas, ed. 1995. *Contested territory: Border disputes at the edge of the former Soviet empire.* Brookfield, Vt.: E. Elgar.

Foucault, Michael. 1980. *Power/Knowledge. Selected interviews and other writings.* Ed. C. Gordon. Brighton, UK: Harvester Press.

Fox, Richard G., ed. 1990. *Nationalist ideologies and the production of national cultures.* Num. 2 of the *American Ethnological Society Monograph Series.* Washington, D.C.: American Anthropological Association.

Fraenkel, Eran, and Christina Kramer, eds. 1993. *Language contact—language conflict.* New York: P. Lang.

Freeman, T. W., Marguerita Oughton, and Philippe Pinchemel, eds. 1977. *Geographers: Biobibliographical studies.* Vol. 1. London: Mansell.

Fukuyama, Francis. 1992. *The end of history and the last man.* New York: Free Press.

Fulbrook, Mary, ed. 1993. *National histories and European history.* Boulder, Colo.: Westview Press.

Fyfe, Hamilton. 1940. *The illusion of national character.* London: Watts and Company.

Gallagher, Michael. 1995. How many nations are there in Ireland? *Ethnic and Racial Studies* 18 (October): 715-39.

Gallegos, Bee, ed. 1994. *English: Our official language?* New York: Wilson.

Galton, Francis. 1883. *Inquiries into human faculty and its development.* London: Macmillan.

Garraty, John A., and Peter Gay. 1972. *The Columbia history of the world.* New York: Harper and Row.

Geary, Patrick J. 1988. *Before France and Germany: The creation and transformation of the Merovingian World.* New York: Oxford University Press.

———. 2002. *The myth of nations: The medieval origins of Europe.* Princeton, N.J.: Princeton University Press.

Gelfand, Lawrence E. 1963. *The inquiry: American preparations for peace, 1917-1919.* New Haven, Conn.: Yale University Press.

Gellner, Ernest. 1983. *Nations and nationalism.* Ithaca, N.Y.: Cornell University Press.

Germany "Lied der Deutschen" (Song of the Germans). http://david.national-anthems.net/de.htm (11 November 2003).

Gerth, H. H., and C. Wright Mills. 1948. *From Max Weber: Essays in sociology.* London: Routledge and Kegan Paul.

Giddens, A. 1987. *Nation-state and violence.* Cambridge: Polity.

Gilbert, Felix. 1979. *The end of the European era, 1890 to the present.* 2d ed. New York: W.W. Norton.

Gildea, Robert. 1987. *Barricades and borders: Europe 1800-1914.* Oxford: Oxford University Press.

GilFillan, S. C. 1924. European political boundaries. *Political Science Quarterly* 39 (September): 458-84.

Gillies, Alexander. 1945. *Herder.* Oxford: Basil Blackwell.

Gilmore, Myron P. 1952. *The world of humanism: 1453-1517.* New York: Harper and Row.

Glassner, Martin Ira, and Chuck Fahrer. 2004. *Political geography.* 3d ed. New York: John Wiley and Sons.

Glauber, Bill. 1997. Britain might leave Scotland to the Scots. *Baltimore Sun,* 25 July, 17A.

Glazer, Nathan, and Daniel P. Moynihan. 1975. *Ethnicity: Theory and experience.* Cambridge, Mass.: Harvard University Press.

Gottman, Jean. 1973. *The significance of territory.* Charlottesville: University Press of Virginia.

Gramsci, Antonio. 1971. *Selections from the prison notebooks.* Ed. and trans. Quintin Hoare and Geoffrey Nowell Smith. New York: International.

Graubard, Stephen R., ed. 1991. *Eastern Europe . . . Central Europe . . . Europe.* San Francisco: Westview.

Gray, Steven. 2002. Language tells Luxembourg's story: Movement to preserve country's culture is based on expanding the written use of the native tongue. *Washington Post,* 29 November, A40.

Green, Robert W., ed. 1973. *Protestantism, capitalism, and social science: The Weber thesis controversy.* 2d ed. Lexington, Mass.: D.C. Heath and Company.

Greenberg, Robert D. 1996. The politics of dialects among Serbs, Croats, and Muslims in the former Yugoslavia. *East European Politics and Societies* 10 (3): 393-415.

Greenfield, Liah. 1992. *Nationalism: Five roads to modernity.* Cambridge, Mass.: Harvard University Press.

Greengrass, Mark, ed. 1991. *Conquest and coalescence: The shaping of the state in early modern Europe.* London: Arnold Press.

Greer, Thomas H., and Gavin Lewis. 1997. *A brief history of the Western world.* New York: Harcourt Brace College Publishers.

Gregory, D., and J. Urry, eds. 1985. *Social relations and spatial structures.* New York: St. Martin's Press.

Grosby, Steven. 1995. Territoriality: The transcendental, primordial feature of modern societies. *Nations and Nationalism* 1(2): 143-62.

Grotius, Hugo. 1925. *De jure belli ac pacis libritres.* Vol. 2. Trans. Francis W. Kelsey. In *The classics of international law.* Ed. James Brown Scott. Oxford: Clarendon Press.

Guibernau, Monserrat. 1996. *Nationalisms: The nation-state and nationalism in the twentieth century.* Cambridge, Mass.: Polity Press, Blackwell.

———. 1999. *Nations without states: Political communities in a global age.* Malden, Mass.: Polity Press.

Guibernau, Monserrat, and John Hutchinson, eds. 2001. *Understanding nationalism.* Oxford: Polity Press, Blackwell.

———, eds. 2004. *Nations and nationalism, special issue: History and national destiny: Ethnosymbolism and its critics* 10 (1-2/January-April): 1-209.

Gurr, Andrew. 1981. *Writers in exile: The identity of home in modern literature.* Atlantic Highlands, N.J.: Humanities Press.

Gyekye, Kwame. 1997. *Tradition and modernity: Philosophical reflections on the African experience.* New York: Oxford University Press.

Hall, John A., ed. 1998. *The state of the nation: Ernest Gellner and the theory of nationalism.* New York: Cambridge University Press.

Halsted, John B., ed. 1969. *Romanticism.* New York: Walker and Company.

Hamm, Michael F. 1998. Chronology. *Nationalities Papers* 26 (1): 165-75.

Hammond-Tooke, David. 1970. Tribal cohesion and the incorporative process in the Transkei, South Africa. Chap. 10 in *From tribe to nation in Africa: Studies in incorporation processes.* Ed. Ronald Cohen and John Middleton. Scranton, Penn.: Chandler.

Hampson, Norman. [1968] 1987. *The Enlightenment: An evaluation of its assumptions, attitudes and values.* Reprint, London: Penguin.

Harris, Chauncy D. 1993. New European countries and their minorities. *Geographical Review* 83 (July): 301-20.

Hartshorne, Richard. 1950. The functional approach in political geography. *Annals of the Association of American Geographers* 40: 95-130.

Haugen, Arne. 2003. *The establishment of national republics in Central Asia.* New York: Palgrave-Macmillan.

Haugen, Einar, J. Derrick McClure, and Derick Thompson, eds. 1980. *Minority languages today.* Edinburgh, Scotland: University Press.

Haushofer, Karl. 1927. *Geopolitik des Pazifischen Ozeans: Studien über die Wechselbeziehung zwischen Geographie und Geschichte.* 2d ed. Berlin: Kurt Vowinckel.

———. 1931. *Geopolitik der Pan-Ideen.* Berlin: Zentral-Verlag.

————. 1937. *Deutscher Volksboden und deutsches Volkstum in der Tschecho-slowakei: Eine geographisch-geopolitische Zusammenschau.* Heidelberg-Berlin: Kurt Vowinckel.

————. 1939. *Grenzen in ihrer geographischen und politischen bedeutung.* Heidelberg: Kurt Vowinckel.

Haushofer, Karl, Erich Ober, Herman Lautensach, and Otto Maul, eds. 1928. *Bausteine zur Geopolitik.* Berlin-Grunewald: Kurt Vowinckel.

Haushofer, Karl, and Kurt Trampler. 1931. *Deutschlands Weg an der Zeiten-wende.* Munich: H. Hugenduble.

Hayes, Carlton Joseph Huntley. 1926-1927. Contributions of Herder to the doc-trine of nationalism. *American Historical Review* 32: 719-36.

————. 1941. *Essays on nationalism.* New York: Macmillan.

————. 1953. *Modern Europe to 1870.* New York: Macmillan.

————. 1959. *Contemporary Europe since 1870.* Rev. ed. New York: Macmil-lan.

————. 1960. *Nationalism: A religion.* New York: Macmillan.

————. 1968. *The historical evolution of modern nationalism.* New York: Rus-sell & Russell.

Heffernan, Michael. 1998. *The meaning of Europe: Geography and geopolitics.* New York: Arnold.

Held, David. 1989. *Political theory and the modern state: Essays on state, power, and democracy.* Stanford, Calif.: Stanford University Press.

Held, David, et al. 1983. *States and societies.* New York: New York University Press.

Herb, Guntram Henrik. 1993. National self-determination, maps, and propa-ganda in Germany, 1918-1945. Ph.D. diss., University of Wisconsin-Madison.

————. 1997. *Under the map of Germany: Nationalism and propaganda 1918-1945.* New York: Routledge.

————. 2004. Double vision: Territorial strategies in the construction of na-tional identities in Germany 1949-1979. *Annals of the Association of American Geographers* 94 (1/March): 140-64.

Herb, Guntram Henrik, and David H. Kaplan, ed. 1999. *Nested identities: Na-tionalism, territory, and scale.* Lanham, Md.: Rowman & Littlefield.

Herr, Friedrich. 1968. *The Holy Roman Empire.* Trans. Janet Sonderheimer. New York: Frederick A. Praeger.

Hinsley, Frances Harry. 1986. *Sovereignty.* 2d ed. London: Watts.

Hirschman, Charles. 1986. The making of race in colonial Malaya: Political economy and racial ideology. *Sociological Forum* 1 (2/Spring): 330-62.

————. 1987. The meaning and measurement of ethnicity in Malaysia: An analysis of census classifications. *Journal of Asian Studies* 46 (3/August): 555-82.

Hobsbawn, Eric J. 1962. *The age of revolution 1789-1848.* New York: World.

————, ed. 1983. *The invention of tradition.* New York: Cambridge University Press.

———. 1987. *The age of empire, 1875-1914.* New York: Pantheon Books.

———. 1990. *Nations and nationalism since 1780: Programme, myth, reality.* 2d ed. Cambridge: Cambridge University Press.

———. 1992. Ethnicity and nationalism in Europe today. *Anthropology Today* 8 (February): 3-13.

Holborn, Hajo. 1969. *A history of modern Germany, 1840-1945.* Princeton, N.J.: Princeton University Press.

Holdrich, Thomas H. 1915a. Political boundaries. *Nineteenth Century* 77: 1119-37.

———. 1915b. Military aspects of a frontier. *Nineteenth Century* 78: 936-47.

———. 1916a. Geographical problems in boundary making. *Geographical Journal* 47: 421-40.

———. 1916b. Political boundaries. *Scottish Geographical Magazine* 32: 497-507.

———. 1918. *Boundaries in Europe and the Near East.* London: Macmillan.

Horne, Donald. 1984. *The great museum: The re-presentation of history.* London: Pluto Press.

Horowitz, D. 1985. *Ethnic groups in conflict.* Berkeley: University of California Press.

Horsman, Reinald. 1987. *Josiah Nott of Mobile: Southerner, physician and racial theorist.* Southern Biography Series. Baton Rouge: Louisiana State University Press.

Hosking, Geoffrey, and George Schöpflin, eds. 1997. *Myths and nationhood.* New York: Routledge.

House, Edward M., and Charles Seymour. 1921. *What really happened at Paris: The story of the Peace Conference, 1918-1919.* New York: Charles Scribner's Sons.

Hroch, Miroslav. 1985. *Social preconditions of national revival in Europe: A competitive analysis of the social composition of patriotic groups among the smaller European nations.* New York: Cambridge University Press.

Hudson, R. A. 1996. *Sociolinguistics.* 2d ed. Cambridge: Cambridge University Press.

Hunter, James M. 1983. *Perspectives on Ratzel's political geography.* Lanham, Md.: University Press of America.

Huntington, Ellsworth. 1907. *The pulse of Asia.* Boston: Houghton Mifflin.

———. 1915. *Civilization and climate.* New Haven, Conn.: Yale University Press.

———. 1924. *The character of races as influenced by physical environment, natural selection, and historical development.* New York: Charles Scribner.

Hutchinson, John. 1994. *Modern nationalism.* London: Fontana.

Huntington, Samuel P. 1996. *The clash of nations and the remaking of the new world order.* New York: Simon and Schuster.

Ignatieff, Michael. 1998. *The warrior's honor: Ethnic war and the modern conscience.* New York: Metropolitan Books.

Ignatiev, Noel. 1995. *How the Irish became white.* New York: Routledge.

Jackson, John Brinckerhoff. 1994. *A sense of place, a sense of time*. New Haven, Conn.: Yale University Press.

Jackson, Peter, and Jan Penrose, eds. 1994. *Constructions of race, place and nation*. Minneapolis: University of Minnesota Press.

James, Harold. 1994. *A German identity: 1770 to the present day*. London: Phoenix.

Jászi, Oszkár. [1929] 1961. *The dissolution of the Habsburg Monarchy*. Chicago: Phoenix Books, University of Chicago Press.

Jenkins, Richard. 1994. Rethinking ethnicity: identity, categorization and power. *Ethnic and Racial Studies* 17 (2): 197-223.

Jethro Tull. 1989. Another Christmas song. *Rock Island*. New York: Capitol Records.

Johnston, R. J. 1991. *A question of place: Exploring the practice of human geography*. Oxford: Blackwell.

Johnston, R. J., David B. Knight, and Eleonore Kofman, eds. 1988. *Nationalism, self-determination and political geography*. New York: Croom Helm.

Jones, Howard Mumford. 1974. *Revolution and Romanticism*. Cambridge, Mass.: Harvard University Press.

Jordan, Terry G. 1996. *The European culture area: A systematic geography*. 3d ed. New York: HarperCollins.

Kaiser, K. 1968. *German foreign policy in transition: Bonn between east and west*. Oxford: Oxford University Press.

Kallis, Aristotle A. 2000. *Fascist ideology: Territory and expansionism in Italy and Germany, 1922-1945*. New York: Routledge.

Kaplan, David H., and Jouni Häkli, eds. 2002. *Boundaries and place: European borderlands in geographical context*. Lanham, Md.: Rowman & Littlefield.

Kasperson, Roger E., and Julian V. Minghi, eds. 1969. *The structure of political geography*. Chicago: Aldine.

Keith, Michael, and Steve Pile, eds. 1993. *Place and the politics of identity*. New York: Routledge.

Kellas, James G. 1991. *The politics of nationalism and ethnicity*. Basingstoke, UK: Macmillan.

Kemiläinen, Aira. 1964. *Nationalism: Problems concerning the word, the concept and classification*. Jyväskylä: Kustanajat.

Kliot, Nurit, and Stanley Waterman, eds. 1991. *The political geography of conflict and peace*. London: Belhaven Press.

Knight, David B. 1982. Identity and territory: Geographical perspectives on nationalism and regionalism. *Annals of the Association of American Geographers* 72 (December): 514-31.

Knippenberg, Hans, and Jan Markusse. 2000. *Nationalising and denationalising European border regions, 1800-2000: Views from geography and history*. Dordrecht, The Netherlands: Kluwer Academic Publishers.

Koch, H. W. 1978. *A history of Prussia*. New York: Longman.

Kohl, Philip L., and Clare Fawcett, eds. 1995. *Nationalism, politics and the practice of archaeology*. New York: Cambridge University Press.

Kohn, Hans. 1955. *Nationalism: Its meaning and history.* New York: Van Nostrand.

———. 1960. *Pan-Slavism: Its history and ideology.* New York: Vintage Books.

———. 1962. *The age of nationalism: The first era of global history.* New York: Harper and Brothers.

———. 1967a. *The idea of nationalism: A study in its origins and background.* 2d ed. New York: Collier-Macmillan.

———. 1967b. *Prelude to nation-states: The French and German experience, 1789-1815.* New York: Van Nostrand.

Kosiński, Leszek A. 1969. Changes in the ethnic structure in East-Central Europe. *Geographical Review* 59: 388-402.

Kratochwil, Friedrich. 1986. Of systems, boundaries, and territoriality: An inquiry into the formation of the state system. *World Politics* 39 (October): 27-52.

Kristof, Ladis. 1959. The nature of frontiers and boundaries. *Annals of the Association of American Geographers* 49 (3/September): 269-82.

Kühl, Stefan. 2002. *The Nazi connection: Eugenics, American racism, and German National Socialism.* New York: Oxford University Press.

Kupchan, Charles A., ed. 1995. *Nationalism and nationalities in the new Europe.* Ithaca, N.Y.: Cornell University Press.

Lampe, John R. 1996. *Yugoslavia as history: Twice there was a country.* Cambridge: Cambridge University Press.

Lansing, Robert. 1921. *The peace negotiations: A personal narrative.* New York: Houghton Mifflin.

Lendvani, Paul. 2003. *The Hungarians: 1000 years of victory and defeat.* London: Hurst.

Leone, Bruno. 1986. *Nationalism: Opposing viewpoints.* Rev. ed. St. Paul, Minn.: Greenhaven Press.

Lewin, Percy Evans. 1916. *The German road to the east: An account of the "Drang nach Osten" and of the Teutonic aims in the Near and Middle East.* London: Heinemann.

Link, Arthur S., ed. 1984. *The papers of Woodrow Wilson.* Princeton, N.J.: Princeton University Press.

Lithuanian Independence Day. 1991. *US Department of State Dispatch,* 25 February, 2 (8): 134.

Livingstone, David N. 1992. *The geographic tradition: Episodes in the history of a contested enterprise.* Oxford: Blackwell.

Lloyd George. David. 1939. *Memoirs of the peace conference.* 2 vols. New Haven, Conn.: Yale University Press.

Lockridge, Laurence S. 1989. *The ethics of Romanticism.* New York: Cambridge University Press.

Lowenthal, David. 1961. Geography, experience, and imagination: Towards a geographical epistemology. *Annals of the Association of American Geographers* 51 (September): 241-60.

Loy, William G. 1989. Geographic names in geography. (Presidential address) *Yearbook, Association of Pacific Coast Geographers* 51: 7-24.

Lyall, Sarah. 1997. With gusto, Scots say yes to their own parliament. *New York Times,* 12 September, A3.

Lyde, Lionel W. 1915. Types of political frontiers in Europe. *Geographical Journal* 45: 126-45.

———. 1916. River frontier in Europe. *Scottish Geographical Magazine* 32: 545-55.

———. 1924. *The continent of Europe.* London: Macmillan.

Lyon, Judson M. 1994. The Herder syndrome: A comparative study of cultural nationalism. *Ethnic and Racial Studies* 17 (2/April): 224-37.

Macartney, Carlile A., and A. W. Palmer. 1962. *Independent Eastern Europe: A history.* New York: Macmillan, St. Martin's Press.

MacKenzie, David. 1977. The background: Yugoslavia since 1964. In *Nationalism in the USSR and Eastern Europe in the era of Brezhnev and Koygin.* Ed. George W. Simmonds. Detroit: University of Detroit Press.

Mackenzie, William James Millar. 1978. *Political identity.* New York: St. Martin's Press.

MacKinder, Halford J. 1904. The geographical pivot of history. *Geographical Journal* 23: 421-37.

———. 1919. *Democratic ideals and reality.* New York: Henry Holt.

Malmberg, Torsten. 1980. *Human territoriality.* The Hague, The Netherlands: Mouton.

Mamatey, Victor S., and Radomír Luža, eds. 1973. *A history of the Czechoslovak republic, 1918-1948.* Princeton, N.J.: Princeton University Press.

Mann, Michael. 1984. The autonomous power of the state: Its origins, mechanism and results. *European Journal of Sociology* 25: 185-213.

Martin, Geoffrey. 1977. Isaiah Bowman. In vol. 1 of *Geographers: Biobibliographical studies.* Ed. T. W. Freeman, Marguerita Oughton, and Philippe Pinchemel. London: Mansell.

Martin, Geoffrey J., and Preston E. James. 1993. *All possible worlds: A history of geographical ideas.* 3d ed. New York: John Wiley and Sons.

Martin, Lt.-Col. Lawrence. 1924. *The treaties of peace 1919-1923, Vol. I: Containing the Treaty of Versailles, the Treaty of St. Germain-en-Laye and the Treaty of Trianon.* New York: Carnegie Endowment for International Peace.

Martin, Terry. 2001. *The affirmative action empire: Nations and nationalism in the Soviet Union, 1923-1939.* Ithaca, N.Y.: Cornell University Press.

Marx, Karl. [1867] 1977. *Das Kapital.* Ed. Friedrich Engels. New York: New World Paperback.

Marx, Karl, and Friedrich Engels. [1848] 1968. *The Communist Manifesto.* Including *Principles of Communism* by Friedrich Engels. Trans. Paul M. Sweezy. New York: Modern Reader Paperbacks.

Masters, Roger D. 1968. *The political philosophy of Rousseau.* Princeton, N.J.: Princeton University Press.

Matthew, Donald. 1983. *Atlas of medieval Europe.* New York: Facts on File.

Mayer, Arno J. 1967. *Politics and diplomacy of peace making: Containment and counterrevolution at Versailles, 1918-1919.* New York: Alfred A. Knopf.

Mayo, James M. 1988. War memorials as political memory. *Geographical Review* 78 (January): 62-75.

McCrum, Robert, William Cran, and Robert MacNeil. 1987. *The story of English.* New York: Elisabeth Sifton—Viking.

McDougall, Walter A. *1997. Promised land, crusader state: The American encounter with the world since 1776.* New York: Houghton Mifflin.

McNeill, William. 1985. *Polyethnicity and national unity in world history.* Toronto: University of Toronto Press.

Meinig, D. W. 1979. *Symbolic landscapes.* In *The interpretation of ordinary landscapes: Geographical essays.* Ed. D. W. Meinig. New York: Oxford University Press.

Mellor, Roy E. H. 1975. *Eastern Europe: A geography of Comecon countries.* New York: Columbia University Press.

Michael-Titus, C. 1976. *In search of "cultural genocide."* London: Panopticum Press.

Micklethwait, John, and Adrian Woolridge. 2000. *A future perfect: The challenge and hidden promise of globalization.* New York: Crown Business.

Mikesell, M. W. 1983. The myth of the nation-state. *Journal of Geography* 82: 257-60.

Miller, David. 1995. *On nationality.* Oxford: Clarendon Press.

Miller, David Hunter. 1924. *My diary at the conference of Paris.* 21 vols. New York: Appeal Printing Co., privately printed.

Milner-Gulland, Robin, and Nikolai Dejevsky. 1991. *Cultural atlas of Russia and the Soviet Union.* New York: Facts on File.

Morse, David. 1982. *Romanticism: A structural analysis.* Totowa, N.J.: Barnes and Noble Books.

Mortenson, Eric. 1992. Concentration camp survivor honors his German heritage. *Register Guard* (Eugene, Oregon), C 1 and 6.

Muir, Richard. 1975. *Modern political geography.* New York: John Wiley and Sons.

Mülhberger, Detlef, ed. 1987. *The social basis of European fascist movements.* New York: Croom Helm.

Murphy, Alexander B. 1988. *The regional dynamics of language differentiation in Belgium: A study in cultural-political geography.* University of Chicago Department of Geography Research Paper no. 227.

———. 1989. Territorial policies in multi-ethnic states. *Geographical Review* 79 (October): 410-21.

———. 1990. Historical justifications for territorial claims. *Annals of the Association of American Geographers* 80 (December): 531-48.

———. 1991a. Territorial ideology and international conflict: The legacy of prior political formations. Chap. 9 in *The political geography of conflict and peace.* Ed. Nurit Kliot and Stanley Waterman. London: Belhaven Press.

————. 1991b. Regions as social constructs: The gap between theory and practice. *Progress in Human Geography* 15 (March): 23-35.

————. 1993. Emerging regional linkages within the European Community: Challenging the dominance of the state. *Tijdschrift voor economische en sociale gografie* 84 (2): 103-18.

————. 1996. The sovereign state system as political-territorial idea: Historical and contemporary consideration. In *State sovereignty as social construct.* Ed. Thomas J. Biersteker and Cynthia Weber. Cambridge: Cambridge University Press.

Murphy, David Thomas. 1997. *The heroic earth: Geopolitical thought in Weimar German, 1918-1933.* Kent, Ohio: Kent State University Press.

Murray, Alexander, ed. 1998. *Sir William Jones, 1746-1797: A commemoration.* Oxford: Oxford University Press.

Nairn, Tom. 1981. *The break-up of Britain: Crisis and neo-nationalism.* 2d ed. New York: Verso.

————. 1997. *Faces of nationalism: Janus revisited.* New York: Verso.

Nemoianu, Virgil. 1984. *The taming of Romanticism.* Cambridge, Mass.: Harvard University Press.

Nettl, Paul. 1967. *National anthems.* 2d ed. Trans. Alexander Gode. New York: Frederick Ungar.

Niedermuller, Peter, ed. 2001. *Europe: Cultural construction and reality.* Copenhagen: Museum Tusculanum Press, University of Copenhagen.

Noble, George Bernard. 1968. *Policies and opinions at Paris, 1919: Wilsonian diplomacy, the Versailles peace, and French public opinion.* New York: Howard Fertig.

Norris, Robert E., and L. Lloyd Haring. 1980. *Political geography.* Columbus, Ohio: Charles E. Merrill.

Nott, Josiah C., and George R. Gliddon. 1854. *Types of mankind: or, ethnological researches, based upon the ancient monuments, paintings, sculptures, and crania of races, and upon their natural, geographical, philological, and biblical history: Illustrated by selections from the inedited papers of Samuel George Morton, M.D., and by professor L. Agassiz, LL.D.; W. Usher, M.D.; and professor H.S. Patterson, M.D.* Philadelphia: Lippincott, Grambo and Company.

Nowak, Karl Friedrich. [1924] 1970. *The collapse of Central Europe.* Trans. P. Lochner and E. W. Dickes. Westport, Conn.: Greenwood.

Offices of the Historian and of Public Communication. 1991. Brief history of the State Department, 1861-95. *US Department of State Dispatch,* 18 February, 2 (7): 119-20.

O'Grady, Joseph, ed. 1967. *The immigrants influence on Wilson's peace policies.* Lexington: University of Kentucky Press.

Oinas, Felix J., ed. 1978. *Folklore, nationalism, and politics.* Columbus, Ohio: Slavica.

Okey, Robin. 1986. *Eastern Europe 1740-1985: Feudalism to communism.* 2d ed. London: Hutchinson.

O'Loughlin, John. 1986. Spatial models of international conflict: Extending current theories of war behavior. *Annals of the Association of American Geographers* 76 (March): 63-80.

Osborne, R. H. 1967. *East-Central Europe.* New York: Frederick A. Praeger.

Owen, David. 1995. *Balkan Odyssey.* New York: A Harvest Book, Harcourt, Brace, and Company.

Özkirimli, Umut. 2000. *Theories of nationalism: A critical introduction.* New York: St. Martin's Press.

———. 2003. The nation as an artichoke? A critique of ethnosymbolist interpetrations of nationalism. *Nations and Nationalism* 9 (3/July): 339-55.

Paasi, Anssi. 1996. *Territories, boundaries, and consciousness: The changing geographies of the Finnish-Russian border.* Chichester, UK: John Wiley and Sons.

———. 2003. Territory. Chap. 8 in *A companion to political geography.* Ed. John Agnew, Katharyne Mitchell, and Gerard Toal. Malden, Mass.: Blackwell.

Palmer, Alan. 1970. *The lands between: A history of East-Central Europe since the Congress of Vienna.* New York: Macmillan.

———. 1992. *The decline and fall of the Ottoman Empire.* New York: M. Evans.

Palumbo, Michael, and William O. Shanahan, eds. 1981. *Nationalism: Essays in honor of Louis L. Snyder.* Westport, Conn.: Greenwood.

Parti Québécois. http://www.uni.ca/pq.html (4 August 2003).

Paulston, Christina Bratt, and Donald Peckham, eds. 1998. *Linguistic minorities in Central and Eastern Europe.* Philadelphia: Multilingual Matters.

Pearcy, G. Etzel, Russell H. Fifield, and Associates. 1948. *World political geography.* New York: Thomas Y. Crowell.

Pearson, Raymond. 1983. *National minorities in Eastern Europe 1848-1945.* London: Macmillan.

———. 1994. *The Longman companion to European nationalism, 1789-1920.* London: Longman.

Peckham, Morse, ed. 1965. *Romanticism: The culture of the nineteenth century.* New York: George Braziller.

Pei, Mario. 1965. *The story of language.* New York: J.B. Lippincott.

Penrose, Jan. 2002. Nations, states and homelands: Territory and territoriality in nationalist thought. *Nations and Nationalism* 8 (3): 277-97.

Penrose, Jan, and Joe May. 1991. Herder's concept of nation and its relevance to contemporary ethnic nationalism. *Canadian Review of Studies in Nationalism* 28 (1-2): 165-78.

Perkins, Edward J. 1992. Aggression by the Serbian regime. *US Department of State Dispatch,* 8 June, 3 (23): 448.

Perman, D. 1962. *The shaping of the Czechoslovak state: Diplomatic history of the boundaries of Czechoslovakia, 1914-1920.* Leiden, The Netherlands: E. J. Brill.

Petrovich, Michael Boro. 1976. *A history of modern Serbia, 1804-1918.* 2 vols. New York: Harcourt Brace Jovanovich.

Pickles, John, and Jeff Woods. 1992. South Africa's homelands in the age of reform: The case of QwaQwa. *Annals of the Association of American Geographers* 82 (4/December): 629-52.

Piirainen, Timo, ed. 1994. *Change and continuity in Eastern Europe.* Brookfield, Vt.: Dartmouth.

Plantinga, Leon. 1984. *Romantic music: A history of musical style in nineteenth-century Europe.* New York: Norton.

Popkewitz, Thomas S., and Marie Brennan, eds. 1998. *Foucault's challenge: Discourse, knowledge, and power in education.* New York: Teachers College Press, Columbia University

Porter, Roy, and Mikuláš Teich, eds. 1988. *Romanticism in national context.* Cambridge: Cambridge University Press.

Poulsen, Thomas M. 1995. *Nations and states: A geographic background to world affairs.* Englewood Cliffs, N.J.: Prentice Hall.

Pounds, Norman J. G. 1951. The origin of the idea of natural frontiers in France. *Annals of the Association of American Geographers* 41 (2/June): 146-57.

———. 1954. France and "Les Limites Naturelles" from the seventeenth to the twentieth centuries. *Annals of the Association of American Geographers* 44 (1/March): 51-62.

———. 1961. *Geographical essays on Eastern Europe.* Bloomington: Indiana University Press.

———. 1963. *Political geography.* New York: McGraw-Hill.

———. 1969. *Eastern Europe.* Chicago: Aldine.

———. 1990. *An historical geography of Europe.* Cambridge: Cambridge University Press.

Pounds, Norman J. G., and Sue Simons Ball. 1964. Core-Areas and the development of the European state system. *Annals of the Association of American Geographers* 54 (March): 24-40.

Powell, E. Alexander. 1928. *Embattled borders: Eastern Europe from the Balkans to the Baltic.* New York: Century.

Pratt, Jeff C. 2003. *Class, nation and identity: The anthropology of political movements.* London: Pluto Press.

Pred, Allan. 1984. Place as historically contingent process: Structuration and the time-geography of becoming places. *Annals of the Association of American Geographers* 74 (June): 279-97.

Prestowitz, Clyde. 2003. *Rogue nation: American unilateralism and the failure of good intentions.* New York: Basic Books.

Pringle, Dennis. 1985. *One island, two nations? A political geographic analysis of the national conflict in Ireland.* New York: John Wiley and Sons.

Public Broadcasting System. *Race: The power of illusion. Go Deeper: Racial Timeline.* http://www.pbs.org/race/000_General/000_00-Home.htm (9 September 2003).

Races of Europe, The. 1918. *National Geographic* 34 (6/December): 441-536.

Rajchman, Marthe. 1944. *Europe: An atlas of human geography.* New York: William Morrow.

Ramm, Agatha. 1984a. *Europe in the nineteenth century: 1789-1905.* Vol. 1. New York: Longman.

———. 1984b. *Europe in the twentieth century: 1905-1970.* Vol. 2. New York: Longman.

Randall, Richard R. 2001. *Place names: How they define the world–and more.* Lanham, Md.: Scarecrow Press.

Ratzel, Friedrich. 1882. *Grundzüge der Anwendung der Erdkunde auf die Geschichte.* Vol. 1 of *Anthropolgeographie.* Stuttgart, Germany: J. Engelhorn.

———. 1891. *Die geographische Verbreitung des Menschen.* Vol. 2 of *Anthropolgeographie.* Stuttgart, Germany: J. Engelhorn.

———. 1896a. Die Gesetze des räumlichen Wachstums der Staaten. *Petermanns Mitteilungen* 42: 97-107.

———. 1896b. The territorial growth of states. *Scottish Geographical Magazine* 12 (7/July): 351-61.

———. 1897. *Politische Geographie, oder die Geographie der Staaten, des Verkehrs, und der Krieges.* Munich, Germany: R. Oldenbourg.

———. 1969. The laws of spatial growth of states. Chap. 2 in *The structure of political geography.* Ed. Roger E. Kasperson and Julian Minghi. Chicago: Aldine.

Read, Conyers. 1969. *The Tudors: Personalities and practical politics in sixteenth century England.* New York: Norton.

Reardon, Douglas. 1998. Ethnic cleansing for peace? A critical analysis of the American role in the expulsion of ethnic Germans after World War II. Ph.D. diss., University of Maryland, College Park.

Relph, Edward. 1976. *Place and placelessness.* London: Pion Lion.

Rich, Norman. 1977. *The age of nationalism and reform, 1850-1890.* 2d ed. New York: Norton.

Richards, Robert J. 2002. *The Romantic conception of life: Science and philosophy in the age of Goethe.* Chicago: University of Chicago Press.

Riedlmayer, Andras. 1994. *Killing memory: Bosnia's cultural heritage and its destruction.* Produced and edited by Anne Walsh. 42 min. videocassette. Haverford, Penn.: Community of Bosnia Foundation.

———. 1995a. *Killing memory: The targeting of Bosnia's cultural heritage.* Testimony presented at a hearing of the Commission on Security and Cooperation in Europe. U.S. Congress, April 4. http://www.haverford.edu/relg/sells/killing.html.

———. 1995b. Erasing the past: The destruction of libraries and archives in Bosnia and Herzegovina. *Middle East Studies Association Bulletin* 29 (1): 7-11.

Roark, Michael O. 1993. Homelands: A conceptual essay. *Journal of Cultural Geography* 13 (Spring/Summer): 5-11.

Robins, Keith. 1984. *The First World War.* Oxford: Oxford University Press.

Robinson, Arthur H. 1982. *Early thematic mapping in the history of cartography.* Chicago: University of Chicago Press.

Rodman, Margaret C. 1992. Empowering place: Multilocality and multivocality. *American Anthropologist* 94 (September): 640-56.

Rodriguez, Richard. 2003. "Blaxicans" and other re-invented Americans. *Chronicle of Higher Education,* 12 September, B 10-12.

Rotberg, Robert I., ed. 1978. *The mixing of peoples: Problems of identity and ethnicity.* Stamford, Conn.: Greylock.

Rosenberg, Michael. 1990. The mother of invention: Evolutionary theory, territoriality, and the origins of agriculture. *American Anthropologist* 92 (June): 399-415.

Rossiter, Clinton. 1956. *The first American Revolution: The American colonies on the eve of independence.* New York: Harcourt, Brace.

Rot, Nikola, and Nenad Havelka. 1973. *Nacionalna vezanost i vrednosti kod srednjoškolske omladine.* Belgrade: Institut za psihologiju, Institut drustvenih nauka.

Rothchild, Joseph. 1989. *Return to diversity: A political history of East Central Europe since World War II.* New York: Oxford University Press.

Rugg, Dean S. 1985. *Eastern Europe.* New York: Longman.

Rupnik, Jacques. 1989. *The other Europe.* New York: Pantheon.

———. 1994. Europe's new frontiers: Remapping Europe. *Daedalus* 123 (Summer): 91-114.

Rushdie, Salman. 1991. *Imaginary homelands: Essays and criticism 1981-1991.* London: Granta Books.

Sack, Robert David. 1980. *Conceptions of space in social thought.* Minneapolis: University of Minnesota Press.

———. 1981. Territorial bases of power. Chap. 3 in *Political studies from spatial perspectives: Anglo-American essays on political geography.* Ed. Alan D. Burnett and Peter J. Taylor. New York: John Wiley and Sons.

———. 1986. *Human territoriality: Its theory and history.* New York: Cambridge University Press.

———. 1993. The power of place and space. *Geographical Review* 83 (July): 326-29.

Sahlins, Peter. 1990. Natural frontiers revisited: France's boundaries since the seventeenth century. *American Historical Review* 95 (December): 1423-51.

Samuel, Raphael, and Gareth Stedman Jones, eds. 1982. *Culture ideology and politics: Essays for Eric Hobsbawn.* London: Routledge and Kegan Paul.

Schama, Simon. 1996. *Landscape and memory.* New York: Vintage Books.

Schechtmann, Joseph B. 1963. *Postwar population transfers in Europe.* Philadelphia: University of Pennsylvania Press.

Schifter, Richard. 1991. Human rights in Yugoslavia. *US Department of State Dispatch,* 4 March, 2 (9): 152-53.

Schleicher, K., ed. 1993. *Nationalism in education.* Frankfurt, Germany: Peter Lang.

Schöpflin, George. 1991. National identity in the Soviet Union and East Central Europe. *Ethnic and Racial Studies* 14 (January): 3-14.

———. 2000. *Nations, identity, power.* New York: New York University Press.

Schöpflin, George, and Nancy Wood, eds. 1989. *In search of Central Europe.* Cambridge: Polity Press.

Schulze, Hagen, ed. 1987. *Nation-building in Central Europe.* New York: Berg.

———. 1996. *States, nations, and nationalism: From the Middle Ages to the present.* Translated from German by William E. Yuill. Cambridge, Mass.: Blackwell.

Schwarzmantel, J. J. 1987. *Structures of power: An introduction to politics.* New York: St. Martin's Press.

———. 2003. *Citizenship and identity: Towards a new republic.* New York: Routledge.

Segesvary, Victor. 2003. *World state, nation states, or non-centralized institutions?: A vision of future politics.* Lanham, Md.: University Press of America.

Semple, Ellen Churchill. 1911. *Influences of geographic environment on the basis of Ratzel's system of anthropo-geography.* New York: Henry Holt.

Seton-Watson, Hugh. 1956. *The East European revolution.* New York: Frederick A. Praeger.

———. 1962. *Eastern Europe between the wars 1918-1941.* 3d ed. New York: Harper and Row.

———. 1975. *The "Sick Heart" of Europe.* Seattle: University of Washington Press.

———. 1977. *Nations and states: An enquiry into the origins of nations and the politics of nationalism.* Boulder, Colo.: Westview.

———. 1981a. *The making of a new Europe: R. W. Seton-Watson and the last years of Austria-Hungary.* Seattle: University of Washington Press.

———. 1981b. *Language and national consciousness.* London: Oxford University Press.

———. 1985. What is Europe, where is Europe? From mystique to politique. *Encounter* 65 (July/August): 9-17.

Seton-Watson, Hugh, and Christopher Seton-Watson. 1981. *The making of a new Europe.* Seattle: University of Washington Press.

Seymour, Charles. 1951. *Geography, justice, and politics at the Paris conference of 1919.* New York: The American Geographical Society.

———. 1965. *Letters from the Paris Peace Conference.* New Haven, Conn.: Yale University Press.

Shafer, Boyd C. 1955. *Nationalism: Myth and reality.* New York: Harcourt, Brace and World.

———. 1972. *Faces of nationalism: New realities and old myths.* New York: Harcourt Brace Jovanovich.

Shapiro, Michael J. 1997. *Violent cartographies: Mapping cultures of war.* Minneapolis: University of Minnesota Press.

Sharp, Alan. 1991. The *Versailles settlement: Peacemaking in Paris, 1919.* New York: St. Martin's Press.

Shepherd, William R. 1929. *Historical atlas.* 7th ed. New York: Henry Holt and Company.

Silber, Laura, and Allan Little. 1997. *The death of Yugoslavia.* London: Penguin.

Singleton, Fred. 1985. *A short history of Yugoslav peoples.* New York: Cambridge University Press.

Situation in the Baltics. 1991. *US Department of State Dispatch,* 28 January, 2 (4): 58-59.

Smith, Anthony D. 1979. *Nationalism in the twentieth century.* New York: New York University Press.

———. 1981a. *The ethnic revival.* Cambridge: University of Cambridge Press.

———. 1981b. States and homelands: The social and geopolitical implications of national territory. *Millennium* 10 (Summer): 187-202.

———. 1981c. War and ethnicity: The role of warfare in the formation of self-images and cohesion of ethnic communities. *Ethnic and Racial Studies* 4 (October): 375-97.

———. 1983. *Theories of nationalism.* 2d ed. New York: Harper and Row.

———. 1984a. Ethnic myths and ethnic revivals. *European Journal of Sociology* 25 (November): 283-305.

———. 1984b. National identity and myths of ethnic descent. *Research in Social movements, Conflict and Change* 7: 95-130.

———. 1985. *Ethnie* and nation in the modern world. *Millennium* 14 (Spring): 127-42.

———. 1986a. Conflict and collective identity: Class, *ethnie,* and nation. In *The theory and practice of international conflict resolution.* Ed. E. E. Azar and J. W. Burton. Brighton, G.B.: Wheatsheaf.

———. 1986b. *The ethnic origins of nations.* New York: Basil Blackwell.

———. 1991. *National identity.* Reno: University of Nevada Press.

———. 1994. The problem of national identity: Ancient, medieval and modern? *Ethnic and Racial Studies* 17 (3): 375-99.

———. 1996. Culture, community and territory: The politics of ethnicity and nationalism. *International Affairs* 72 (3): 445-58.

———. 1998. *Nationalism and modernism: A critical survey of recent theories of nations and nationalism.* New York: Routledge.

———. 1999. *Myths and memories of the nation.* Oxford: Oxford University Press.

———. 2001. *Nationalism: Theory, ideology, history.* Cambridge: Polity Press.

Smith, Graham, ed. 1995. *Federalism: The multiethnic challenge.* New York: Longman.

Smith, Helmut Walser. 1995. *German nationalism and religious conflict: Culture, ideology, politics, 1870-1914.* Princeton, N.J.: Princeton University Press.

Smith, Justin H. 1907. *Our struggle for the fourteenth colony: Canada and the American Revolution.* 2 vols. New York: G.P. Putnam's Sons.

Snyder, Louis L., ed. 1964. *The dynamics of nationalism.* New York: Van Nostrand.

———. 1976. *The varieties of nationalism, a comparative view.* Hinsdale, Ill.: Dryden Press.

———. 1978. *Roots of German nationalism.* Bloomington: Indiana University Press.

———. 1990. *Encyclopedia of nationalism.* Chicago: St. James Press.

———. 1992. *Contemporary nationalisms: Intensity and persistence.* Armonk, N.Y.: M.E. Sharpe.

Soja, Edward W. 1971. *The political organization of space.* Commission on College Geography Resource Paper Number 8. Washington, D.C.: Association of American Geographers.

———. 1989. *Postmodern geographies: The reassertion of space in critical social theory.* New York: Verso.

Song, Miri. 2003. *Ethnicity and identity.* Malden, Mass.: Blackwell.

Sopher, David E. 1967. *Geography of religions. Foundations of cultural geography series.* Englewood Cliffs, N.J.: Prentice Hall.

Sörlin, Sverker. 1999. The articulation of territory: Landscape and the constitution of regional and national identity. *Norsk Geografisk Tidsskrift* 53 (3): 103-12.

Sötér, I., and I. Neupokoyeva, eds. 1977. *European Romanticism.* Budapest, Hungary: Akadémiai Kiadó.

Stalin, Joseph V. 1994. The Nation. Chap. 2 in *Nationalism.* Ed. John Hutchinson and Anthony D. Smith. New York: Oxford University Press.

Starkey, David. 2001. *Elizabeth: The struggle for the throne.* New York: HarperCollins.

Steinberg, S. H. 1966. *Five hundred years of printing.* New York: Penguin.

Stewart, George R. 1945. *Names on the land.* New York: Random House.

Stewart, Pamela J., and Andrew Strathern, eds. 2003. *Landscape, memory and history.* London: Pluto Press.

Stone, John, and Rutledge Dennis, eds. *Race and ethnicity: comparative and theoretical approaches.* Malden, Mass.: Blackwell.

Storey, David. 2001. *Territory: The claiming of space.* New York: Prentice Hall.

Strayer, Joseph Reese. 1970. *On the medieval origins of the modern state.* Princeton, N.J.: Princeton University Press.

Stuckey, Tom. 2002. Appeals court scraps redistricting plans: Governor's proposal violates constitution. *Cumberland Times News,* 12 June, B1-B2.

Suny, Ronald Grigor, and Michael D. Kennedy, eds. 1999. *Intellectuals and articulation of the nation.* Ann Arbor: University of Michigan Press.

Suny, Ronald Grigor, and Terry Martin, eds. 2001. *A state of nations: Empire and nation-making in the age of Lenin and Stalin.* Oxford: Oxford University Press.

Symmons-Symonolewicz, Konstantin. 1985. The concept of nationhood: Towards a theoretical clarification. *Canadian Review of Studies in Nationalism* 12 (Fall): 215-22.

Tardieu, André. 1921. *The truth about the treaty.* Forward by Edward M. House. Introduction by Georges Clemenceau. Indianapolis: Bobbs-Merril.

Tatalovich, Raymond. 1995. *Nativism reborn? The official English language movement and the American states.* Lexington: University of Kentucky Press.

Taylor, Alan John Percivale. 1957. *The struggle for the mastery of Europe: 1848-1918.* Oxford: Clarendon Press.

———. 1976. *The Habsburg monarchy, 1809-1918: A history of the Austrian Empire and Austria-Hungary.* Chicago: University of Chicago.

Taylor, Peter J. 1993. Contra political geography. *Tijdschrift voor Economische en Sociale Geografie* 84: 82-90.

———. 1994. The state as container: Territoriality in the modern world-system. *Progress in Human Geography* 18: 151-62.

———. 1996. Embedded statism and the social sciences: Opening up to new spaces. *Environment and Planning A* 28: 1917-28.

Taylor, Peter, and Colin Flint. 2000. *Political geography: World economy, nation-state, and locality.* 4th ed. Essex, England: Prentice Hall.

Taylor, Peter, and John House, eds. 1984. *Political geography: Recent advances and future directions.* London: Croom Helm.

Temperely, Harold W. V., ed. [1921] 1969. *A history of the Paris Peace Conference.* 6 vols. London: Henry Frowde and Hodder and Stoughton.

———. 1928. How the Hungarian frontiers were drawn. *Foreign Affairs* 6 (3/April): 432-47.

Thane, Pat, Geoffrey Crossick, and Roderick Floud, eds. 1984. *The power of the past: Essays for Eric Hobsbawn.* Cambridge: Cambridge University Press.

Thernstrom, Stephan, ed. 1980. *Harvard encyclopedia of American ethnic groups.* Cambridge, Mass.: Harvard University Press.

Thompson, Charles Thaddeus. 1920. *The peace conference day by day: A presidential pilgrimage leading to the discovery of Europe.* Introductory letter by Colonel E. M. House. New York: Brentano's.

Thompson, Dorothy. 1990. *Queen Victoria: The woman, the monarchy, and the people.* New York: Pantheon.

Tihany, Leslie Charles. 1976. *A history of Middle Europe: From the earliest times to the age of the world wars.* New Brunswick, N.J.: Rutgers University Press.

Tipton, Frank B., and Robert Aldrich. 1989a. *An economic and social history of Europe, 1890-1939.* Baltimore: Johns Hopkins University Press.

———. 1989b. *An economic and social history of Europe, from 1939 to the present.* Baltimore, Md.: Johns Hopkins University Press.

Tivey, Leonard, ed. 1981. *The nation-state: The formation of modern politics.* New York: St. Martin's.

Toynbee, Arnold J. 1915. *Nationality and the war.* Toronto: J.M. Dent and Sons.

Tuan, Yi-Fu. 1974. *Topophilia: A study of environmental perception, attitudes, and values* Englewood Cliffs, N.J.: Prentice Hall.

————. 1977. *Space and place: The perspective of experience.* Minneapolis: University of Minnesota Press.

————. 1980a. The significance of the artifact. *Geographical Review* 70 (October): 462-72.

————. 1980b. Rootedness vs. sense of place. *Landscape* 24 (1): 3-8.

————. 1991. Language and the making of place: A narrative-descriptive approach. *Annals of the Association of American Geographers* 81 (December): 684-96.

Ó Tuathail, Gearóid. 1996. *Critical geopolitics: The politics of writing global space.* Minneapolis: University of Minnesota Press.

Tunnard, Christopher, and Howard Hope Reed. 1955. *American skyline: The growth and form of our cities and towns.* Boston: Houghton Mifflin.

Tunstall, Graydon Allen. 1993. *Planning for war against Russia and Serbia: Austro-Hungarian and German military strategies, 1871-1914.* Boulder, Colo.: Social Science Monographs.

Turnock, David. 1978. *Studies in industrial geography: Eastern Europe.* Boulder, Colo.: Westview.

————. 1988. *The making of Eastern Europe: From earliest times to 1815.* New York: Routledge.

————. 1989a. *The human geography of Eastern Europe.* New York: Routledge.

————. 1989b. *Eastern Europe: An Economic and Political Geography.* New York: Routledge.

————. 2002. *The human geography of East-Central Europe.* New York: Routledge.

Tutweiler, Margaret. 1991. US Policy towards Yugoslavia. *US Department of State Dispatch,* 3 June, 2 (22): 395-96.

United States Department of Treasury. *Fact Sheets: Currency & Coins: History of "In God We Trust."* http://www.treas.gov/education/fact-sheets/currency/in-god-we-trust.html (15 July 2003).

Urbansky, Andrew B. 1968. *Byzantium and the Danube frontier: A study of the relations between Byzantium, Hungary, and the Balkans during the period of the Comneni.* New York: Twayne.

U.S. Census Bureau. 2001. *Census 2000 shows America's diversity.* http://www.census.gov/Press-Release/www/2001/cb01cn61.html (28 July 2003).

U.S. Recognition of former Yugoslav Republics. 1992. *US Department of State Dispatch,* 13 April, 3 (15): 287.

Vagts, Alfred. 1959. *A history of militarism, civilian and military.* Rev. ed. New York: Free Press.

Vale, Lawrence J. 1992. *Architecture, power, and national identity.* New Haven, Conn.: Yale University Press.

Van Den Berghe, Pierre. 1978. Race and ethnicity: A sociobiological perspective. *Ethnic and Racial Studies* 1 (4): 401-11.

————. 1981. *The ethnic phenomenon.* New York: Elsevier.

Van der Kiste, John. 1986. *Queen Victoria's children.* Gloucester, UK: Alan Sutton.

————. 1993. *Crowns in a changing world: The British and European monarchies 1901-1936.* London: Grange Books.

Vandersluis, Sarah Owen. 2000. *The state and identity construction in international relations.* New York: St. Martin's Press.

Vladislav, Jan. 1990. Exile, responsibility, destiny. In *Literature in exile,* ed. John Glad. Durham, N.C.: Duke University Press.

Wachtel, Andrew Baruch. 1998. *Making a nation, breaking a nation: Literature and cultural politics in Yugoslavia.* Stanford, Calif.: Stanford University Press.

Wade, Nicholas. 2003. Y chromosomes sketch new outline of British history. *New York Times,* 27 May, F2.

Wagner, Philip L. 1996. *Showing off: The Geltung hypothesis.* Austin: University of Texas Press.

Wagner, Philip L., and Marvin W. Mikesell, eds. 1962. *Readings in cultural geography.* Chicago: University of Chicago Press.

Walicki, Andrzej. 1982. *Philosophy and Romantic nationalism: The case of Poland.* Oxford: Clarendon Press.

————. 1997. Intellectual elites and the vicissitudes of <Imagined Nation> in Poland. *East European Politics and Societies* 11 (2): 227-53.

Walters, E. Garrison. 1990. *The other Europe: Eastern Europe to 1945.* New York: Dorset Press.

Walworth, Arthur. 1977. *America's moment: 1918, American diplomacy at the end of World War I.* New York: Norton.

————. 1986. *Wilson and the peacemakers: American diplomacy at the Paris Peace Conference, 1919.* New York: Norton.

Wanklyn, Harriet. 1961. *Friedrich Ratzel: A biographical memoir and bibliography.* Cambridge: Cambridge University Press.

Ware, Kallistos (Timothy). 1964. *The Orthodox Church.* New York: Penguin.

Warren, W. L. 1973. *Henry II.* Berkeley: University of California Press.

Weber, Eugen. 1976. *Peasants into Frenchmen: The modernization of rural France, 1870-1914.* Stanford, Calif.: Stanford University Press.

Weber, Max. [1947] 1997. *The theory of social and economic organization.* Trans. A. R. Henderson and Talcott Parsons. New York: Free Press.

————. 1978. *Economy and society: An outline of interpretive sociology.* Ed. Guenther Roth and Claus Wittich. Trans. Ephraim Fischoff et al. Berkeley: University of California Press.

————. 2002. *The Protestant ethic and the spirit of capitalism.* 3d Roxbury ed. Introduction and translation by Stephen Kalberg. Los Angeles: Roxbury.

Wellens, Koen. 1998. What's in a name? The Premi in southwest China and the consequences of defining ethnic identity. *Nations and Nationalism* 4 (1): 17-34.

Whittlesey, Derwent. 1944. *The earth and the state.* New York: Henry Holt.

Williams, Colin H. 1985. Conceived in bondage—called unto liberty: Reflections on nationalism. *Progress in Human Geography* 9 (September): 331-55.

———, ed. 1988. *Language in geographic context.* Philadelphia: Multilingual Matters.

Williams, Colin H., and Anthony D. Smith. 1983. The national construction of social space. *Progress in Human Geography* 7 (December): 502-18.

Williams, Raymond. 1976. *Keywords: A vocabulary of culture and society.* New York: Oxford University Press.

Wilson, William A. 1973. Herder, folklore, and Romantic nationalism. *Journal of Popular Culture* 6 (Spring): 819-35.

Wixman, Ronald. 1980. *Language aspects of ethnic patterns and processes in the north Caucasus.* University of Chicago Department of Geography Research Paper no. 191. Chicago: University of Chicago Press.

———. 1981. Territorial Russification and linguistic Russianization in some Soviet Republics. *Soviet Geography: Review and Translation* 22 (10): 667-75.

———. 1984. Demographic Russification and linguistic Russianization of the Ukraine: 1959-1979. In *Geographical Studies on the Soviet Union.* Ed. George Demko et al. Chicago: University of Chicago Press, Geography Research Series no. 211.

Wolff, Larry. 1994. *Inventing Eastern Europe: The map of civilization on the mind of Enlightenment.* Stanford, Calif.: Stanford University Press.

Woloch, Isser. 1982. *Eighteenth-Century Europe, tradition and progress 1715-1789.* New York: Norton.

Wood, Anthony. 1984. *Europe: 1815-1960.* 2d ed. Essex, England: Longman.

Wood, Ellen Meiksins. 1999. *Capitalism: A longer view.* New York: Verso.

Wood, William B. 2001. Geographic aspects of genocide: A comparison of Bosnia and Rwanda. *Transactions, Institute of British Geographers* 26 (1): 57-75.

Woodward, Colin. 1996. Slips of the tongue can incite lashing by locals in former Yugoslavia. *The Christian Science Monitor*, 13 August.

Woolf, Stuart. 1991. *Napoleon's integration of Europe.* New York: Routledge.

Wright, John Kirkland. 1928. *The geographical basis of European history.* New York: Henry Holt.

Zeman, Zbyněk A. B. 1971. *Twilight of the Habsburgs: The collapse of the Austro-Hungarian Empire.* New York: American Heritage.

Zivojurovic, Dragon R. 1969. The Vatican, Woodrow Wilson, and the dissolution of the Hapsburg Monarchy, 1914-1918. *East European Quarterly* 3 (March): 31-70.

Zoellick, Robert B. 1991. Soviet disunion: The American response. *US Department of State Dispatch*, 4 March 2, (9): 144-49.

Index

281

Reno, Janet, 129
Rhine River, 130, 158, 197, 208, 211, 216
Rhône River, 135
Riedlmayer, Andras, 48
Rodriguez, Richard, 32, 52-53
Rogane, Ted, 29, 62n8
Roman Catholics, 25, 44, 74, 105, 107, 114, 126, 138-39, 146, 166, 189-91, 194, 196, 199, 200, 223, 229
Roman Empire, 95
Romania, 25, 68, 103-5, 157, 194, 197, 200-201, 203, 210, 218-19, 228, 235-37, 239-40
Romanov dynasty, 196
Romans, 130, 147, 162
Romanticism. *See* Romantic nationalism
Romantic nationalism, 12-13, 153-69, 223-24, 226. *See also* patriotism
Romantic philosophy. *See* Romantic nationalism
Rome, 140, 190, 200
Rousseau, Jean-Jacques, 149, 161
Russia, 3, 95, 108, 165-66, 192-93, 196-204, 207, 219-22, 225-26, 229-30, 234, 237, 239, 241, 243. *See also* Soviet Union
Russification, 83, 165, 230, 243
Russo-Turkish War, 200
Ruthenia(ns), 219-20, 226, 234, 237
Rwanda, 2

Salonica (Thessaloníki), 236
Sanskrit, 155-56
Santayana, George, 18, 126
Sarajevo, 202
Sardinia, 136
Saxe-Coburg, 197
Saxe-Coburg-Gotha, 198
Saxe-Meiningen, 197
Schaumburg-Lippe, 197
Schleswig-Holstein, 197
Schweitzer, Albert, 46
Scotland, 79
Scots, 23-24, 30-31
Second World War, 4, 92, 125, 234-41, 243-44
self-determination, 208-12, 234
Semple, Ellen Churchill, 184-85

Seneca, 251
Serbia, 81, 96, 192, 194, 199, 202, 215, 224-26, 236, 239
Serbs, 26, 34, 56-57, 68-69, 105, 107, 215, 223-24, 228-29, 237
seventeenth century, 136-46
Sicilians, 32
Sicily, 136, 224
Silesia, 212, 220
simultaneity, 125, 178
site identification, 9, 59
sixteenth century, 136-46
Slavic, 220
Slavs, 141, 163, 165, 199, 200, 239. *See also* South Slavs
Slazacy (Slonzaks), 82, 212
Slovakia, 72, 244
Slovaks, 141, 165, 218-19, 226, 234, 237, 239
Slovenes, 165, 167, 224-25, 228, 236
Slovenia, 4, 34, 70, 96. *See also* Yugoslavia
Slavonians, 223
Smith, Anthony, 122, 162
socialism, 173n19, 187-89, 230-31
socialist nation, 230
Social Security, 84
Somalia, 35
Sopher, David, 38
South Africa, 102
South Carolina, 89
Southeast Asia, 31, 86, 99, 102
South Ossetia, 96
South Slavs, 211, 222-26
South Tyrol, 216
Southwest Asia, 2, 3, 5, 18, 19n1, 99, 204
sovereignty, 69-70
soviet nation, 230
Soviet Union, 1, 4, 5, 42, 68, 71, 79, 96, 100, 108, 177, 229, 233-37, 241, 243-44. *See also* Russia
Spain, 31, 96, 98, 141, 171n9, 197, 214
Spanish, 24, 98, 171n9, 182
spatial disjunctions, 95-96
Spencer, Herbert, 181, 185
Stalin, Joseph, 231, 237, 241
Stalingrad, 240
state, 3, 4, 10, 22, 27, 65-71; artificial, 99